THE
PROVENCE
COOKBOOK

ALSO BY PATRICIA WELLS

The Paris Cookbook

L'Atelier of Joël Robuchon

Patricia Wells at Home in Provence

Patricia Wells' Trattoria

Simply French

Bistro Cooking

The Food Lover's Guide to France

The Food Lover's Guide to Paris

THE
PROVENCE
COOKBOOK

*175 Recipes and a Select Guide
to the Markets, Shops, & Restaurants
of France's Sunny South*

PATRICIA WELLS

HarperCollins*Publishers*

HarperCollins books may be purchased for educational, business, or sales promotional use.
For information, please write: Special Markets Department, HarperCollins Publishers Inc.,
10 East 53rd Street, New York, NY 10022.

FIRST EDITION

Photographs © 2004 by Patricia Wells
Designed by Joel Avirom and Jason Snyder
Design assistant: Meghan Day Healey

Printed on acid-free paper

Library of Congress Cataloging-in-Publication Data

Wells, Patricia.
    The Provence cookbook / Patricia Wells.—1st ed.
        p. cm.
    ISBN 0-06-050782-9
        1. Cookery, French—Provençal style. 2. Cookery—France—Provence. I. Title.

TX719.2.P75W47 2004
641.5944'9—dc22

2003056977

04 05 06 07 08 ❖/RRD 10 9 8 7 6 5 4 3 2

To Walter, my husband and best friend.
Thank you for always waving that magic wand, improving our little kingdom.
With gratitude for a truly remarkable past, a stellar present,
and in anticipation of a future together without end.

Contents

ACKNOWLEDGMENTS

I WANT TO THANK EVERYONE who makes our life in Provence that much more joyful.

Special thanks to friends in our "neighborhood," people always ready to share friendship and good times, including Johanne Killeen and George Germon, Devon Fredericks and Eli Zabar, Sheila and Julian More, Carole Allen and Fred Feinsilber, Colette and Jean-Claude Viviani.

I want to thank two special friends, Steven Rothfeld and Andrew Axilrod, whose travels each summer make for fine winter memories and keep me supplied with laughter and good thoughts all year long.

Thank you to my friends the merchants: Josiane and Christian Deal at the cheese shop Lou Canestéou; Eliane and Aymar Berenger at our fish shop, Poissonnerie des Voconces; Josiane and Corinne Meliani, our produce purveyors at Les Gourmandines; butcher Franck Peyraud at Boucherie La Romane; and baker Denis Lefèvre at Le Pain des Moissons. Special thanks to Hervé Poron for his friendship as well as his truffle generosity, and to Jean-Louis Martin and Susy Seysson in Maussane-les-Alpilles.

Thank you to my friends the restaurateurs: Guy and Tina Julien at La Beaugravière; Jean-Louis and Mireille Pons at Le Bistrot du Paradou; Flora and Raoul Reichrath at Le Grand Pré; Marlies and Johannes Sailer at L' Oustalet; and Sophie and Serge Ghoukassian at Chez Serge.

Winemaker friends are too numerous to mention here, but I want to say special thanks to our winemaker, Ludovic Cornillon and his wife, Eliane, for making such a splendid and ever-enjoyable wine. Thanks, too, to all the folks at Château du Beaucastel and Château La Nerthe in Châteauneuf-du-Pape, and to all the winemakers of Vacqueyras and Gigondas who have given such pleasure over the years.

Thank you, Elisabeth de Lesparda, for careful attention to the manuscript. At HarperCollins, I want to thank Califia Suntree for keeping tabs on everything and knowing how to gently nudge; and of course my friend and editor Susan Friedland, for making the entire experience a treat and a joy. Thank you all.

Special thanks to Rita and Yale Kramer, without whom we would never have discovered Chanteduc.

INTRODUCTION

SOON MY HUSBAND, Walter, and I will celebrate our twentieth year as owners—I should really say caretakers—of our rewarding little farmhouse in northern Provence. The property is known as Chanteduc—the song of the owl—and is made up of a splendid spread of grapevines, oaks, pines, and olive trees, as well an endless blue-sky view of the Provençal countryside. I cannot imagine a patch of land that could offer more happiness. Much of the reward comes from the precious bounty the earth here provides. It is one of paradox, for I can speak the word "earth" but barely the word "soil." How can this rocky, seemingly forsaken land give us such richness? Bold and fruity red wine with a touch of wild cherry, plump black olives, precious figs that seem to drip with honey, and all manner of herbs and vegetables, from my prized Russian variety of tomatoes to my cherished caper bush.

But that's just home ground. This book is more than a scrapbook of our twenty years huddled around the fire in winter and beneath the oak tree in summer. It is the story of farmers and winemakers, tradesmen, shopkeepers, and restaurateurs, the men and the women who bake our bread, age our cheese, press our olives, unearth our truffles. It is a window into *my* Provence, a very specific part of northern Provence, a world filled with lavender fields, fruit orchards, olive groves, and endless stretches of vines. It is home to some of the finest vineyards in the world, those of the Southern Rhône, including the famed Châteauneuf-du-Pape, as well as my favorite Vacqueyras and Gigondas, and the lesser known Tavel and Lirac.

I live more than half of each year here, much of it spent touring markets, shops, restaurants, farms, in search of the freshest and finest of the season, sniffing out a new variety of potato or a just-released variety of strawberry, making friends with almost everyone I meet, snatching recipes and sharing a few of my own. Vendors laugh as I gasp when I see the first-of-season fresh white shell beans—*cocos blancs*—a signal that I can add Provençal vegetable soup, or *pistou*, to my weekly repertoire. And when the fishmonger sees me coming, he is sure to point out the rarity of a special Mediterranean species. Chefs bring me into the kitchen to sniff a freshly unearthed truffle, and my winemakers delight in squeezing a perfectly ripe grape, its juice running free and fragrant.

In ways that only people who share a special passion can, we feed upon one another, understanding that we will all become equally excited and grateful for a perfectly ripe and flawless grape harvest, about a particularly successful truffle hunt, a second season's crop of figs, or the beauty of an olive tree laden with a record bounty of ripe fruit. I know that we all feel equally fortunate to reap such harvests, and share mutual disappointment when the rains, excessive heat or drought, even hail, derail plans for a perfect season.

In this book I have tried to share the fruits of my own labors, both in touring the region and in the kitchen. This is a volume of Provençal customs and lore, of personal tips on kitchen organization, talk of cheese as well as wine. Market life plays a huge role in final enjoyment and so I have tried to shed a glimpse of light on that welcome ritual.

Food is nothing if it is looked upon only as an ingredient or a crop. It must be appreciated in its natural state, savored, and sometimes transformed—with minimal intervention—until it arrives at our table to be shared and appreciated by family and friends. As I have been taught by experience, the ingredient is best enjoyed when the least has been done to it. Over the years, my food has become simpler and simpler. I want a pear cake to taste of pears, not of sugar or honey. I like tomatoes to star in a tomato salad and for nothing to overwhelm the sweet flavor of fresh red tuna. Chicken should be meaty and not camouflaged with creams or butters, and nothing can beat the flavor of sweet fresh almonds baked into a crispy giant cookie-cake. Each recipe is here for a reason, has a personal story, and is connected to a human being. Please, come into my kitchen and share with me the sunshine of Provence, the fruits of many labors. Appreciate and enjoy.

PATRICIA WELLS
CHANTEDUC
OCTOBER 2003

THE
PROVENCE
COOKBOOK

CHANTEDUC RAINBOW OLIVE COLLECTION

SAVORY ROSEMARY-PARMESAN MADELEINES

SUMMER HERB BREAD

HAZELNUT, GRUYERE, AND ROSEMARY BISCUITS

SAUTEED ALMOND-STUFFED DATES

NIÇOISE FIGS STUFFED WITH FENNEL SEEDS AND WALNUTS

APPETIZERS, STARTERS, AND FIRST COURSES
Les Hors-d'Oeuvre et les Entrées

BLACK OLIVE AND DRIED FIG SPREAD

BLACK TRUFFLE OPEN-FACED SANDWICHES

ROASTED PROVENÇAL CHICKPEAS

PROVENÇAL CHICKPEA SPREAD WITH CUMIN

GARDEN EGGPLANT-CUMIN SPREAD

TUNA AND OLIVE SPREAD

Bar à Thym, Montbrun-les-Bains

CHANTEDUC RAINBOW OLIVE COLLECTION

Camaïeu d'Olives de Chanteduc

*T*he olive vendors at our outdoor markets in Provence offer an extravagant collection of olives in all colors and sizes, with an endless variety of flavorings. There are miniature black olives from Nice, our own wrinkled black Tanche olives from Nyons, the famed cracked olives from Maussane-les-Alpilles, flavored with wild fennel, and colossal green olives from Greece, as well as mixtures seasoned with hot pepper flakes, paired with plumped dried fava beans, or stirred with golden bits of preserved lemons. I make my own mixture, combining many varieties, then boosting the flavor and color even more by adding bay leaves, lemon or orange rind, hot peppers, and fennel seeds. The combinations are endless, so use this recipe as a simple jumping-off point for your own rainbow collection.

1 cup extra-virgin olive oil

½ cup best-quality red wine vinegar

30 fresh bay leaves

5 plump cloves garlic, peeled, green germs removed, thinly sliced

Wide strips of rind from 2 lemons or 2 oranges, preferably organic

1 teaspoon hot red pepper flakes

1 teaspoon fennel seeds

4 cups olives, preferably a mix of French brine-cured black olives, green Picholines in fennel, green pimiento-stuffed olives, and tiny black Niçoise olives

In a large saucepan, combine the oil, vinegar, bay leaves, and garlic. Heat over low heat just until warm. Remove from the heat and add the lemon or orange rinds and the red pepper flakes. Add the olives and toss to coat them with the liquid. Transfer to a large airtight container. Refrigerate—shaking the container regularly to redistribute the liquid—for at least 2 hours and up to 2 weeks.

4 CUPS OLIVES

BY WORLD STANDARDS, France is a tiny producer of olives and olive oil, accounting for only 0.2 percent of the world's production and way behind the top producers, including Spain at 38 percent and Italy at 23.7 percent. But in the past twenty years French interest in growing olive trees, curing olives, and pressing olives for oil, as well as consuming the fruits of that labor, has increased dramatically. Today France can count almost 3 million trees and 130 olive-oil mills. During these twenty years, consumption of olive oil has almost tripled nationwide.

Some of the country's best-known olives—and the first olive in France to be awarded its own *appellation d'origine contrôlée*—come from the village of Nyons in northern Provence, a region known as the Drôme Provençale. This is as far north as olives grow in the world, and the region has only a single variety of olive, the Tanche—a big, plump, wrinkled olive that was first planted by the Romans and is known as the "black pearl."

People unfamiliar with olive culture are often surprised to find that there are not green olive trees and black olive trees. Green olives are simply unripe olives; as the olive matures on the tree, it turns from green and smooth to black and wrinkled, with many color and texture stages in between. Over time, olive growers and consumers have learned that some olives are best picked green and preserved for eating, some can be used for both eating and pressing for oil, and some reach a peak of flavor only when left on the tree to ripen and turn black. For example, the slender green Lucques variety is best picked a brilliant green, then used for either curing or pressing. In the same way, the Tanche variety is picked only when black and ripe, then cured in either salt or a salt brine, or pressed for oil. Other favorite eating varieties in France include the tiny Niçoise olive known as Cailletier, the artichoke-flavored green olive from the Haute Provence known as Aglandau, the peppery green Picholine from Languedoc, and the famed black Salonenque, cured with wild fennel, from the Vallée des Baux.

For more information, contact or visit:
Institut du Monde de l'Olivier
40, place de la Libération
26110 Nyons
Telephone: 04 75 26 90 90
Fax: 04 75 29 90 94
E-mail: *monde-olivier@wanadoo.fr*

Olive vendors, Vaison-la-Romaine

SAVORY ROSEMARY-PARMESAN MADELEINES

Petites Madeleines Salées au Romarin et au Fromage

When I mentioned the idea of savory *madeleines* to one of my best friends, cookbook author Susan Herrmann Loomis, she was quite excited. She and I have been *madeleine* lovers ever since we walked the streets of Paris in the 1980s researching *The Food Lover's Guide to Paris*. I make the sweet, cookielike *madeleines* nearly every week during my cooking classes, and love their crunch, daintiness, and neat shell-like form. So when I first sampled savory *madeleines* at the hand of Anne-Sophie Pic of the restaurant Pic in Valence, I knew I had fertile ground for research. And this is what I came up with: tiny savory bites filled with cheese and fragrant rosemary. Serve them warm or at room temperature as appetizers that welcome a nice glass of bubbly, such as the Provençal Clairette de Die.

1 Preheat the oven to 425 degrees F.

2 In a food processor or blender, combine the flour, baking powder, salt, egg, and yogurt, and blend thoroughly. Add the cheese and herbs and blend.

EQUIPMENT: A food processor or blender; 24 miniature nonstick *madeleine* molds.

⅓ cup unbleached all-purpose flour

1 teaspoon baking powder

¼ teaspoon fine sea salt

1 large egg, lightly beaten

⅓ cup nonfat plain yogurt

¼ cup (1 ounce) freshly grated Parmigiano-Reggiano or Swiss Gruyère cheese

1 tablespoon finely minced fresh rosemary leaves or fresh chives

Restaurant Pic
Anne-Sophie Pic
285, avenue Victor Hugo
26000 Valence
Telephone: 04 75 44 15 32
Fax: 04 75 40 96 03
Web: *www.pic-valence.com*

3 Spoon the batter into the *madeleine* molds. Place the molds in the center of the oven and bake until firm and golden, about 10 minutes. Remove the molds from the oven and let the *madeleines* cool in the molds for about 10 minutes before turning them out on a rack to cool further. Serve warm or at room temperature. Store securely in a plastic bag at room temperature for up to 3 days.

24 MINIATURE MADELEINES

Wine Suggestion: Try a bubbly Clairette de Die from the village of Die in the Drôme Provençale. This low-alcohol wine (usually 8 percent as opposed to an average 12 percent alcohol for most wines) is made from the white Clairette grape and is a pleasant summer aperitif that is only slightly sweet and never cloying.

MISE EN PLACE, OR EVERYTHING IN ITS PLACE

I'VE LONG NOTICED that when people get flustered in the kitchen, it's due to lack of organization. Cluttered counters, sinks overflowing with dirty dishes, refrigerators stuffed to the gills: a sure invitation to disaster.

The French have a system of kitchen organization called *mise en place,* meaning quite simply "everything at hand." In my cooking classes and even when I cook alone at home, I insist on rigid organization. I have a collection of Provençal trays, and each recipe—whether I am testing or retesting or cooking for the fun of it—gets a tray, with all the ingredients carefully measured out. I make a list of everything that has to be done for that meal, and work systematically through the list. It makes for satisfying, efficient work in the kitchen, and I find it incredibly calming.

There are other reasons to make *mise en place* part of your life. There is nothing worse than getting halfway into a recipe, only to find that you need six eggs but have only five in the house. Just as bad is to slip a cake in the oven, then realize that you forgot to add the melted butter.

SUMMER HERB BREAD

Cake aux Fines Herbes

*I*n Provence one finds an entire repertoire of full-flavored quick breads—breads the French call *cake*, the most common being the black-olive–studded *cake aux olives*. This bread—inspired by a stroll through my herb garden—is golden, light, moist, and fragrant. It is also versatile, for you can enjoy it from breakfast through dinnertime. I serve it as a first course, cut into thin slices and teamed up with a Spicy Tomato, Fennel, and Orange Sauce (page 318). I toast it and enjoy it for breakfast, or I serve the toast with the cheese course at dinner. It can also be cut into tiny cubes, speared with a toothpick, and served as a welcoming appetizer. Don't be surprised by the 2 tablespoons of mustard in the bread; it won't blow your head off!

EQUIPMENT: A food processor or blender; a nonstick 1-quart rectangular bread pan.

1 cup unbleached all-purpose flour

2 teaspoons baking powder

½ teaspoon fine sea salt

3 large eggs, lightly beaten

1 cup nonfat plain yogurt

2 tablespoons imported French mustard

½ cup (2 ounces) freshly grated Parmigiano-Reggiano or Swiss Gruyère cheese

¼ cup finely minced fresh mint leaves

¼ cup finely minced fresh chives

¼ cup finely minced fresh thyme leaves

1 Preheat the oven to 425 degrees F.

2 In a food processor or blender, combine the flour, baking powder, salt, eggs, yogurt, and mustard; blend thoroughly. Add the cheese and herbs and blend.

3 Pour the batter into the bread pan. Place the pan in the center of the oven and bake until firm and golden, about 45 minutes. Remove the pan from the oven and turn the bread out onto a rack to cool.

4 Serve at room temperature. As an appetizer, slice the bread, cut into cubes, and spear with a toothpick. Arrange the cubes on a small serving platter. As a first course, cut the bread into thin slices, place each slice on a small plate, and serve with a spoonful of tomato sauce alongside. Or, serve toasted for breakfast or with cheese. Store securely in a plastic bag at room temperature for up to 3 days.

I LOAF, ABOUT 12 SLICES

HAZELNUT, GRUYERE, AND ROSEMARY BISCUITS

Biscuits au Fromage, Romarin et Noisettes

*T*hese warm and tidy little biscuits of herbs, cheese, and nuts always receive a welcome smile from my guests. There's something about the fragrant sconelike treats that make people feel at home. As the French would say, *tant mieux,* or all the better! That's the purpose of inviting people into your home in the first place. While I like these best served warm from the oven, they can be made an hour or so ahead if time or oven space poses a problem. Sometimes I turn them into little sandwiches, slicing the biscuits in half and stuffing them with a pitted olive, some black-olive spread, or even a bit of mustard.

1 Preheat the oven to 450 degrees F.

2 In a large bowl, combine the flour, baking powder, and salt; stir to blend. With a fork, rub the butter into the mixture until it resembles bread crumbs. Add the hazelnuts, rosemary, and two thirds of the cheese; stir to combine. Add the milk and stir until a soft dough forms, adding additional milk as necessary.

EQUIPMENT: 2 nonstick baking sheets; a 2-inch round pastry cutter.

1 cup unbleached all-purpose flour

2 teaspoons baking powder

½ teaspoon fine sea salt

1 tablespoon unsalted butter, chilled

¼ cup hazelnuts, finely chopped

½ cup fresh rosemary leaves, finely chopped

1 cup (4 ounces) finely grated Swiss Gruyère cheese (or any hard grating cheese)

¾ cup nonfat milk, plus more as needed

EGG WASH:

1 egg yolk, lightly beaten with 1 teaspoon water

3 In a small bowl, combine the egg yolk and water and stir to blend.

4 Roll out the dough on a lightly floured surface until about ½ inch thick. Using the pastry cutter, cut out rounds of dough. (Re-roll the scraps only once or the biscuits may be tough.) Place the rounds of dough side by side on the baking sheets. Brush the tops of the rounds with the egg wash. Sprinkle the tops with the remaining cheese.

5 Place the baking sheets in the oven and bake until the biscuits are a deep golden brown, about 10 minutes. Transfer the biscuits to a wire rack to cool. Serve warm or at room temperature.

ABOUT 36 BISCUITS

MEASURE, THEN CHOP? Depending upon the ingredient, it is usually easier to measure stemmed herbs or nuts, then chop them. So when a recipe calls for a quantity of "stemmed herbs or nuts, chopped," it means just that: measure first, chop second.

SAUTEED ALMOND-STUFFED DATES

Dates Fourrées aux Amandes

I am eternally in search of different and unusual appetizers that will both surprise and please my guests. One morning a student in my cooking class in Provence shared this recipe, one that was an instant hit with family and friends. The combination of sweet and salty, soft and crunchy, awakens the palate and makes one actually salivate, setting the stage for a fine meal to come.

EQUIPMENT: A large nonstick frying pan.

24 whole dates

24 whole blanched almonds

2 teaspoons extra-virgin olive oil

Fleur de sel or fine sea salt to taste

At Christmastime in Provence, my organic market offers fresh dates from Iran—almost black, super-moist, and oh so sweet. Depending upon the season, I use either fresh or dried dates. The dates can be prepared several days ahead and stored in an airtight container until they are sautéed.

1 Pit a date but do not cut all the way through. Stuff with an almond. Press the date closed. Repeat with the remaining dates.

2 Heat the oil in the frying pan over moderate heat. Add the dates and brown very lightly, 2 to 3 minutes. Remove from the heat, season with a touch of salt, and transfer to a serving platter. Serve immediately, offering guests toothpicks and cocktail napkins.

Appetizers, Starters, and First Courses

Niçoise Figs Stuffed with Fennel Seeds and Walnuts

Figues Sèches Farcies aux Noix et aux Graines de Fenouil

Years ago in a little shop in Nice I found these tasty stuffed figs. Their version consisted of delicious dried figs stuffed with fennel seeds and walnuts, then wrapped in fig leaves. My version is a bit simpler: I merely slice the figs partway open, stuff them with a freshly cracked walnut and a few fennel seeds, then press them closed. I layer them in a large canning jar with fresh bay leaves tucked between the figs. They are delicious as an instant appetizer with a glass of Beaumes-de-Venise, as a touch of fruit to serve with the cheese course, or as a quick and simple dessert.

EQUIPMENT: A 1-quart airtight container.

24 dried figs

1 tablespoon fennel seeds

24 freshly cracked walnut halves

24 bay leaves, preferably fresh

Halve each fig, leaving the fruit still attached at the bottom. Stuff each fig with a few fennel seeds and a walnut half. Press each fig closed. In a 1-quart container, layer the figs and the bay leaves. Cover securely and let cure for at least 1 week before serving. The figs will keep, stored in the airtight container, for several months. To serve, arrange the bay leaves on a platter and place the figs on top. The bay leaves are for decoration and should not be consumed.

24 STUFFED FIGS

Black Olive and Dried Fig Spread

Pâté d'Olives Noires et Figues Sèches

*B*lack olives and dried figs are among my favorite foods, and both fruits grow naturally on our property in Provence—so the idea of combining the two is obvious. I adore the chunky nature of this sweet and salty combination. Serve it with toasted Black Olive Fougasse (page 266) as a welcome and out-of-the-ordinary appetizer.

EQUIPMENT: A food processor or blender.

½ cup best-quality French brine-cured black olives, pitted

½ cup dried figs, stem ends trimmed, cut into tiny cubes

In a food processor or blender, combine the olives and the cubed figs. Blend, but allow the mixture to remain a bit chunky. Transfer to an airtight container. Store, refrigerated, for up to 1 week.

I CUP

Herve Poron, the Truffle King

IN A WORLD THAT REVERES truffles above all other things gastronomic, it must feel pretty wonderful to be Hervé Poron, Provence's truffle king. Driving past his small and modern truffle-preserving factory just off a country road outside the village of Vaison-la-Romaine, you would never imagine what this modest building housed. More than 30 tons of truffles pass through his hands each year. Of that, some 10 to 15 tons of fragrant, pungent, pervasively aromatic "black diamonds" unearthed in the hills and villages in the region are brought to his cannery from November to March. About 25 percent of the latter are sold fresh, mostly to restaurants, while the rest are preserved in glass jars or tins and later sold to restaurants and to other canneries and food producers. The same tonnage of white truffles is sold

Hervé Poron, Truffle King

during the summer months. Poron also imports top-quality dried morels from India, selling about 1 ton a month. France, of course, is Poron's largest market, with healthy sales also in the United States, Japan, and Germany.

Plantin

84110 Puymeras
Telephone: 04 90 46 41 44
Fax: 04 90 46 47 04
E-mail: *herve@plantin.com*

BLACK TRUFFLE OPEN-FACED SANDWICHES

Tartines aux Truffes

*T*hese fragrantly delicious open-faced sandwiches are always a highlight of our winter truffle workshop in Provence. It is one of the best ways to appreciate and savor a truffle, whether it's a winter black or a summer white variety.

1 Preheat the broiler.

2 Place the bread on a baking sheet and spread with the Truffle Butter. Grill the bread lightly on one side.

3 Layer each slice of toast with a layer of the marinated truffle slices. Return to the broiler just until the truffles warm slightly, about 30 seconds. Remove from the oven. Season with *fleur de sel*. Serve immediately.

8 SERVINGS

8 slices best-quality sourdough bread or brioche, crusts trimmed and discarded

Several teaspoons Truffle Butter (page 320)

2 or 3 fresh black truffles (about 2 ounces total), thinly sliced and marinated in Truffle Oil (page 319)

Fleur de sel

Wine Suggestion: This elegant starter demands a bubbly glass of Champagne, preferably a vintage one from the house of Veuve Clicquot.

The Truffle Wars of Provence

The truffle wars, you might call them. Wars over prices. Wars over quantity and quality. Wars over whose truffles these really are.

We have a small oak tree–framed vineyard where those strange and rare, fragrant and mysterious black truffles can be found at the edges of the vines from late November to early March. As is the case with the varied wild mushrooms that grow in our woods, all the locals truly believe these truffles are *theirs*. As foreigners we may own the property, but that's a mere legality. The locals have a birthright.

In the early years poachers came up when we were in residence on weekends or holidays, digging around the vineyards with playful mutts with names like Pénélope or Dynamo. We would go out and join the fun, watching as the dogs would assuredly point a paw to a spot in the chalky soil, and we would begin digging. Sometimes we would unearth a treasure—anywhere from the size of an olive to one bigger than a golf ball—and there were days we gathered enough to really experiment with these precious underground wonders.

Now, as truffles get more and more rare and more and more expensive, the playful digging has stopped. Poachers are bolder. They comb the vineyard when we are there and when we are not and most often hand over "our" half as a much-begrudged token.

Actually, if the truffle as it is today did not exist, the French would have to find a worthy substitute. The black truffle has all the qualities of a much-sought-after commodity. It is rare. Man has not been able to reproduce it. It is coveted gastronomically. It can be hunted in secret. And best of all—even in declared markets such as one finds in the village of Richerenches on Saturday or Carpentras on Friday morning—it is still sold out of trunks of cars, the treasures secreted away in old pillowcases made of thick ticking material. An under-the-counter, thumb-your-nose-at-the-Feds cash business—what could be better!

But it does get better. For the same qualities that apply to finding and selling or buying a truffle apply to cooking it. Or not cooking it. In the kitchen, there are few ingredients as tricky. Or with such potential for disaster. Which is why so few cooks, or chefs for that matter, manage to get it right. Assuming that you have a perfect specimen—a truffle that is firm and not spongy, fragrant, and big enough to matter—you can still get yourself in a lot of trouble and turn that expensive luxury into a great big nothing.

It's hard to believe, but what is most appealing about a truffle is its texture. It is crunchy, what the French call *croquant*. And it's in that crunch that you release into your mouth, through your olfactory sense, the earthy, woodsy, magical fragrance of the truffle. Cook a truffle and you lose both crunch and aroma. Slice it and serve it raw and you still are not there. The truffle needs a companion: a touch of olive oil and a sprinkling of French *fleur de sel* are best, for they provide just enough moisture, just enough seasoning, to help the truffle shine.

ROASTED PROVENÇAL CHICKPEAS

Pois Chiches de Provence Grillés

*T*hese delightful roasted chickpeas are as crunchy as peanuts and make a marvelous appetizer or snack any time of the day. I particularly love to season them with ground cumin and freshly ground black pepper, for a spicy hit. But feel free to vary the seasoning according to your mood: with curry powder, hot pepper flakes, or a personal blend of spices.

EQUIPMENT: A nonstick baking sheet.

One 15-ounce can chickpeas, drained, rinsed, and dried in a towel

2 teaspoons fine sea salt

2 teaspoons ground cumin

1 teaspoon freshly ground black pepper

1 Preheat the oven to 450 degrees F.

2 Place the chickpeas in a large bowl. Toss with the salt, cumin, and black pepper. Transfer the seasoned chickpeas to the baking sheet in a single layer. Place the baking sheet in the center of the oven and bake until golden, about 40 minutes, tossing from time to time to keep chickpeas from burning.

3 Remove the baking sheet from the oven and transfer the chickpeas to a shallow bowl to cool. Store in a sealed container at room temperature for up to 1 week.

8 SERVINGS

PROVENÇAL CHICKPEA SPREAD WITH CUMIN

Purée de Pois Chiches au Cumin

*A*t Chanteduc, my Provençal assortment of appetizers usually includes home-cured green and black olives, toasted almonds, and this appealing spread or dip. I prepare this with canned chickpeas (which some call garbanzo beans), adding a good dose of freshly squeezed lemon juice, smooth and creamy sesame paste, and a touch of cumin. The spread is great for toast, crackers, or with ribs of fresh celery.

Combine all the ingredients in a food processor or blender. Blend until smooth. Taste for seasoning. Store in a sealed container in the refrigerator for up to 1 week.

1½ CUPS

EQUIPMENT: A food processor or blender.

One 15-ounce can chickpeas, drained (reserve liquid) and rinsed

¼ cup freshly squeezed lemon juice, or to taste

2 tablespoons sesame paste (tahini)

1 teaspoon fine sea salt

1 tablespoon water or liquid from the canned chickpeas

1 teaspoon cumin seeds

GARDEN EGGPLANT‑CUMIN SPREAD

Purée d'Aubergines au Cumin

There are certain vegetables that thrive in my garden, and one of them is eggplant. Each summer, a few hearty plants produce a healthy batch of shiny purplish‑black elongated eggplants, helping to enhance my ever‑growing repertoire of recipes. This is a cumin‑flecked variation on the Middle Eastern *baba ghanouj*, and is a favored summertime appetizer. I like to pick the eggplants when they are still small— weighing less than 8 ounces—for their flavor is more delicate.

EQUIPMENT: A food processor or blender.

4 small eggplants (each about 8 ounces), rinsed and dried

1 plump clove garlic, peeled, halved, green germ removed

1 tablespoon sesame paste (tahini)

2 tablespoons freshly squeezed lemon juice

1 teaspoon fine sea salt

1 teaspoon cumin seeds

1 Preheat the oven to 450 degrees F.

2 With a meat fork, prick the eggplants all over. Place the eggplants directly on an oven rack in the center of the oven. (Placing them directly on the rack allows the air to circulate as the eggplants cook—they roast rather than steam.) Place a baking sheet on another rack beneath the eggplants to collect any juices. Roast until the eggplants are soft and collapsed, about 25 minutes. There is no need to turn them.

3 Remove the rack with the eggplants from the oven. Place the eggplants on a clean work surface, and with a sharp knife, trim off the stem ends and discard. Cut the eggplants in half lengthwise. With a small spoon, scrape out the pulp; then discard the skins. Transfer the pulp to a food processor or blender. Add the garlic, sesame paste, lemon juice, salt, and cumin seeds and blend thoroughly. Taste for seasoning. Transfer to a bowl and serve as an appetizer with an assortment of raw vegetables or crisp bread. Store in a sealed container in the refrigerator for up to 3 days.

1½ CUPS

DO YOU FIND EGGPLANT BITTER? There are few issues as charged as that of the bitterness in eggplants. To salt and weight or not to salt and weight to extract the bitterness? Years ago, when I was working with chef Joël Robuchon, he was adamant about *not* salting eggplant. Robuchon insisted that only old, soft eggplants were bitter, and the freshest and firmest eggplants exhibited only the freshest, mildest flavor. After growing several varieties of eggplant in my garden, this is my conclusion: truly fresh eggplant has no bitterness whatsoever and is best used immediately, garden to table. The most flavorful variety is the long, thin, dark purple type. Eggplants that are round and bulbous are less flavorful.

The question many still ask is, If I buy an eggplant at the supermarket, do I still salt it? If you can't get perfectly fresh eggplant, go without. Choose another vegetable!

TUNA AND OLIVE SPREAD

Thoïonade

The markets of Provence provide a wealth of inspiration. Colorful stands feature as many as twenty-five varieties of olives—cured in salt, mixed with herbs or garlic, cured in brine, flavored with wild fennel, to name just a few—as well as delicious olive-based spreads made for spreading on crackers and serving with a glass of rosé at aperitif time. This is just one of the many variations inspired by those markets.

In the bowl of a food processor or blender, combine all the ingredients. Process to form a thick paste, adding additional oil if necessary to form a smooth purée. Taste for seasoning. The spread can be stored, covered and refrigerated, for up to 1 week.

1½ CUPS

VARIATION: Along the same lines, prepare a more pungent sardine-based spread, or *sardinade*, substituting a 3¾-ounce can of best-quality sardines cured in olive oil for the canned tuna.

EQUIPMENT: A food processor or blender.

1 cup best-quality French brine-cured black olives (such as Nyons), pitted

2 tablespoons capers in vinegar, drained

2 tablespoons dry red wine

2 plump cloves garlic, peeled, green germs removed, minced

½ teaspoon freshly ground black pepper, or to taste

One 7-ounce can best-quality tuna in olive oil (do not drain)

1 to 2 tablespoons extra-virgin olive oil, as necessary

Olive vendors, Vaison-la-Romaine

each culture has its own
repertoire of appetizer

OF TAPENADE AND OTHER SPREADS

spreads and dips, based on ingredients close at hand. In Provence, the olive—along with tomatoes, anchovies, artichokes, tuna, and mushrooms—forms the base for many of these hors-d'oeuvre designed for spreading on toast as an appetizer or tossing into pasta for a quick, efficient meal. Tapenade—which comes from the Provençal word for capers, or *tapeno*—is the most famous of them all, with the classic version composed of pitted black olives, capers, anchovies, mustard, garlic, thyme, black pepper, and olive oil blended to a smooth purée. In Marseille, the classic version includes rum, since boats used to leave the port loaded with goods and return with rum. During the past few years cooks have gotten more and more creative, making tapenade with green olives, almonds, and a touch of pastis, or combining green or black olives with everything from dried tomatoes to anchovies to sardines. Modern spreads might include a mix of sun-dried tomatoes, fresh tomatoes, mozzarella, garlic, and oil, or even slightly nutty versions based on the prize artichoke blended with garlic, lemon juice, olive oil, and black pepper. No matter how you make them, these spreads are part of a timeless moment of pleasure.

"The aperitif which lasts becomes a veritable meal,
in a sort of waltz of delicacies enjoyed one by one."
—JEAN-LOUIS MARTIN, MAUSSANE-LES-ALPILLES

Appetizers, Starters, and First Courses

MIREILLE'S TOMATO, GREEN PEPPER, OLIVE,
AND ANCHOVY SALAD

BISTROT DE FRANCE GARLIC SALAD

THE POURCEL BROTHERS' GRILLED
CHERRY TOMATO SALAD WITH BALSAMIC VINAIGRETTE

RAOUL'S SUMMER TRUFFLE SALAD

SALAD OF TOMATOES, PINE NUTS, AND BASIL

SUNDAY SALAD OF GREENS, OLIVE TOASTS,
AND MINT-INFUSED FRESH CHEESE

SALADS
Les Salades

COUSCOUS SALAD WITH MINT, PARSLEY, AND TOMATOES

BROCCOLI, AVOCADO, AND PISTACHIOS WITH PISTACHIO OIL

SALAD OF TOMATOES, LEMONS, CROUTONS, CAPERS, AND BASIL

CHANTEDUC SALAD OF GARDEN SORREL AND FRESH MINT

AUTUMN SALAD: WILD MUSHROOMS, PARMESAN, AND ARUGULA

BELGIAN ENDIVE, BROCCOLI, POTATO,
AND GOAT CHEESE SALAD

WINTER SALAD: BELGIAN ENDIVE, YELLOW PEPPER,
FENNEL, AND BLUE CHEESE

Mixed salad greens at the Velleron market

MIREILLE'S TOMATO, GREEN PEPPER, OLIVE, AND ANCHOVY SALAD

La Salade Provençale de Mireille

One Friday in August a friend and I headed for some of our familiar haunts: the olive oil mill in Maussane-les-Alpilles and our favorite pottery shop, Lis Amélie. We couldn't resist a lunch stop at Le Bistrot du Paradou, since we knew that aïoli would be on the menu that day. As we entered the bustling bistro our eyes lit up when we saw that each table was set with this lovely fresh salad: Mireille Pons had lined pottery bowls with lettuce leaves, then arranged in them tomatoes, green peppers, anchovies, and olives, dressed with the complex and fruity olive oil from Maussane. This is the time to bring out your very best oil, since it is a star of this salad.

Layer the bottom of a large, shallow bowl with the lettuce leaves. Carefully arrange the tomatoes on top of the lettuce leaves. Scatter the pepper strips, shallots, parsley, and chives on top of the tomatoes. Drizzle with the oil and season with salt. Arrange the anchovies in a crisscross pattern on top of the tomatoes and peppers. Scatter the olives on top. Allow guests to serve themselves, seasoning with coarsely ground black pepper as desired.

4 SERVINGS

12 large lettuce leaves (such as Boston lettuce, or use arugula), washed and dried

4 semi-ripe tomatoes, cored and cut crosswise into thin slices

1 green bell pepper, trimmed, seeds removed, cut into thin strips

2 shallots, peeled and cut into thin rings

¼ cup fresh parsley leaves

¼ cup finely minced fresh chives

2 to 3 tablespoons fruity extra-virgin olive oil

Fleur de sel

12 anchovy fillets in olive oil, drained

12 brine-cured black olives, preferably from Nyons

A peppermill, for the table

Le Bistrot du Paradou
Jean-Louis and Mireille Pons
13125 Le Paradou
Telephone: 04 90 54 32 70

SOMETIME IN THE EARLY 1980s I bought a bottle of olive oil from the boutique at restaurant L'Oustaù de Baumanière in Les Baux-de-Provence and took it home to my kitchen. The first time I used it, I poured a few tablespoons of the oil into a frying pan and turned on the heat. I turned my back for a second, but soon I stopped in my tracks. I could not believe the aroma wafting through the air—sweet, nutty, complex, intense! I took the frying pan off the stove and just inhaled deeply. I examined the bottle and was determined to track down the mill the next time I was in Provence. It turned out to be oil from the now-famed cooperative Moulin Jean-Marie Cornille in the village of Maussane-les-Alpilles.

This oil, from a mill that dates from 1610, is different in many ways. Most oils around the world are pressed from a single variety of olive, generally one that over time has proved to fare well in the soil and weather of the region. The oil from Moulin Jean-Marie Cornille is pressed from five different varieties of olives—Salonenque, Grossane, Béruguette, Picholine, and Verdale—making what I like to call the Châteauneuf-du-Pape of oil, since Châteauneuf-du-Pape wines can be made with as many as thirteen varieties of grapes. Contributing to a symphony of flavors, each variety of olive brings a different quality to the oil: The Salonenque lends a slight anise taste. The Béruguette gives special qualities of preservation. The Verdale and Picholine bring a grassy flavor, while the Grossane helps to soften the flavors.

The olives are harvested from mid-November to mid-January, but unlike other mills that press the olives immediately, the Maussane cooperative stores the olives in a cool attic for at least a day, with the belief that these ripe and healthy fruits will begin to ferment just a bit before they are crushed, adding yet another desirable layer of taste to the final product.

The olives—about 1,000 tons a year—are pressed in the old-fashioned way: between granite stones. It takes some 10 pounds of olives to yield a single quart of oil, and when one realizes that an olive tree in the area will produce about 20 pounds of olives, that means only 2 quarts per tree! Precious nectar, for sure!

Moulin "Jean-Marie Cornille"
Rue Charloun-Rieu
13520 Maussane-les-Alpilles
Telephone: 04 90 54 32 37 and 04 90 54 38 12
Fax: 04 90 54 30 28
Web: *www.moulin-cornille.com*

Moulin Jean-Marie Cornille,
Maussane-les-Alpilles

BISTROT DE FRANCE GARLIC SALAD

Salade à l'Ail Bistrot de France

When you are in the mood for a real garlic bomb, this is the recipe to turn to! It's a favorite at the super-popular Bistrot de France, an always-crowded, lively spot in the city of Apt. The salad is a mixture of soft butter lettuce, curly frisée, romaine, a touch of celery leaves, and—the secret weapon—tons of minced garlic. Almost everyone in the restaurant orders this copious starter, and when you place your order you are asked if you want it "with or without" garlic. The salad is served with a side portion of the creamiest, runniest artisanal Banon goat's milk cheese, the famous disk made near the village of Banon not far from Apt. I love the Bistrot de France all year round, but especially in the winter months when scrambled eggs are made with truffles, cabbages are stuffed with truffles, and there's wild bull stew *(gardiane de taureau de Camargue)*, as well as *aïoli*—salt cod and vegetables in a garlic-rich mayonnaise—every Friday, the day that this largely Catholic country generally feasts on fish rather than meat. The restaurant also offers some good wines from the Lubéron as well as from Vacqueyras.

3 plump cloves garlic, peeled, halved, green germs removed

About 6 cups (5 ounces) loosely packed mixed greens, such as butter lettuce, frisée, and romaine, washed, dried, and torn into bite-size pieces

½ cup celery leaves, torn into small pieces

Classic Vinaigrette to taste (page 323)

Fine sea salt to taste

Freshly ground black pepper to taste

1 ripe Banon cheese or other soft goat cheese (about 4 ounces)

Braids of garlic

Rub a large salad bowl all over with half a garlic clove. Mince the remaining garlic and toss it into the bowl. Add the lettuce and celery leaves, drizzle with the dressing, and toss until all the leaves are evenly coated with dressing and the garlic is well distributed. Season with salt and pepper. Serve, allowing guests to spoon portions of the ripe Banon on top of the salad. Serve with plenty of toasted country bread.

4 SERVINGS

Bistrot de France
67, place Bouquerie
84400 Apt
Telephone: 04 90 74 22 01

THE POURCEL BROTHERS' GRILLED CHERRY TOMATO SALAD WITH BALSAMIC VINAIGRETTE

La Salade de Tomates-Cerises des Frères Pourcel

*D*epending upon the year, we grow some twenty varieties of tomatoes in our garden at Chanteduc. Most are old varieties, and some are more prolific than others; each year I change the lineup, noting those I love most or love less. Cherry tomatoes of many hues—brilliant red, bright orange, lime green, golden-glow yellow, and yellowish orange—proliferate, and that's when I turn to this amazingly simple and always satisfying salad, which I first sampled at the Compagnie des Comptoirs. This trendy, beautiful restaurant, located within the ancient walls of Avignon, was created by Jacques and Laurent Pourcel, who also have a Michelin three-star restaurant, Le Jardin des Sens, in Montpellier. The Avignon restaurant is located in a restored 15th-century cloister, making for a vast courtyard and abundant indoor dining space. When I prepare this salad at home, I grill the tomatoes over quick-burning grapevine clippings, or *sarments de vigne*, which give the tomatoes a smoky flavor. Serve the salad on clear glass plates for a clean, refreshing presentation.

4 cups salad greens (a mixture of arugula and lettuce)

4 tablespoons finely minced fresh chives

Several tablespoons Balsamic Vinaigrette (page 323)

4 branches of cherry tomatoes (about 6 tomatoes per branch)

Fleur de sel for garnish

La Compagnie des Comptoirs

Laurent and Jacques Pourcel
83, rue Joseph Vernet
84000 Avignon
Telephone: 04 90 85 99 04
Fax: 04 90 85 89 24

1 Preheat a grill or a broiler.

2 Place the salad greens and chives in a bowl and toss with a little vinaigrette. Evenly distribute the salad among four salad plates. Set aside.

3 Place the branches of cherry tomatoes directly on the grill or under the broiler and cook just until they are warmed and some are beginning to burst. Transfer each branch to a salad plate. Drizzle with the remaining vinaigrette. Garnish with *fleur de sel* and serve immediately.

4 SERVINGS

Wine Suggestion: The first time I sampled this, we drank a rosé from the outstanding vineyard of Château Puech Haut, Coteaux du Languedoc. The white, rosé, and red are all a must.

RAOUL'S SUMMER TRUFFLE SALAD

La Salade aux Truffes d'Eté de Raoul

*T*his is a regal salad, rich with the flavor of the white summer truffles of Provence, well-aged Parmigiano-Reggiano cheese, and fresh garden greens flavored with a light olive oil, such as that from the nearby village of Nyons. Raoul Reichrath, Dutch chef-owner of Le Grand Pré restaurant in the village of Roaix, created this perfect August salad. If you can't find truffles, substitute a few top-quality fresh mushrooms. Note that this salad contains no lemon juice or vinegar for the dressing, allowing the truffles— or mushrooms—to star, along with top-quality olive oil.

In a large salad bowl, combine the truffles, cheese, and lettuce and toss to blend. Add the oil and chives, and toss to evenly coat the greens with oil. Season with salt. Carefully arrange the salad on four salad plates and serve immediately.

4 SERVINGS

2 summer truffles (each about 2 ounces), scrubbed and thickly sliced (or substitute mushrooms)

About 20 strips of Parmigiano-Reggiano cheese (preferably aged 24 months), shaved with a vegetable peeler

4 cups fresh lettuce, such as romaine, ribs removed, torn into 3-inch squares

About 3 tablespoon mild olive oil, such as oil from Nyons

1 tablespoon finely minced fresh chives

Fleur de sel to taste

Le Grand Pré

Flora and Raoul Reichrath
Route de Vaison (D 975)
84110 Roaix
Telephone: 04 90 46 18 12
E-mail: *legrandpre@walka9.com*

Flora and Raoul Reichrath, Le Grand Pré

Wine Suggestion: Flora Reichrath, Raoul's wife and the restaurant's *sommelière*, suggests a sweet red wine here, a signature *vin doux naturel* from the village Cave de Rasteau 1998.

Tomatoes of Every Hue

WHEN WE BEGAN OUR vegetable garden in
earnest a few years ago, beginner's enthusiasm
took over. We counted no fewer that twenty
varieties of tomatoes in every color and size,
including the traditional St.-Pierre (small, round,
red, and productive), the workhorse of the
Provençal family vegetable garden. Soon our
palates were tempted by other varieties we had
seen in the markets, especially an heirloom
variety the locals call La Russe, a gigantic, deep-
red type whose dense, sweet, and juicy
specimens easily weigh 2 pounds.

Some tomatoes—especially the pear-shaped
Jaune St.-Vincent—I love just for their looks,
and others—such as the elongated paste tomato
called *Dix Doigts de Naples* ("Ten Fingers from
Naples")—I have to love just for their names.
It's only the black and purple varieties that I
like less than the others: they tend to turn
mushy, and I prefer a red, green, yellow, and
orange palette for my salads.

Each morning from late June to September,
and each day at noon, I take a trip to the
garden to see what I might harvest for breakfast
or lunch. I pick whatever is ripe, no matter the
color, size, or variety. Sometimes I peel and slice
the tomatoes for salad; sometimes I just cut
each tomato into wedges and toss them with a
sprinkle of salt, a drizzle of oil, and a shower of
fresh basil. The only constant is true pleasure,
pure satisfaction.

My favorite varieties:

Red Tomatoes
La Russe
Paola
Dix Doigts de Naples
Money Maker
Coeur de Boeuf
Rouge des Andes

Yellow Tomatoes
Jaune St.-Vincent
Banana Legs
Yellow Stuffer

Orange Tomatoes
Valencia
Coeur de Boeuf Orangé

Green Tomatoes
Evergreen

Striped Tomatoes
Tigerella
Striped Germain

Miniature Tomatoes
Barbaniaka
Poire Rouge
Pêche Rouge
Poire Jaune
Mirabelle Jaune
Cerise Cocktail
Délice du Jardinier
Prune Noir
Green Grape
Tomate-Cerise

SALAD OF TOMATOES, PINE NUTS, AND BASIL

Salade de Tomates, Pignons de Pin, et Basilic

On the theory that "what grows together, goes together," I look out my kitchen window and find the makings of this marvelous salad: myriad varieties of tomatoes and basil from the *potager,* and pine nuts from our towering parasol pines. (Okay, I don't harvest the pine nuts, but they do inspire!) A good pine nut oil is best, but good walnut or hazelnut oil is far from a shabby substitute. Even a very green herbaceous olive oil, like those from the Alpes de Haute-Provence, would not be out of place here.

Layer the sliced tomatoes on a large platter, overlapping as necessary. Season with salt. Sprinkle with the pine nuts and the basil. Drizzle with the lemon juice and oil. Season gently again with salt, then generously with pepper. Let sit for 5 to 10 minutes to allow the flavors to mellow. Serve as a first course or as part of a buffet.

6 TO 8 SERVINGS

6 ripe tomatoes (about 1½ pounds), cored, peeled, and sliced lengthwise

Fleur de sel or fine sea salt to taste

½ cup pine nuts, toasted

1 cup fresh basil leaves, cut into a *chiffonnade*

1 tablespoon freshly squeezed lemon juice

¼ cup pine nut oil (or substitute walnut, hazelnut, or olive oil)

Freshly ground black pepper to taste

SUNDAY SALAD OF GREENS, OLIVE TOASTS, AND MINT-INFUSED FRESH CHEESE

*Salade Verte du Dimanche aux Toasts d'Olives
et Fromage Frais à la Menthe*

*N*early every Sunday for the past twenty years I have spent the morning—and sometimes all day—at the vast antiques market in the village of L'Isle-sur-la-Sorgue. It is an addictive ritual, as it always seems there is some item we are in search of, whether it's a towel with the initials of a friend whose birthday is near, a different tablecloth for entertaining, a new piece of silver, or a set of antique bowls. We rarely stop for lunch, but when we do, it's usually at one of the outdoor cafés where the meal won't take hours, for we go to Isle to shop, not to eat. One Sunday I was pleasantly surprised to be served this tasty salad, a mound of greens flanked by a pair of toast points spread with tapenade and two dollops of fresh sheep's milk cheese—in Provence it is known as *brousse,* in Italy it is known as ricotta—infused with finely chopped fresh mint. This has become a staple in our home ever since, for we can never get enough green salad.

About 6 cups (5 ounces) loosely packed mixed greens such as frisée, radicchio, and oak-leaf lettuce, washed, dried, and torn into bite-size pieces

Several tablespoons Classic Vinaigrette (page 323)

Fine sea salt to taste

Freshly ground white pepper to taste

4 slices sourdough bread, toasted

½ cup Olive Purée from Nyons (page 311)

1 recipe Mint-Infused Fresh Cheese (page 257)

Café du Village
Village des Antiquaires
84800 L'Isle-sur-la-Sorgue
Telephone: 04 90 20 72 31

1 In a large salad bowl, combine the greens and toss to mix. Add enough vinaigrette to evenly coat the greens with the dressing. Season with salt and pepper. Taste for seasoning.

2 Transfer the salad to large dinner plates. Halve each slice of toast. Spread each piece of toast with olive purée. Arrange two slices of toast on either side of each plate. Place two small mounds of the cheese on the opposite sides of each plate. Serve immediately.

4 SERVINGS

Couscous Salad with Mint, Parsley, and Tomatoes

Salade de Couscous à la Menthe, Persil et Tomates

Come summer, I love nothing better than to spend the cool mornings in the kitchen, preparing a grand buffet of vegetable salads for lunch. This salad, an easy, appealing combination of quick-cooking couscous, mint, parsley, and tomatoes, is always included in the assortment. Note that here I find it easier to measure the parsley and mint as whole leaves, then mince them.

In a large, shallow bowl, combine the couscous and salt. Toss with a fork to blend. Add the oil and fluff until the grains are evenly separated and coated with oil. Add the water and continue to fluff. Set aside and occasionally fluff and toss the grains until all the liquid has been absorbed, about 10 minutes. Add the lemon juice, parsley, mint, and tomatoes and toss to blend. Taste for seasoning. The salad can be stored, covered and refrigerated, for up to 2 days.

8 SERVINGS

1 cup instant couscous

1 teaspoon fine sea salt

1 tablespoon extra-virgin olive oil

1⅓ cups water

5 tablespoons freshly squeezed lemon juice

2 cups loosely packed fresh parsley leaves, finely minced

4 cups loosely packed fresh mint leaves, finely minced

4 medium tomatoes, cored, peeled, seeded, and chopped

Salads

37

BROCCOLI, AVOCADO, AND PISTACHIOS WITH PISTACHIO OIL

Brocoli, Avocat, Pistaches et Huile de Pistache

There are days when I simply crave broccoli, and on one of those days I created this salad, which has become a favorite in our household and with students in my cooking classes. I love the green on green—the broccoli with the avocado—and the texture and sweetness added by the pistachios and pistachio oil.

1 tablespoon freshly squeezed lemon juice

½ teaspoon fine sea salt

¼ cup pistachio oil, pine nut oil, almond oil, or extra-virgin olive oil

3 tablespoons coarse sea salt

8 ounces broccoli florets (about 2 cups)

1 ripe avocado

¼ cup salted pistachios, coarsely chopped

Fleur de sel to taste

Freshly ground black pepper to taste

1 In a small jar, combine the lemon juice and fine sea salt, and stir to blend. Add the oil, cover the jar, and shake to blend.

2 Prepare a large bowl of ice water.

3 Bring a large pot of water to a boil over high heat. Add the coarse sea salt and the broccoli. Boil, uncovered, until the broccoli is crisp-tender, 3 to 4 minutes. Immediately drain the broccoli and plunge the florets into the ice water so they cool down as quickly as possible and retain their crispness and bright green color. (The vegetable will cool in 1 to 2 minutes. After that, it will soften and begin to lose crispness and flavor.) Transfer the broccoli to a colander and drain.

4 Halve, peel, and very thinly slice the avocado. Arrange a mound of broccoli in the center of a serving plate. Arrange the avocado slices in a circle around the broccoli. Sprinkle with the pistachios. Drizzle with the lemon and oil mixture, then season with salt and pepper. Let infuse 3 to 4 minutes before serving as a first course or a vegetable course.

4 SERVINGS

DOES YOUR OIL GO RANCID?

THE ONLY GOOD NEWS about oil going rancid is that it is usually *not* your fault. Let's begin with olive oil, the most common oil we use today. In the best of circumstances, the oil is pressed from fruit that is good condition without blemishes and within a few hours of harvest. It is pressed in a mill in which the materials are clean and hygienic, and it is transferred to equally hygienic containers to age and/or decant. If any of these conditions are not perfect, the oil could already be rancid before you open the container. I always advise consumers to buy the smallest size bottle or container possible—say a 1-pint bottle—until you are sure that this is an oil you like and you will want to purchase again. Even once an oil has been deemed a favorite in your home, I still advise purchasing the oil in 1-quart glass containers, which is my habit. I never transfer the oil to another container (that's an invitation to rancidity) and generally keep it on my kitchen counter, since oil is used rapidly in my home. If I am going to be away for any length of time—more than two weeks—I store the oil in the refrigerator.

Nut and seed oils—such as pistachio, almond, pine nut, hazelnut, walnut, peanut, and sesame—are another story. While most good-quality olive oil is cold-pressed, meaning no heat is applied to extract the oil from the olives, almost all nut and seed oils undergo some sort of heating to extract the oil. The heating breaks down the nuts and seeds, making the oil more fragile—and more likely to go rancid with time. I store *all* nut and seed oils in the refrigerator. The day I open the bottle, I write the date on the label. I try to use walnut oil (the most fragile of them all) within six months and the others within a year.

SALAD OF TOMATOES, LEMONS, CROUTONS, CAPERS, AND BASIL

Salade de Tomates, Citron, Croûtons, Câpres et Basilic

*T*his summer salad is composed of some of the season's greatest hits: Meyer lemons from our little trees, a giant Russian variety of tomatoes, and tiny Provençal basil from the garden; whole-grain bread from the village baker; and capers from our little shrub that now produces an abundant supply. And when my caper supply has dwindled, I love to make this with the giant caper berries that form once the flower has bloomed and fallen to the ground. Slicing the lemon paper-thin turns it into an almost sweet fruit, with its tasty juices mingling with the juices of the sweet tomatoes and soaking into the crunchy toasted cubes of bread.

EQUIPMENT: A mandoline or very sharp knife.

1 lemon

4 firm, ripe medium tomatoes (about 1 pound), cored and sliced lengthwise

4 slices whole-grain bread, toasted and cut into cubes

½ cup capers in vinegar (or substitute caper berries in vinegar), drained

1 cup fresh basil leaves

¼ cup extra-virgin olive oil

2 tablespoons best-quality homemade vinegar

Fine sea salt to taste

With a mandoline, cut the lemon into paper-thin slices, shaving the slices directly into a large, shallow bowl to catch all the juices. Layer the sliced tomatoes on top of the lemon. Sprinkle with the bread cubes. Scatter the capers and basil on top. Drizzle with the oil and vinegar. Season with salt. Toss to evenly coat the ingredients. Let sit for 5 to 10 minutes to allow flavors to mellow, then serve as a first course or as part of a buffet.

4 TO 6 SERVINGS

I CAN GET PRETTY EXCITED about the littlest things, and having a productive caper bush is an idea that makes me really excited. I've never known anyone who grew her own capers, but some ten years ago I planted a caper bush—native to Provence—and waited. And waited. And waited. The caper bush is a perennial that comes to life late in the spring, so each spring I would worry that the shrublike plant, with its prickly tendrils that spread out in every direction, was dead. But year after year it came back, and slowly it began to produce those tiny green buds we know as capers. I have a chalkboard in my kitchen that reads PICK CAPERS DAILY!, for if you don't get at the buds each day, they will flower (the most elegant purple and white), and if you are lucky, those flowers will then produce giant fruits—what we know as caper berries. I don't know why, but my bush never gets to the berry stage. After the buds flower, the little stem that seems to be the beginning of a berry falls off.

Once I began picking the capers I had to cure them. I love salted capers, so I carefully covered my daily harvest (then twenty or thirty tiny buds each morning from May to July) with the best coarse sea salt. I waited and waited, and nothing happened. They were just green and very salty. Then I found instructions in an old French cookbook for curing the buds in vinegar. I cured them in every kind of vinegar, from the best homemade red wine vinegar to vintage cider vinegar and even the cheapest white distilled vinegar from the supermarket. The distilled vinegar won hands down, and now that's the way I cure capers. I bring a little jar of vinegar right to the shrub each morning, and drop in the firm green buds. On a good day I can harvest up to 2 cups of capers. Within a day or two they are ready for eating, to toss in salads, serve on pasta, or add to sauces.

CHANTEDUC SALAD OF GARDEN SORREL AND FRESH MINT

Salade Chanteduc à l'Oseille et à la Menthe Fraîche

I can't imagine how many recipes have been created during a simple, pensive walk to and from my garden. This one—now a Monday lunch classic in all of my classes in Provence—came to mind as I was returning with a handful of sorrel from the *potager*. There, the tangy, pleasingly bitter leaves of sorrel are in residence year-round so no matter what, there will be salad on the table! Then I passed a newly planted mint garden that contained no fewer that fifteen varieties. I snipped here and there, added them to the sorrel, and bingo! I hit upon a brilliant marriage of sweet and bitter, a combination that always surprises the palate. I cut both greens into a *chiffonnade*, making for a more delicate, elegant salad. Also, since garden sorrel can be strong and bitter to some palates, cutting it into a *chiffonnade* softens the blow. Serve this in tiny portions, like a little shrub or *buisson*—as the French would say— thinking of it as more of a condiment than a salad.

About 4 cups (3 ounces) loosely packed sorrel leaves, washed, dried, and cut into a *chiffonnade*

About 1 cup fresh mint leaves, cut into a *chiffonnade*

Classic Vinaigrette to taste (page 323)

Fine sea salt to taste

Freshly ground white pepper to taste

In a large bowl, combine the sorrel and mint, and toss lightly to blend. Drizzle with the vinaigrette and toss until all the leaves are evenly coated with dressing. Arrange in a little mound on small individual salad plates. Season with salt and pepper. Serve.

4 SERVINGS

HOW CAN YOU NOT LOVE something that will grow year-round in your garden? Sorrel—that astringent, spinach-like perennial that people either love or hate—seems to relish the Provençal soil and climate. The Romans and Greeks included sorrel at all their banquets, and it has long had medicinal uses to help aid digestion, among other virtues. I am a longtime member of the I Love

Sorrel Club, and so I slip the French *oseille* into salads whenever I can. I almost always cut the green into a *chiffonnade*, or ribbons. To do this, simply pile about twenty stemmed, washed, and dried leaves of sorrel on top of one another. Roll them lengthwise like a cigar. With a sharp knife, cut the roll crosswise into thin ribbons. Dress and serve in tiny mounds.

Autumn Salad: Wild Mushrooms, Parmesan, and Arugula

Chanterelles, Pieds-de-Moutons et Roquette au Parmesan

This dish—with variations found all over France—was first sampled at the hands of Laurent and Jacques Pourcel, the twins known for their Michelin three-star restaurant in Montpellier. There is a lot going on here, so the dish has unlimited possibilities. I have made this with mixed wild mushrooms as well as domestic mushrooms, with equal success and appeal. When roasting a chicken, I always reserve a bit of the juices and freeze them for uses such as this one. Alternatively, I reduce homemade chicken stock over high heat until it forms a thick glaze. The only requirement is that the dish be served warm, so that the cheese and the arugula begin to melt and wilt, exuding a lovely aroma as the dish is served.

1 In a large skillet, heat 2 tablespoons of the olive oil over high heat until hot but not smoking. Cook each variety of mushroom separately, cooking just until the mushrooms begin to give up their juices, about 2 minutes. Add the remaining oil as needed.

2½ tablespoons extra-virgin olive oil

1 pound mixed mushrooms, to include chanterelles and sheep's foot mushrooms (or use portobello or domestic white or brown mushrooms), cleaned and trimmed

¼ cup reserved chicken juices (or use a meat or poultry demi-glace, or chicken stock reduced to a thick glaze)

Sea salt to taste

12 strips (about 2 ounces) of Parmigiano-Reggiano cheese, shaved with a vegetable peeler

12 leaves of arugula, tossed in olive oil

Le Jardin des Sens
Laurent and Jacques Pourcel
11, avenue St.-Lazare
34000 Montpellier
Telephone: 04 99 58 38 38
Fax: 04 99 58 38 39
E-mail: *contact@jardindessens.com*

2 Wipe out the skillet, and in the same skillet, gently rewarm the mushrooms all together, tossing with the chicken juices or reduced stock. Taste for seasoning.

3 Mound the mushrooms on warmed plates and carefully arrange the strips of cheese and the arugula leaves on top of the mushrooms. Serve immediately.

4 SERVINGS

Wine Suggestion: A good fruity white wine, preferably one made from the Viognier grape. A Condrieu from Yves Cuilleron would be heavenly.

Belgian Endive, Broccoli, Potato, and Goat Cheese Salad

Salade d'Endives, de Brocoli, et de Pommes de Terre au Fromage de Chèvre

*W*inter vegetables are often given a once-over, especially when it comes to salads. My husband, Walter, and I are big salad eaters, especially at lunchtime, and I created this winter salad for those cool but sunny Provençal winter days when we lunch in the kitchen by the warmth of the fireplace.

1 In a large bowl, combine the steamed broccoli, potatoes, endive, cheese, and olives and toss to blend. Season to taste with salt and pepper.

2 Place the vinegar and salt to taste in a small bowl. Whisk to dissolve the salt. Add the oil and whisk to blend. Add the pepper. Taste for seasoning.

3 Pour the dressing over the salad ingredients and toss to thoroughly coat the vegetables and cheese. Taste for seasoning. Serve.

4 SERVINGS

NOTE: To steam the vegetables, bring 1 quart of water to a simmer in the bottom of a vegetable steamer. Place the vegetables on the steaming rack. Place the rack over the simmering water, cover, and steam until the vegetables can be pierced with a sharp knife, 10 to 15 minutes, depending upon the size of the vegetables. (You may have to add water from time to time to keep the steamer from running dry.) Drain, and let cool.

8 ounces broccoli florets (about 2 cups), steamed

8 ounces small, yellow-fleshed potatoes (about 4), steamed, peeled, and thinly sliced on the diagonal

1 Belgian endive, trimmed and thinly sliced on the diagonal

2 ounces fresh but firm goat cheese (such as Sainte-Maure), crumbled (about ½ cup)

About 10 green olives, pitted and chopped

Sea salt

Finely ground black pepper

THE DRESSING:

2 teaspoons best-quality red wine vinegar (or substitute freshly squeezed lemon juice)

Fine sea salt

1 tablespoon extra-virgin olive oil

Freshly ground black pepper to taste

Winter Salad: Belgian Endive, Yellow Pepper, Fennel, and Blue Cheese

Salade d'Endives à la Fourme d'Ambert

Walter's favorite winter salad is Belgian endive. I keep the vegetable on hand at all times, and while most often I serve it as a simple chopped salad dressed with our everyday vinaigrette, every now and then I feel a need to embellish just a bit, and I turn it into a main course. This version also includes his favorite cheese, the creamy Fourme d'Ambert from the Auvergne. So I get double points!

1 Place the lemon juice and salt in a bottle. Cover and shake to dissolve the salt. Add the oil and shake to blend. Taste for seasoning. The vinaigrette can be stored at room temperature or in the refrigerator for several weeks. Shake again at serving time to create a thick emulsion.

2 In a large bowl, combine the bell pepper, fennel, and Belgian endive and toss to blend. Add the cheese and toss again.

THE DRESSING:

2 teaspoons freshly squeezed lemon juice

Sea salt to taste

2 tablespoons walnut oil (or substitute olive oil)

1 yellow bell pepper, trimmed, seeds removed, cut into thin strips

1 large fennel bulb, trimmed and thinly sliced

1 Belgian endive, trimmed and thinly sliced

¼ cup crumbled blue cheese (such as Fourme d'Ambert)

Sea salt

Finely ground black pepper

3 Pour the dressing over the salad ingredients and toss to coat the vegetables and cheese. Season generously with salt and pepper and serve.

4 SERVINGS

Salads

CREAMY ZUCCHINI AND FRESH LEMON VERBENA SOUP

FRESH PROVENÇAL VEGETABLE SOUP

LIGHT BASIL SAUCE

THE LAFONTS' MUSSEL SOUP

CHILLED TOMATO SOUP WITH GOAT CHEESE
AND OLIVE PUREE

THE POURCEL BROTHERS' CHILLED LENTIL GAZPACHO
WITH FRESH MINT

SOUPS

Les Soupes et les Potages

LEEK, POTATO, AND TRUFFLE SOUP

PUMPKIN SOUP WITH TRUFFLES AND PUMPKIN SEED OIL

WINTER GRAIN AND BEAN SOUP WITH TOMATOES
AND ROSEMARY

CAMARGUE RICE AND CURRIED LENTIL SOUP

WINTER CARROT AND STAR ANISE SOUP

VEGETARIAN CHILI

CREAMY ZUCCHINI AND FRESH LEMON VERBENA SOUP

Velouté de Courgettes à la Verveine

This is the sort of recipe everyone loves—long on flavor, short on labor, low in calories, and fat-free. It is amazing how creamy the soup appears, yet there is not an ounce of fat. The additional burst of refreshing flavor supplied by the fresh lemon verbena makes it a perfect summer soup. If lemon verbena is not within reach, fresh mint is a worthy substitute.

1 Bring about 3 cups of water to a simmer in the bottom of a vegetable steamer. Place the zucchini and the sprigs of lemon verbena on the steaming rack. Place the rack over the simmering water, cover, and steam until the zucchini is soft, about 10 minutes.

2 Drain, discarding the sprigs of lemon verbena. Transfer the zucchini to a food processor or blender and purée. Once the purée has cooled, add the yogurt or *fromage blanc* and blend. Taste for seasoning. Transfer to a bowl and refrigerate until serving time. (The soup can be made up to 8 hours in advance.)

3 At serving time, reblend the soup to a smooth purée with an immersion blender, food processor, or blender. Taste again for seasoning. To serve, ladle the soup into the bowls and garnish with the *chiffonnade* of fresh lemon verbena.

8 SERVINGS

EQUIPMENT: A vegetable steamer; a food processor or blender; an immersion blender.

2½ pounds fresh zucchini, trimmed and cubed

Several sprigs fresh lemon verbena, plus 24 leaves for garnish, cut into a *chiffonnade* (or use fresh mint leaves)

4 cups plain nonfat yogurt or nonfat *fromage blanc*

Fine sea salt to taste

Round zucchini

I DON'T THINK I HAD ever seen
a live *verveine,* or lemon verbena,
plant before moving to Provence in

VERVEINE/LEMON VERBENA

the early 1980s. And I didn't have a good opinion of this herb, which is abused
in dried form and stuffed into tiny sachets to be sold in cafés as an *infusion de
verveine.* Most often it is insipid, and the resulting liquid tastes no more exciting
than infused dirt.

But, oh, snip a fresh plant—or just swish your hand over it as you walk by—
and you are in another world! The aroma is deep and dense, like a lemon tree on
a high! With its dense, spiky leaves the color of spring and its tiny mauve-toned
flowers, this perennial shrub can grow up to 16 feet tall in Provence. It is one of
those shrubs that emerges late in the spring, and after a cold Provençal winter,
one will think it has indeed given up. But, no, more often than not the lemon
verbena plants survive and then thrive in the dry heat of summer. I have planted
lemon verbena all over the place: in the vegetable garden, where it thrives, as well
as along the entry to the house, so that on a dark evening I need walk only a few
steps to clip the herb for tea infusions, for a favorite sorbet, or for snipping into
a *chiffonnade* and scattering over a chilled zucchini soup.

PROVENÇAL WISDOM

*"In the summertime, if you drink lemon verbena tea all day long,
you will never be bitten by a mosquito."*

FRESH PROVENÇAL VEGETABLE SOUP

Soupe au Pistou

*T*his is an abbreviated version of the more traditional *soupe au pistou*, a fresh vegetable soup that generally includes green beans, carrots, potatoes, pumpkin, zucchini, onions, garlic, tomatoes, and fresh white beans *(cocos blancs)* or fresh cranberry beans *(cocos rouges)* or both. I love the simplicity and beauty of this dish—green and orange, red and white—gathering just the zucchini, pumpkin, green beans, white beans, and tomatoes. Sometimes I think that *soupe au pistou* is just an excuse to anoint the soup with giant dollops of the gorgeous green *sauce au pistou* or Light Basil Sauce. But who needs an excuse? In the heat of summer I serve this both chilled and hot. I always make a large batch, for the soup freezes very well. (For best results do not add the *sauce au pistou* or the cheese before freezing, for the resulting texture and color will be less pleasant.)

1 In the stockpot, combine the oil, garlic, bouquet garni, and salt. Stir to coat with the oil. Sweat over moderate heat until the garlic is fragrant and soft, 3 to 4 minutes. Add the fresh or prepared dried beans and the pumpkin. Stir to coat with the oil. Cover and cook over low heat for 5 more minutes.

Cocos rouges, *red shell beans*

Wine Suggestion: I can't think of anything better than Domaine de la Mordorée's Tavel rosé, a wine that has great power and depth but is still light enough to quaff under the summer's sun.

2 Add the zucchini, tomatoes, tomato paste, green beans, cold water, and salt to taste. Simmer gently, partially covered, until the beans are tender, about 30 minutes. (Cooking time will vary according to the freshness of the beans. Add additional water if the soup becomes too thick.)

3 Remove and discard the bouquet garni. If serving chilled, refrigerate and keep chilled until serving time. At serving time, spoon the soup into chilled or warmed shallow soup bowls. Place a very large basil leaf or a very small lettuce leaf on the edge of the soup plate, and place a spoonful of basil sauce inside the leaf. Garnish with chopped fresh tomato, more basil leaves, and *fleur de sel*. Pass the remaining basil sauce and the cheese to swirl into the soup.

12 SERVINGS

NOTE: If using dried beans, rinse the beans, picking them over to remove any pebbles. Place the beans in a large bowl, add boiling water. Cover, and set aside for 1 hour. Drain the beans, discarding the water. Proceed with step 1.

EQUIPMENT: A large, heavy-bottomed stockpot.

2 tablespoons extra-virgin olive oil

4 plump cloves garlic, peeled, halved, green germs removed, minced

1 bouquet garni: several bay leaves and sprigs of thyme wrapped with the green part of a leek and securely fastened with cotton twine, or secured in a wire mesh ball

Sea salt to taste

2 pounds fresh small white beans in the pod, shelled, or 1 pound dried small white beans (such as cannellini, Great Northern, or marrow beans), soaked (see Note)

1 pound pumpkin, peeled and cubed

1½ pounds small zucchini, trimmed and cut into matchsticks

1½ pounds tomatoes, cored, peeled, seeded, and chopped

2 tablespoons tomato paste

1½ pounds green beans, trimmed at both ends and quartered lengthwise

2 quarts cold water

Several large fresh basil leaves or small lettuce leaves, for garnish

1 recipe Light Basil Sauce (page 56)

1 large tomato, cored, peeled, seeded, and chopped, for garnish

Fleur de sel to taste

1 cup (4 ounces) freshly grated Parmigiano-Reggiano cheese

Soups

BOUQUET GARNI

TRADITIONALLY, A BOUQUET GARNI—most often made up of dried or fresh herbs and usually including thyme, parsley, and bay leaf—is wrapped with the green part of a leek and tied securely with cotton twine. For the past several years I have used instead a wire mesh tea infuser. I have a collection of sizes and shapes, measuring from 2 inches to 10 inches round. When I prepare a soup, I choose the size ball that will fit the bill and stuff the ball with the herbs and spices that go with the soup. With a fine-mesh ball, little bits of herb won't end up in your soup. Nor will you forget to remove the tea ball at serving time!

DURING THE 1890s, the little train that went from Orange to the village of Buis-les-Baronnies (long known as the main market for *tilleul,* or linden blossoms) was not only a fabulous

 *LE COCO DE MOLLANS/ WHITE BEANS FROM MOLLANS-SUR-OUVEZE*

method of transportation for the locals but also a boon for agriculture. All sorts of products could go from tiny villages to the big city of Orange, and then be shipped quickly by train to Lyon and Marseille and beyond.

One local product whose producers profited from the train was the special white bean or *coco de Mollans,* from the tiny perched village of Mollans-sur-Ouvèze in the Drôme Provençale. In its heyday, the village farmers produced some 1,000 tons annually. The nutty, smooth, and soft white bean encased in a pale green pod is an essential ingredient in the ever-popular Provençal dish known as *soupe au pistou.* The locals believed that it was not only the soil of Mollans that was special but the climate as well, for the valleys below are protected from the mighty mistral wind, creating a bean that is more moist than its counterparts subjected to the fierce winds of Provence.

When the train from Orange to Buis-les-Baronnies stopped running in the 1950s, the Mollans bean farmers lost their market, and the crop was reduced to next to nothing, with beans soon found at only a few weekly peasant markets in the area. But in the early 1990s, farmers decided to re-popularize the legume, and today the locals are again producing some 1,000 tons a year. The bean is found in markets in the late summer and early fall, and is distinguished by the bright blue and green banner displayed across its packing crate. The beans area always sold in the pod, with five to six beans per pod. The farmers have created a syndicate to promote the bean and have set up agricultural standards. Someday—maybe ten or twenty years down the road—they hope to obtain their own *appellation d'origine contrôlée,* a national guarantee of quality for the tasty legume.

A banner for cocos blancs, *white shell beans, of Mollans-sur-Ouvèze*

*Soups*

55

Light Basil Sauce

Sauce Légère au Basilic

*T*here are many days, particularly in the heat of summer, when I want the hit of basil and the texture of the sauce, but with a bit less fat. So I created this light sauce, which I use regularly in place of the traditional basil sauce known as *pistou*. While its most traditional use is as a sauce for the Provençal vegetable soup known as *soupe au pistou* (page 52), I put it on everything. I use it as a sauce for pasta, dab it on pizza along with tomato sauce, pair it with poached fish, and swirl it in a soup.

4 plump cloves garlic, peeled, halved, green germs removed, minced

⅛ teaspoon fine sea salt

4 cups loosely packed fresh basil leaves and flowers

6 tablespoons extra-virgin olive oil

BY HAND: Place the garlic and salt in a mortar and mash with a pestle to form a paste. Be patient and work slowly and evenly. Add the basil little by little, pounding and turning the pestle with a grinding motion to form a paste. Slowly add the oil, turning the pestle with a grinding motion until all the oil has been used. The sauce will not form an emulsion like a mayonnaise, but, rather, the basil leaves will remain suspended in the oil. Taste for seasoning. Stir again before serving.

IN A FOOD PROCESSOR: Place the garlic, salt, and basil in the bowl of a food processor and process to a paste. With the machine running, slowly pour the oil through the tube and process again. Taste for seasoning. Stir again before serving.

Transfer to a small bowl. (The sauce can be stored, covered and refrigerated, for 3 days or frozen for up to 6 months. Bring to room temperature and stir again before serving.)

⅔ CUP; TWELVE
1-TABLESPOON SERVINGS

ORIGINS The word *pistou* comes from the Latin word *pestare*, which means "to crush."

EXPRESSIONS *Semer du basilic:* a French expression for slandering others.

CUSTOMS A Provençal custom: Place a basil plant in the window, and you will not be attacked by mosquitoes, flies, or bats in the summer months!

I THINK I HAVE a lot of basil plants, with eight different varieties lined up in my vegetable garden, but once you realize that there are some 400 varieties of basil in the world, my collection seems pretty meager. This aromatic, mentholated plant is a dream: it can be used as is to flavor salads, pounded into a rich sauce when combined with olive oil and salt for a lofty *sauce au basilic,* slipped between layers of tomatoes for a perfect salad dressed with a vinaigrette, and even used as the base of a vinaigrette itself.

Tiny-leafed basil

One of the two basic green basils one finds in Provence is the highly perfumed, piquant, tiny-leafed variety known as *Le Marseillais,* and it is the best in my book for a brilliantly flavored *sauce au pistou* and for tucking into salads. There's also the large-leafed *Genovaise,* great for scattering over tomatoes. And for drama, I like to use the large-leafed purple variety in a tomato salad that includes tomatoes of every hue. I reserve Thai and lemon basils for delicately flavored vegetables such as zucchini.

We don't think of basil as a "sweet" plant, but it actually cuts the acidity of tomato, lemon, and vinegar, which is why it is often paired with them. Tiny leaves are sweeter than larger leaves, and if one searches, one finds varieties that hint of lemon, anise, thyme, jasmine, ginger, and even cloves.

Basil is fragile, and there is no point in using it any other way than fresh, for it loses its vibrant personality if it is cooked, dried, or frozen. Always add basil at the last moment, for it darkens once it comes into contact with an acid such as lemon juice or vinegar.

Soups

THE LAFONTS' MUSSEL SOUP

La Soupe aux Moules des Lafont

*E*dmond and Arlette Lafont have been selling fish in Provence since April 1957. They have a thriving business, offering the very freshest line-caught fish as well as shellfish harvested from Brittany and Provence, sold from their fish trucks that tour the markets of the region. I have been buying fish from them since 1984, and I admit that even in Paris it is hard to find seafood as brilliantly fresh as theirs. The Lafonts kindly loaned me their family cookbook, and from it I gleaned this pleasing soup recipe. This is a soothing, simple soup, golden with saffron and pasta, punctuated by the sweetness of the mussels and the lactic hit of cheese.

EQUIPMENT: Two large saucepans with lids; a fine-mesh sieve; dampened cheesecloth.

2 pounds mussels

1 tablespoon extra-virgin olive oil

2 onions, peeled, halved lengthwise, and thinly sliced

Fine sea salt

1 bottle white wine

1 quart mineral water

¼ teaspoon saffron threads

8 ounces small pasta, such as *orzo* or *rosmarino*

1 cup (4 ounces) freshly grated Parmigiano-Reggiano cheese

Freshly ground black pepper

1 Thoroughly scrub the mussels, and rinse with several changes of water. If an open mussel closes when you press on it, then it is good; if it stays open, the mussel should be discarded. Debeard the mussels. (Do not do this more than a few minutes in advance or the mussels will die and spoil. Note that in some markets mussels are cleaned, in that the small black beards have been clipped off but not entirely removed. These mussels do not need further attention.) Set aside.

2 In a large saucepan, combine the oil, onions, and a pinch of salt and stir to blend. Sweat—cook, covered, over low heat until soft but not browned—for about 3 minutes. Set aside.

3 Pour the wine into another large saucepan. Bring to a boil and boil, uncovered, for 5 minutes. Add the mussels, cover, and cook just until the mussels open, about 5 minutes. Do not overcook. Discard any mussels that do not open. Transfer the mussels to a large bowl. Place a sieve over a bowl and line the sieve with several thicknesses of dampened cheesecloth. Carefully strain the liquid through the sieve.

4 Transfer the strained liquid to the pan with the onions. Add the water and saffron, and bring to a boil. Add the pasta and cook until al dente.

5 Meanwhile, remove the mussels from their shells, discarding the shells. Place the mussels in a small bowl and set aside.

6 To serve, taste the soup for seasoning. Ladle the soup into warmed shallow soup bowls. Spoon the mussels into the center of the bowls. Sprinkle with pepper and cheese and serve.

6 TO 8 SERVINGS

The Lafonts are at the following markets in Provence, 8:30 a.m. to noon:

MONDAY: Bollène

TUESDAY: Vaison-la-Romaine

THURSDAY: Sablet and Orange

FRIDAY: Mirabel-aux-Baronnies

SATURDAY: Vaison-la-Romaine

CHILLED TOMATO SOUP WITH GOAT CHEESE AND OLIVE PUREE

Potage Glacé à la Tomate au Fromage de Chèvre et Crème d'Olives

What better way to announce the summer flavors of Provence than with ripe red tomatoes, pure white goat cheese, and deep black olive purée? The flavors are equally appealing, all tied together with the sweet touch of fresh mint. This dish is at its refreshing best served very cold.

1 Place the soup bowls in the refrigerator to chill.

2 In a food processor or a blender, combine the tomatoes, lemon juice, olive oil, and salt. Purée. Taste for seasoning. Transfer to a bowl and cover securely with plastic wrap. Refrigerate for at least 1 hour and up to 24 hours.

3 At serving time, reblend the soup to a smooth purée with an immersion blender, food processor, or blender. Pour the soup into the soup bowls. Break off a small piece of goat cheese and, with your hands, roll the cheese into a tiny ball. Place the ball of cheese on top of the soup in the center of the bowl. Place a tiny dollop of olive purée alongside the goat cheese. Garnish with mint and serve.

8 SERVINGS

EQUIPMENT: A food processor or blender.

10 to 12 medium fresh tomatoes (about 3 pounds), cored, peeled, seeded, and chopped

2 tablespoons freshly squeezed lemon juice

1 tablespoon extra-virgin olive oil

2 teaspoons fine sea salt

8 teaspoons soft, fresh goat cheese

8 teaspoons Olive Purée from Nyons (page 311)

12 fresh mint leaves, cut into a *chiffonnade*

Wine Suggestion: A chilled white wine from Les Baux-de-Provence, such as the Mas de la Dame, promising the scents of Provence and opulent fruit.

ON PEELING TOMATOES: Years ago, Italian cooking teacher Marcella Hazan introduced me to her method of peeling fresh tomatoes, and I have used it ever since. With a sharp knife, remove the core of the tomato. With a vegetable peeler, peel the tomato using a back-and-forth sawing motion. In recipes such as this—where the tomato is not cooked—it is essential to peel the tomato in this manner to preserve its flavor and texture. In recipes where the tomato will be cooked, you might prefer to remove the peel by plunging the (uncored) tomato in boiling water for 1 minute and then slipping off the skin.

THE POURCEL BROTHERS' CHILLED LENTIL GAZPACHO WITH FRESH MINT

La Crème de Lentilles en Gaspacho
à la Menthe Fraîche des Frères Pourcel

I first sampled this mysterious soup at Jacques and Laurent Pourcel's restaurant in Paris, La Maison Blanche. I say "mysterious" because no matter how I tried, I could not figure out what the specific, nuanced flavor was in the soup. I later discovered that the secret ingredient was just a few drops of peppermint extract. It is amazing how this refreshing flavor perks up the flinty nature of dark green lentils. At both La Maison Blanche and Le Jardin des Sens, the twin brothers' Michelin three-starred restaurant in Montpellier, they serve this soup chilled, in tiny espresso cups. I have often spent time with them in their kitchen and am a huge fan of their style: just the right blend of modern and classic, with a youthful touch.

EQUIPMENT: 8 espresso cups; a large heavy stockpot with a lid; a food processor or blender; a food mill fitted with the finest blade.

1 carrot, peeled and finely cubed

1 onion, peeled, halved, and thinly sliced

1 leek, white part only, washed and cut into thin rounds

2 teaspoons extra-virgin olive oil

Fine sea salt to taste

1 cup French lentils, preferably *lentilles du Puy*, rinsed and drained

1 quart Homemade Chicken Stock (page 325), or more as needed

1 or 2 drops peppermint extract

12 fresh mint leaves, cut into a *chiffonnade*

1 Place the espresso cups in the refrigerator.

2 In the stockpot, combine the vegetables, oil, and salt and stir to coat with the oil. Sweat—cook, covered, over low heat until soft but not browned—for about 3 minutes. Add the lentils and stock. Cook, covered, over low heat until the lentils are soft, about 20 minutes. Add additional stock or water as necessary.

3 Purée the lentil mixture in a food processor or blender. Pass it through the food mill into a large bowl. Add the peppermint extract. Be cautious—the flavor of mint should not be overpowering. Cover the bowl securely with plastic wrap. Refrigerate for at least 1 hour and up to 24 hours.

4 At serving time, whisk the soup with a fork to blend once again. Pour into the chilled espresso cups. Garnish with mint and serve.

8 ESPRESSO-CUP SERVINGS

Le Jardin des Sens
Laurent and Jacques Pourcel
11, avenue St.-Lazare
34000 Montpellier
Telephone: 04 99 58 38 38
Fax: 04 99 58 38 39
E-mail: *contact@jardindessens.com*

Soups

Leek, Potato, and Truffle Soup

Potage Parmentier aux Truffes

*A*ll root vegetables—especially potatoes, leeks, and turnips—seem to marry well with the earthy pungency of truffles. Poor man, rich man—why not?

1 Trim the leeks at the roots and split them lengthwise for easier cleaning. Rinse well under cold running water. Transfer to a bowl of cold water and soak for 5 minutes to get rid of any excess dirt. When all the grit has settled to the bottom of the bowl, remove the leeks and dry thoroughly. Chop coarsely and set aside.

2 In the stockpot, combine the butter, a pinch of salt, and the leeks and sweat—cook, covered, over low heat until soft but not browned—for about 3 minutes. Add the cubed potatoes and milk and cover. Simmer gently, stirring often, for another 10 minutes. Taste for seasoning.

3 Process the mixture in a food processor or a blender, or with an immersion blender, until smooth. Return the soup to the pot, increase the heat to high, and bring to a gentle boil. Using a slotted spoon, skim off any impurities that may rise to the surface. Add pepper. Taste for seasoning.

4 To serve, ladle the soup into warmed soup bowls. Serve immediately, allowing guests to shave fresh truffles over their soup.

EQUIPMENT: A large stockpot with a lid; a food processor, blender, or immersion blender; a truffle slicer or small mandoline.

2 medium leeks, white and tender green parts

3 tablespoons unsalted butter

Sea salt

1 pound potatoes (3 medium), peeled and cubed

2 quarts whole milk

Freshly ground white pepper to taste

1 fresh black truffle (about 2 ounces), cleaned

THE PROVENCE COOKBOOK

Pumpkin Soup with Truffles and Pumpkin Seed Oil

Velouté de Potiron aux Truffes et Huile de Courge

*O*ne January afternoon our winemaker, Ludovic Cornillon, and I hosted a luncheon for employees and distributors of our wine, imported in the U.S. by our friend Kermit Lynch in Berkeley, California. We set up a huge heated tent on the property to accommodate the twenty-five guests, and we crossed our fingers. There was snow on the ground; it poured buckets all morning, and I envisioned the service staff holding umbrellas as they served the meal. Miraculously, at noon, the clouds vanished, the sun shone bright, and by the time dessert was to be served, a beautiful rainbow sparkled in the eastern sky! This velvety pumpkin soup is particularly gorgeous when served in clear white bowls, showered with a few shavings of fragrant black truffles and just a drizzle of deep green pumpkin seed oil. Do use fresh pumpkin for this dish, not canned: the flavors will be fresher and more alive. And please don't use Halloween pumpkins for this soup, for they're too watery and tasteless.

EQUIPMENT: A 6-quart stockpot with a lid; a food processor, blender, or immersion blender; a truffle slicer or small mandoline.

2 pounds pumpkin or butternut squash, peeled and cubed

1 quart Homemade Chicken Stock (page 325)

Sea salt to taste

Freshly ground white pepper to taste

1 fresh black truffle (about 2 ounces), cleaned and cut into thin rounds

About 1 teaspoon pumpkin seed oil, pistachio oil, or walnut oil

1 In the stockpot, combine the pumpkin and stock and bring to a boil over high heat. Cover and boil until the pumpkin is soft, about 15 minutes.

2 Purée the mixture in a food processor, blender, or with an immersion blender until smooth. (The soup may be prepared ahead of time up to this point. Cool and refrigerate.)

3 At serving time, return the mixture to the stockpot and bring to a boil again. With a flat-mesh sieve, skim off any scum that rises to the top. Taste for seasoning. Serve immediately, in warmed shallow soup bowls, garnished with truffles and pumpkin seed oil.

4 SERVINGS

Soups

OF POTIRON AND POTIMARRON

HOW CLEVER OF THE French to sell their *courge d'hiver*—which we call winter squash—by the handy *tranche,* or slice. I find that I use the vegetable far more often than I would if I had to purchase a huge, imposing squash.

The four most common types of winter squash found in Provence are the Muscade de Provence, a squash with a sandy orange-hued peel and dense, exuberant orange flesh; the small—4- to 5-pound—Potimarron, with its bulbous onion shape and shiny, deep orange exterior; the Potiron, which could be mistaken for a Citrouille, or Halloween pumpkin, but is smaller, less round, and with denser flesh; and the Courge Musquée, or butternut squash, which looks like a giant pear, with a golden exterior and salmon-colored flesh.

I use squash throughout the year, adding it cubed to vegetable soups in the summer, and alone as a great winter soup laced with a bit of fresh black truffles.

In the Potager du Roi, in Versailles, one finds more than fifty varieties of squash and pumpkins. Here are some of the most popular found in France, and their general uses:

MUSCADE DE PROVENCE Loved for its musky aroma and thick, dense flesh, this all-purpose squash is great in soups, as a vegetable purée, or in desserts.

POTIRON—EUROPEAN PUMPKIN Used mostly for soups, gratins, flans, and cakes.

POTIMARRON—HOKKAÏDO, RED KURI, OR COURGE DE CHINE Sweet, with a fine texture; used in making confiture or jams, savory cakes, and tarts.

COURGE MUSQUÉE—BUTTERNUT SQUASH Popular in soups, steamed or roasted as a vegetable, or American-style, in a tart or pie. Loved for its buttery flavor, thus the name.

Potimarron, a variety of squash

BUTTERCUP Simply roasted.

CITROUILLE—HALLOWEEN PUMPKIN OR JACK'O'LANTERN
Decorative, carved for Halloween.

PÂTISSON—PRIEST'S BONNET OR ISRAELI ARTICHOKE Tiny summer
squash, usually pickled.

COURGERON OR COURGE POIVRÉE—ACORN SQUASH Simply baked and
enjoyed for its delicate taste of almonds and walnuts.

> *When you feel as though your head is going to burst,*
> *you might say you have a head like a pumpkin,*
> *or "la tête comme une citrouille!"*

Winter Grain and Bean Soup with Tomatoes and Rosemary

Soupe d'Epeautre, Haricots, Tomates et Romarin

*D*o you want to fill your kitchen with the warming aroma of rosemary? Then head in there and make this filling winter soup, which will warm your bones as well as your soul. One winter's Saturday I had just come back from the market with a new crop of the wheat-like grain *épeautre*, or spelt, and while making bread and dessert I decided to put this soup on to cook. It filled the kitchen with the woodsy perfume of fresh rosemary. My husband, Walter, adores soup and managed to devour this in record time.

1 Place the *épeautre* and beans in the sieve and rinse under cold running water. Set aside.

EQUIPMENT: A fine-mesh sieve; a food processor or blender; a large stockpot with a lid.

1 cup *épeautre* (spelt, or substitute wheat berries)

1 cup dried kidney beans

1 cup dried cranberry beans

2 tablespoons extra-virgin olive oil

Several large sprigs fresh rosemary, wrapped securely in cheesecloth

Sea salt

One 28-ounce can peeled Italian plum tomatoes in their juice, tomatoes and juice puréed in a food processor or blender

About 2½ quarts cold water

Extra-virgin olive oil, for the table

2 In the stockpot, combine the *épeautre*, beans, oil, rosemary, and 1 teaspoon sea salt. Add the puréed tomatoes and 2 quarts of the cold water. Simmer, covered, over low to moderate heat until the grains are tender, about 45 minutes, adding additional water as necessary. (Cooking time will depend upon the freshness of the grains—older grains take longer to cook.) Remove and discard the rosemary. Taste for seasoning. (This soup is even more delicious the second day, after the flavors have had time to ripen.)

3 Serve piping hot, drizzled with extra-virgin olive oil.

8 SERVINGS

Fresh herbs from Provence

CAMARGUE RICE AND CURRIED LENTIL SOUP

Soupe au Riz de Camargue et aux Lentilles

*R*ice and lentils warm the soul on those chilly days in winter, when I love to spend the day testing recipes as the kitchen fills with the fragrance of grapevine clippings burning in the fireplace. I find a restorative appeal in the warm, dense liquids. We like a bit of spice in our house, so I don't mind going heavy on the curry here. My favorite rice for this recipe is southern France's *riz de Camargue*, a rice that is golden, nutty, fragrant, and flavorful.

1 Place the lentils in the sieve and rinse under cold running water. Set aside.

2 In the stockpot, combine the oil, bouquet garni, onion, carrots, and 1 teaspoon salt. Sweat—cook, covered, over low heat until soft but not browned—for about 3 minutes. Add the stock and bring to a simmer over moderate heat. Add the lentils, rice, and curry powder and stir. Simmer, covered, until the grains are tender, about 20 minutes. (Cooking time will depend upon the freshness of the lentils—older lentils take longer to cook.) Remove and discard the bouquet garni. Taste for seasoning. (This soup is even more delicious the second day, after the flavors have had time to ripen.)

3 Serve piping hot, in warmed soup bowls. At the table, season with a spoonful of yogurt and a sprinkling of cumin.

EQUIPMENT: A fine-mesh sieve; a large stockpot with a lid.

1½ cups French lentils, preferably *lentilles du Puy*, rinsed and drained

2 tablespoons extra-virgin olive oil

1 bouquet garni: several parsley stems, celery leaves, and sprigs of thyme, wrapped in the green part of a leek and securely fastened with cotton twine, or secured in a wire mesh ball.

1 large onion, peeled and thinly sliced

2 large carrots, peeled and finely chopped

Fine sea salt

2 quarts Homemade Chicken Stock (page 325)

½ cup Camargue rice or long-grain brown rice

About 2 teaspoons Homemade Curry Powder (page 326), or more to taste

½ cup nonfat plain yogurt

½ teaspoon ground cumin

THE CAMARGUE—the wild, wet, and sandy patch
of land just south of Arles—is France's rice capital.
Although France has grown rice since the 13th century,
and has tried growing the popular grain all over the country, nature decided
that the soil and climate of the Camargue was best for rice. Here, the often
pesky mistral wind is a boon, for it serves to dry out the rice fields after a rain.
Not surprisingly, the region is as far north as rice is grown in the Northern
Hemisphere. Camargue rice—with production of about 122,000 tons a year—
accounts for only 5.6 percent of European production, far behind that of Spain,
Portugal, or Italy. The most popular type of rice here is long-grain, with my
favorite brand Riz Canavère, a superior long-grain variety that is golden, nutty,
and remains pleasantly firm when cooked.

CAMARGUE RICE

Café du Centre, Villedieu

WINTER CARROT AND STAR ANISE SOUP

Soupe d'Hiver aux Carottes et à l'Anis Etoilé

*T*his gorgeous, fragrant soup offers the most mysterious and delicious medley of flavors. The intense infusion of star anise—that star-shaped spice the French call *badiane*—will amaze you. In winter months, I like to serve this soup in tiny white porcelain espresso cups as my guests arrive and I am putting the finishing touches to the meal.

1 In the stockpot, heat the oil over moderate heat until hot but not smoking. Add the carrots and cook, uncovered, for about 5 minutes. Add the stock and salt. Cover and cook over low heat until the carrots are meltingly tender, about 50 minutes. Remove from the heat. Add the star anise, cover, and infuse for 20 minutes. Remove and discard the star anise.

2 Transfer the mixture in batches to a food processor or a blender and purée. Taste for seasoning. Serve hot, in warmed espresso cups.

8 DEMITASSE SERVINGS

EQUIPMENT: A large stockpot with a lid; a food processor or blender; 8 espresso cups.

1 tablespoon extra-virgin olive oil

1 pound carrots, peeled and cut into 1-inch pieces

3 cups Homemade Chicken Stock (page 325)

Sea salt to taste

4 whole star anise

Wine Suggestion: This elegant soup should be paired with a fine and elegant wine, such as Pierre Gaillard's fruity, spontaneous white Crozes-Hermitage.

VEGETARIAN CHILI

Huit Personnes, Sans Chili

A favorite place to eat in our neighborhood on Sunday evenings is in the charming village square of Villedieu. They didn't name it God's Town for nothing, for the sycamore-filled *place* is right out of central casting, complete with the Café du Centre, with its worn shutters and properly faded sign. One summer the café decided to hold an American-style chili party. By the time we reserved, they were out of chili and we found on our table a little note saying *"Huit Personnes, Sans Chili."* I'll never know how good their chili was, but I love this personal version, one I make whenever I want a bit of spice in my life.

In the soup pot, combine the oil, carrots, leek, red pepper, celery, and salt. Sweat—cook, covered, over low heat until soft but not browned, about 5 minutes. Add the puréed tomatoes, cold water, beans, chili powder, and rice and stir. Simmer, covered, until the flavors are well blended, about 15 minutes. Taste for seasoning.

8 SERVINGS

EQUIPMENT: A food processor or blender.

2 teaspoons extra-virgin olive oil

2 carrots, peeled and cut into thin rounds

1 leek, white part only, washed and cut into thin rounds

1 red bell pepper, stemmed, seeds removed, cut into fine dice

2 ribs celery, cut into thin slices

1 teaspoon fine sea salt

One 28-ounce can peeled plum tomatoes in their juice, puréed in a food processor or blender

1 quart cold water

One 15-ounce can kidney beans, rinsed and drained

4 teaspoons chili powder (or to taste)

2 cups cooked rice

Wine Suggestion: This is where I draw the line at wine, and go for a chilled beer instead.

POUR VOS TOASTS
le TARTARE D'AIGUES
LES RiLLETTES
AUX DEUX SAUMONS
... LLES DE MAQUEREAUX

ECOSSE
ÉLEVÉ
label Rouge
Filets de saumon
PORTION
22
5,7
THON

POACHED SALT COD WITH VEGETABLES AND GARLIC MAYONNAISE

GARLIC MAYONNAISE

TUNA FILLET WITH MEYER LEMONS AND SUMMER SAVORY

MY FISHMONGER'S TUNA DAUBE WITH GREEN OLIVES
AND RED WINE

TANDOORI SHRIMP

QUICK-CURED SARDINES

SEA BASS ROASTED IN A SALT CRUST

SIX-MINUTE COD BRAISED IN SPICY TOMATO SAUCE

FISH AND SHELLFISH

Les Poissons, Coquillages et Fruits de Mer

SIX-MINUTE SALMON BRAISED IN VIOGNIER

PIC'S FRESH CRAB SALAD WITH LIME ZEST

LE GRAND PRE'S SEARED AND ROASTED SALMON
WITH SORREL SAUCE

ELIANE'S BARBECUED MUSSELS

TWO-MINUTE STEAMED SQUID WITH GARLIC, LEMON,
AND PARSLEY

SQUID STEWED IN TOMATOES AND WHITE WINE

MUSSELS WITH PESTO

MUSTARD-MARINATED GRILLED MACKEREL

*Aymar Berenger, Julie Legrand and Eliane Berenger
at La Poissonnerie des Voconces in Vaison-la-Romaine*

POACHED SALT COD WITH VEGETABLES AND GARLIC MAYONNAISE

Grand Aïoli

"Aïoli epitomizes the heat, the power, and the joy of the Provençal sun, but it has another virtue—it drives away flies."
—FRÉDÉRIC MISTRAL, PROVENÇAL POET, 1830–1914

Old customs die hard, and though this very Catholic country of France no longer insists that there be a day without meat, Friday is still a fish day as far as the Provençal diet is concerned. You see fish trucks parked in nearly every village, so that housewives can fill their baskets with sardines and anchovies, mackerel, and sweet, tiny mussels from the Bassin de Thau off the Mediterranean. But the favorite Friday fish of all is salt cod, the main ingredient of the popular one-dish meal known as *aïoli*, which is served with the garlic-rich mayonnaise of the same name. Traditional *aïoli* includes good portions of poached salt cod, which the French call *morue salée*, along with steamed green beans,

carrots, potatoes, cauliflower, and hard-cooked eggs. Some cooks add the local tiny snails known as *petits gris*, and others add cooked beets and steamed artichokes. A proper *aïoli* is served only at lunch, giving the digestive system a good long time to deal with the richness of the sauce. The meal is a festive affair, and often the sauce is served direct from the giant stone or marble mortar and olive-wood pestle essential to every Provençal kitchen. Since it is usually quite hot when *aïoli* is served, it's perfectly fine if everything is at room temperature, but never cold. As one drives around Provence in the summer months, one often see posters tacked on a tree announcing an *Aïoli Géant!* Follow the signs and you are sure to have a festive meal, downed with plenty of chilled local rosé.

Mireille Pons and Pascal Estève in the kitchen at Le Bistrot du Paradou

1 One or 2 days before preparing the final dish—depending upon the saltiness of the fish—place the salt cod in a bowl of cold water and soak, covered, in the refrigerator. Change the water three or four times during the soaking period to remove excess salt. Drain and rinse the fish.

2 Place the cod in a large saucepan. Add fresh cold water to cover, along with the orange zest, fennel branches or quarters, onion pricked with cloves, and peppercorns, and bring just to a simmer over medium heat. Immediately remove the pan from the heat. Cover and let stand for at least 15 minutes. Drain well and discard the flavorings. Scrape any fatty skin off the fish and remove any bones. Tear the fish into large pieces and arrange on a platter.

3 Cooking each vegetable separately, steam the beets, potatoes, and carrots. Peel and halve or quarter the beets and arrange on a separate platter for just the vegetables. Add the potatoes to the platter. Halve the carrots lengthwise and arrange on the platter.

4 Separately blanch, refresh, and drain the cauliflower and green beans. Arrange the cauliflower and beans on the platter. Arrange the eggs around the edges of the platter. Bring the platters to the table and serve with the sauce.

8 SERVINGS

EQUIPMENT: A vegetable steamer; a 6-quart pasta pot fitted with a colander.

2 pounds salt cod

Grated zest of 1 orange

A handful of dried fennel branches or 1 fennel bulb, quartered

1 onion, stuck with 4 whole cloves

6 black peppercorns

1 pound small beets

2 pounds small potatoes, scrubbed but not peeled

1 pound medium carrots, peeled

1 whole cauliflower (about 2 pounds), trimmed and broken into florets

1 pound ultra-fresh small green beans

8 hard-cooked eggs, in their shells

1 recipe Garlic Mayonnaise (page 78)

Wine Suggestion: A rosé is traditional here. You need a wine that has enough personality and force of its own, but one that will also allow the powerful garlic mayonnaise to play its role. I am particularly fond of the Bandol rosé from Domaine Tempier.

Fish and Shellfish

GARLIC MAYONNAISE

Aïoli

I can't imagine a summer season without at least one hit of the pungent Provençal garlic mayonnaise known as *aïoli*. This is the classic garlic mayonnaise for the salt cod preparation known as *Grand Aïoli* (see page 76) and can also be used as one would any mayonnaise.

EQUIPMENT: A mortar and pestle or a food processor or blender.

6 plump cloves garlic, peeled, halved, green germs removed, minced

½ teaspoon fine sea salt

2 large egg yolks, at room temperature

1 cup extra-virgin olive oil

BY HAND: Pour boiling water into a large mortar to warm it; discard the water and dry the mortar. Place the garlic and salt in the mortar and mash together evenly with a pestle to form as smooth a paste as possible. (The fresher the garlic, the easier it will be to crush.)

Add the egg yolks. Stir, pressing slowly and evenly with the pestle, always in the same direction, to thoroughly blend the garlic paste and yolks. Continue stirring, gradually adding just a few drops of the oil, whisking until thoroughly incorporated. Do not add too much oil in the beginning or the mixture will not emulsify. As soon as the mixture begins to thicken, add the remaining oil in a slow and steady stream, whisking constantly. Taste for seasoning. Transfer to a bowl. Cover, and refrigerate for at least 1 hour to allow the flavors to blend. The mayonnaise can be stored, covered and refrigerated, for up to 3 days.

IN A FOOD PROCESSOR OR A BLENDER: Combine the garlic, salt, and egg yolks and process until well blended. With the motor running, very slowly add several tablespoons of oil, processing until the mixture thickens. With the motor still running, slowly add the remaining oil in a steady stream. Taste for seasoning. Transfer to a small bowl. Cover, and refrigerate for at least 1 hour to allow the flavors to blend. The mayonnaise can be stored, covered and refrigerated, for up to 3 days.

ABOUT 1 CUP

Tuna Fillet with Meyer Lemons and Summer Savory

Filet de Thon au Citron Meyer et à la Sarriette

My potted Meyer lemon trees are some of the dearest plants in the garden. I still can't believe that I can grow lemons and have to stop myself from always trying to keep the fruit "for good." If I don't watch myself they'll just hang there until they are overripe and past their prime. I could eat fresh red Mediterranean tuna—*thon rouge*—every few days if given the chance, and so I look forward to creating new ways to prepare it. This thoroughly Provençal creation was inspired by the Meyer lemon trees and the huge patch of summer savory—*sarriette*—that thrives at the edge of my vegetable garden. When lemons are sliced paper-thin on a mandoline they become almost sweet, offering a brilliant, delicious contrast to the rich, densely flavored tuna.

1 With a mandoline or a very sharp knife, slice the lemons into paper-thin slices, shaving the slices directly into a large, shallow bowl to catch all the juices. Add the strips of tuna, olive oil, and herbs. Toss to blend and marinate for 10 minutes.

EQUIPMENT: A mandoline or very sharp knife; a large nonstick skillet.

2 lemons (Meyer lemons if available)

About 12 ounces ultra-fresh tuna fillet, cut into even strips about ¾ inch thick and about 4 inches long

6 tablespoons extra-virgin olive oil

2 tablespoons fresh summer savory leaves (or substitute thyme leaves or rosemary leaves)

4 sprigs fresh summer savory, thyme, or rosemary, for garnish

---

Wine Suggestion: This is a white-wine dish if there ever was one. Try one of the Perrin brothers'—of Château du Beaucastel in Châteauneuf-du-Pape—new Vin de Pays d'Orange, a stunning 50-50 Roussanne-Marsanne blend. Or, other good bets in their line include the white Vieille Ferme Côtes-du-Lubéron or their white California-made Tablas Creek.

2 Heat the skillet over high heat. When hot, remove the tuna from the marinade, drain carefully, and place in the skillet. Working quickly, sear the fish for about 15 seconds on each side for rare tuna, longer for tuna that is well cooked. Immediately transfer the tuna to dinner plates. Spoon the lemons and marinade over the seared tuna. Arrange a branch of herbs alongside for garnish. Serve immediately.

4 SERVINGS

TUNA RED, TUNA WHITE

SINCE THE DAYS of the Romans, the tuna has been a symbol of Provence and the most prized of all fish and shellfish, with its image decorating Roman vases, coins, and mosaics. Today fish shops in Provence offer two kinds of tuna throughout much of the year: the brilliant red-fleshed bluefin tuna, *thon rouge (Thunnus thynnus)*, and the pale-fleshed white longfin *thon blanc (Thunnus alalunga)*, which we know more commonly as albacore tuna, the chicken of the sea that we find preserved in cans.

Mediterranean tuna are indefatigable swimmers—reaching speeds of up to 60 miles an hour—and grow quickly. A baby tuna will grow to a pound in just three months, and in a year it can reach ten pounds in weight.

SARRIETTE, OR SUMMER SAVORY, grows wild in the Mediterranean region and is close in flavor to the better-known rosemary and thyme, but it has a bit more finesse and a bigger punch. With sharp, pointed leaves that fade to an almost dusty green, summer savory finds its way into salads, lentil dishes, and those made with fava beans or chickpeas, as well as stewlike daubes or rabbit and pork dishes. A sprig of *sarriette* is often laid across a disk of mild goat's cheese as a contrast in both flavor and color. Today *sarriette* can be found growing wild all over the region, and in its domesticated state it serves as a super-hearty perennial in the vegetable garden. Historically in Provence, it was considered an aphrodisiac as well as an herb that can ease the effects of flatulence caused by some starchy vegetables.

A generous assortment of dried herbs and spices in the Tuesday market in Vaison-la-Romaine

My Fishmonger's Tuna Daube with Green Olives and Red Wine

Daube de Thon aux Olives Vertes et Vin Rouge

I am lucky enough to have both a fish market—La Poissonnerie des Voconces—and roaming fish trucks that come to the village on Tuesday, market day, as well as on Saturday. Nearly every Saturday morning throughout the year you can find me standing in line at the Lafonts' fish truck on the main square of Vaison-la-Romaine. I've always said that living in France demands a lot of patience and determination, and the Lafont line is a prime example. Shopping there is part social event, part quick course on how to tell the freshness of fish, and part a comedy of errors, as Edmond Lafont cuts and weighs and chats and then forgets the weight and we all roll our eyes and laugh a bit as the weekly process unrolls. The Lafonts kindly shared with me this outstanding tuna *daube,* one that is regularly found on our dinner table all summer long, when fresh French tuna is in season.

The Lafonts are at the following markets in Provence, 8:30 a.m. to noon:

MONDAY: Bollène

TUESDAY: Vaison-la-Romaine

THURSDAY: Sablet and Orange

FRIDAY: Mirabel-aux-Baronnies

SATURDAY: Vaison-la-Romaine

EQUIPMENT: A large heavy-duty casserole with a lid.

2 tablespoons extra-virgin olive oil

2 onions, peeled, halved, and thinly sliced

Sea salt to taste

2 pounds tuna steaks, cut about 2 inches thick

Freshly ground black pepper to taste

2 pounds tomatoes, cored, peeled, seeded, and chopped

10 plump cloves garlic, peeled and halved

4 fresh or dried bay leaves

1 bouquet garni: several parsley stems, celery leaves, and sprigs of thyme, wrapped in the green part of a leek and securely fastened with cotton twine, or secured in a wire mesh ball

1½ cups red wine (such as a Syrah) or Homemade Chicken Stock (page 325)

6 ounces (about 2 cups) pitted green olives

In the casserole, combine the oil, onions, and a pinch of salt and sweat—cook, covered, over low heat until soft but not browned—about 3 minutes. Transfer the onions to a bowl. In the fat remaining in the casserole, sear the tuna over high heat, about 2 minutes per side. Season each side generously with salt and pepper. Add the tomatoes, garlic, bay leaves, bouquet garni, red wine, olives, and the onions. Reduce the heat to very low, cover, and cook until the tuna is very tender, about 1 hour. Serve warm, with steamed rice or spelt *(épeautre)*.

8 SERVINGS

Edmond Lafont in his fish truck, with a wild salmon from Scotland

WHERE'S THAT SHOPPING LIST?

MOST OF US COOKS like to be efficient as we go off to market, carrying a carefully penned list of what we'll need to prepare the next meal. When it comes to fish in Provence, I've found it's best to come with an open mind, ready to pounce on whatever is best and fresh in the market that day. I get some of my best recipes that way, since fish and shellfish generally cook quickly and fishmongers in Provence (or shoppers next to you in line) are always ready and willing to share a quick and easy recipe. But when I know I am going to be preparing a specific dish, I order my fish or shellfish several days in advance, so I am not disappointed.

TANDOORI SHRIMP

Crevettes Tandoori

Our little village of Vaison-la-Romaine has many ethnic restaurants, including Vietnamese, Chinese, West Indian, and at one time, a fabulous Indian spot. I think that I and my friends and neighbors Johanne Killeen and George Germon, of Providence, Rhode Island's famed Al Forno, were about their only faithful customers. Alas, the lovely restaurant full of spice and good times closed for lack of business. I never get enough Indian food, so I am more than happy to make my own. For this recipe I use giant langoustines (like a cross between giant shrimp and delicate lobster) fresh from Brittany, for I find most French shrimp rather tasteless and boring. I also use this tandoori marinade when searing strips of red tuna.

1 In a large shallow bowl, combine all the ingredients for the marinade. Add the langoustines or shrimp and toss to evenly coat the shellfish. Let marinate at room temperature for 10 minutes.

2 Heat the olive oil in the skillet. Add the langoustines or shrimp, searing them evenly on all sides, about 1 minute per side. This will have to be done in batches.

3 Transfer 4 langoustines to the center of a warm dinner plate. Garnish with the basil *chiffonnade*. Repeat for the other three plates. Serve immediately.

EQUIPMENT: A large nonstick skillet.

TANDOORI MARINADE:

2 tablespoons nonfat plain yogurt

2 tablespoons freshly squeezed lemon juice

2 tablespoons minced garlic

2 tablespoons crushed or grated fresh ginger

2 teaspoons dried ground ginger

2 teaspoons roasted cumin seeds

2 teaspoons ground roasted coriander seeds

2 teaspoons ground cardamom

2 teaspoons cayenne pepper

2 teaspoons fine sea salt

16 langoustines or extra-large shrimp, shelled and deveined

3 tablespoons extra-virgin olive oil

About 1 cup fresh basil leaves, cut into a *chiffonnade*

Wine Suggestion: This spicy dish needs a regal white wine to stand up to it: try the white Côtes-du-Rhône from the fine Châteauneuf-du-Pape estate Domaine du Clos du Caillou.

THE PROVENCE COOKBOOK

4 SERVINGS

QUICK-CURED SARDINES

Sardines Crues

We manage to find sparkling fresh sardines in the market almost year-round, and barely a week goes by that I don't fix this protein-rich fish one way or the other. In summer months, quickly marinated sardines are great as an appetizer, set atop grilled country bread that's been drizzled with fruity olive oil.

12 small, very fresh sardines

¼ cup coarse sea salt

6 slices country bread, grilled or toasted

Several tablespoons extra-virgin olive oil

Freshly ground black pepper to taste

Wine Suggestion: Select a wine raised close to the sea, such as a Bandol rosé or a white Picpoul de Pinet.

1 Rinse the sardines gently under cold running water, gently rubbing the scales off. Gently twist the head off each sardine, pulling the guts with it. Discard the head and guts. With your fingertips, gently press down the belly side, pressing the sardine open like a book. With your fingertips, gently pull the central bone head to tail, being careful not to tear the flesh. With scissors, gently detach the bone from the flesh. Discard the bone. Open the sardine flat and cut it into two fillets.

2 Place the fillets in a single layer in a flat, shallow dish. Cover the sardines completely with the salt, then cover with plastic wrap. Refrigerate for 8 hours.

3 To serve, remove the fillets from the salt and wipe dry with paper towels. Drizzle the toast with olive oil. Place 4 sardine fillets atop a slice of bread. Generously season with freshly ground black pepper. Serve immediately as an appetizer.

6 SERVINGS

SEA BASS ROASTED IN A SALT CRUST

Bar en Croûte de Sel

When I want to cook a whole fish, this is my preferred method, for it is quick, foolproof, and festive. There is also magic in the fact that the sea salt and fish come from the same waters! Generally I roast a small fish for a small dinner party, though I have been known to roast an entire salmon (a copper fish poacher is great!) for a group of twenty diners. All you need is super-fresh fish, a few herbs, and a good quantity of coarse salt. Although it's hard to check the doneness of the fish (you *can* stick a knife into it, piercing through the salt crust and into the flesh to see if the fish is flaky), I have always found the timing to be rather foolproof. In fact, you can cook the fish a few minutes more than you might under other conditions, since the salt crust insulates the fish and keeps the flesh nice and moist. Be sure to keep the scales on the fish. They act as a protective moisture barrier and also tend to stick to the salt, so that when you peel away the salt, the skin comes with it. And if you have a truly top-flight olive oil that you save for special occasions, use it now!

EQUIPMENT: An ovenproof baking dish large enough to hold the fish; a mandoline or a very sharp knife.

One 2-pound whole sea bass (or substitute red snapper, porgy, or salmon), gutted, but scales and head left on

Fine sea salt

Freshly ground black pepper to taste

Several fresh or dried bay leaves

Several sprigs fresh rosemary

Several sprigs fresh thyme, plus extra thyme leaves for garnish

7 to 8 cups (about 4 pounds) coarse sea salt or kosher salt

1 lemon

Extra-virgin olive oil

Wine Suggestion: This is where I take out one of my finest whites. Why not a Châteauneuf-du-Pape from Château Rayas or a white Hermitage from J. L. Chave?

1 Preheat the oven to 450 degrees F.

2 Pat the fish dry with paper towels inside and out until there is no trace of blood. If the gills have not been removed, do so to avoid bitterness. Season the cavity of the fish with salt and pepper. Tuck the bay leaves, rosemary, and thyme into the cavity.

3 Evenly spread 1 cup of the salt in the bottom of the baking dish. Place the fish on top of the salt. Pour the remaining salt over the fish to completely cover it from head to tail. The dish should look as though you have a baking dish mounded with nothing but salt. (Do not be concerned if the tail fin extends outside the baking dish. This will not alter the roasting of the fish.)

4 Place the dish in the center of the oven. Bake for 10 minutes per pound, or 20 minutes for a 2-pound fish. Adjust baking times by 5 minutes either way for each ½ pound of fish, 10 minutes more for each additional pound of fish.

5 While the fish roasts, use a mandoline to slice the lemon into paper-thin slices, shaving the slices directly into a bowl to catch all the juices. Set aside.

6 Remove the baking dish from the oven. Allow the fish to rest for 5 minutes to firm up the flesh and make it easier to fillet. Brush away as much salt as possible from the fish, so it will not fall into the flesh when you remove the skin. Using the blade of a sharp knife, gently scrape away and discard the skin from the top fillet of the fish. Remove and discard the herbs from the cavity of the fish.

7 Using the knife, gently trace along the backbone of the fish to release the top fillet. Then, beginning at the head end of the top fillet, cut ½ inch deep down the center along the full length of the fish. Trim off and discard any fat, extraneous flesh and skin from the sides of the fillet; this will make for neater fillets and easier removal. Using two large spoons, gently remove one half of the top fillet in neat pieces and transfer it to a warmed dinner plate. Repeat for the other half of the top fillet. With the spoons, carefully remove and discard the center bone. Repeat for the bottom fillet, dividing it in two and removing the halves of the fillet in pieces. Transfer to two additional warmed dinner plates. Garnish each plate with the thin slices of lemon, a drizzle of olive oil, and a few leaves of fresh thyme. Pass a cruet of olive oil for seasoning.

4 SERVINGS

SEL DE CAMARGUE

AIGUES-MORTES, A LOVELY seaside village along the Mediterranean coast, has been the host to *salins*—or salt marshes—since the days of antiquity. A Roman engineer named Peccius was first given the job of organizing salt production along the shores of Aigues-Mortes. The salt production continued with diverse success over the centuries, depending largely upon whether or not the lands were flooded. In 1856 the Compagnie des Salins du Midi was founded, and to this day they are the largest producer of Mediterranean sea salt in all forms: coarse raw salt, refined raw salt, raw fine sea salt, and refined fine sea salt, as well as the precious *fleur de sel,* or caviar of the sea.

The salt cycle begins in the month of March, when the seawater is dense. Salt water is pumped into a series of reservoirs, where it is left to evaporate, becoming denser and denser from the sunshine of Provence and the mighty mistral winds. By late spring the density of the water may have changed from 2 ounces of salt per quart of seawater to a hefty 8 ounces of salt per quart. Come summer, the liquid in the reservoirs is moved to reservoirs called *cristallisoirs,* where the dense liquid evaporates into cakes of salt as much as 10 inches thick. In September, the single annual salt harvest takes place as the salt workers delicately remove the cakes of salt, breaking them into the crystals we know as *sel de mer.*

FLEUR DE SEL DE CAMARGUE

In the summer months, early in the morning with the help of the sun, and on days that the wind has died down, very tiny crystals form naturally on the surface of the *cristallisoirs,* giving birth to *fleur de sel.* The salt master's art consists of patiently waiting for the perfect moment to carefully, manually, collect what they call "the gift of nature," since a very gentle breeze is all it takes to blow away the fine flakes. We think of *fleur de sel* as a rather modern invention because until the 1980s, it was generally kept as a special treat for the salt masters and the owners of the *salins,* or salt marshes, and not sold commercially.

Six-Minute Cod Braised in Spicy Tomato Sauce

Cabillaud Braisé au Coulis de Tomates Epicé

*M*y six-minute braised salmon (see page 90) was such a success with my students that I decided to expand the repertoire. Here, codfish fillets are simply poached in a rich, homemade tomato sauce. I like to use a nicely spiced sauce. This is lovely served with rice and, if you wish, a garnish of olives.

1 Run your fingers over the top of the fish to detect any tiny bones that remain. Use the tweezers to remove the bones. Cut the cod into four even 8-ounce portions.

2 In the skillet, bring the tomato sauce to a boil over high heat. Instantly reduce the heat to very low and add the cod. Cover and simmer gently until the fish is cooked through, about 6 minutes. Carefully transfer the fish to warmed dinner plates. Spoon sauce over cod. Season to taste with salt and pepper. Garnish with olives and serve.

4 SERVINGS

Wine Suggestion: The tomato sauce calls for a tasty red. I would take our own, Clos Chanteduc, a fine blend of Grenache, Syrah, and Mourvèdre, from winemaker Ludovic Cornillon.

EQUIPMENT: A tweezers; a large skillet with a lid.

2 pounds fresh cod fillet, skin intact

1 quart Spicy Tomato, Fennel, and Orange Sauce (page 318)

Fine sea salt to taste

Freshly ground white pepper to taste

24 olives from Chanteduc Rainbow Olive Collection (page 4; or substitute pitted green olives)

Clos Chanteduc

Ludovic Cornillon
Domaine Saint Luc
26970 La Beaume-de-Transit
Telephone: 04 75 98 11 51
Fax: 04 75 98 19 22
Web: *www.dom-saint-luc.com*
U.S. importer: Kermit Lynch
Wine Merchant, Berkeley, CA;
telephone: (510) 524 1524

Fish and Shellfish

89

Six-Minute Salmon Braised in Viognier

Saumon Braisé au Viognier

One day Eliane Berenger—who runs our village fish shop with her husband, Aymar—suggested braising salmon in a tiny bit of water. I had some opened wine on hand and decided to braise the salmon with one of my favorite whites, one from the Viognier grape. It is a bit of a luxury, I admit, but the wine does impart a touch of fruit that I love. I transplanted some wild fennel from the roadside into my vegetable garden and use it with abandon. The heady fragrance of the fennel seems right at home here with the wine and the salmon. If you don't have fennel branches, wild or domestic, substitute sprigs of fresh rosemary. I like to serve the fish with a touch of pistachio or toasted sesame oil, and olives from my home-cured collection.

EQUIPMENT: A tweezers; a large skillet with a lid.

2 pounds fresh salmon fillet, skin intact

2 cups Viognier wine or other white wine (or substitute water)

Several branches wild or domestic fennel (or substitute sprigs of fresh rosemary)

Several drops of pistachio oil or toasted sesame oil

Fleur de sel

Fennel fronds (or minced rosemary leaves), for garnish

16 olives from Chanteduc Rainbow Olives Collection (page 4; or substitute pitted green olives)

Poissonnerie des Voconces
Eliane and Aymar Berenger
6, rue Maquis
84110 Vaison-la-Romaine
Telephone: 04 90 36 00 84

1 Run your fingers over the top of the salmon fillet to detect any tiny bones that remain. Use the tweezers to remove the bones. Cut the salmon into four even 8-ounce portions.

2 In the skillet, bring the wine to a boil over high heat. Reduce by half. Reduce the heat to a simmer, add the fennel or rosemary branches, and place the fish on top of the herbs. Cover and simmer gently until the fish is cooked through, about 6 minutes. Carefully transfer the fish to warmed dinner plates. Drizzle with pistachio oil and *fleur de sel.* Garnish with fennel fronds and olives. Serve.

4 SERVINGS

Wine Suggestion: I enjoy this with a fresh and fragrant Viognier, such as one made by one of my favorite winemakers, Jean-Pierre Cartier, of Domaine les Goubert in Gigondas.

ON VIOGNIER

I THINK THAT THE FIRST 100 percent Viognier wine I sampled in our part of Provence was that of winemaker Jean-Pierre Cartier of Domaine les Goubert of Gigondas, and to this day his is my favorite. The Viognier grape has been fashionable in Provence for the past twenty years, but is of course best known as *the* single grape that goes into some of France's top appellations to the north of us, including Condrieu, Château Grillet, and some white Saint-Joseph. What I love about the grape—difficult to grow and offering rather low yields and said to be a fickle vine—is its full-bodied, golden nature with an almost haunting bouquet of musky peaches, ripe pears, and even honey. Young, it is delicious as an aperitif, and though most experts feel it does not age, I beg to differ. I have some marvelous Viogniers that have mellowed and matured beautifully, keeping their acidity and losing none of their fruit—more fodder to the argument that in general whites age better than reds.

Fish and Shellfish

91

Pic's Fresh Crab Salad with Lime Zest

La Salade de Crabe au Zeste de Citron Vert de Pic

I first sampled a variation of this crab salad as part of a luxurious dish served at restaurant Pic in Valence, where Anne-Sophie Pic is following in the family's august culinary tradition. Fresh crab meat is such a delicacy and has so much flavor of its own that it is a shame to gild the lily. Serve this on a bed of lettuce or a layer of thinly sliced cucumbers.

In a bowl, combine the crab meat, lime zest, and enough mayonnaise to evenly coat the crab. Taste for seasoning. Arrange a layer of lettuce leaves or thinly sliced cucumbers on four salad plates. Place the crabmeat in a mound atop the lettuce or cucumbers. Serve.

4 SERVINGS

1 pound fresh lump crab meat

Grated zest of 2 limes

5 or 6 tablespoons mayonnaise

Fine sea salt

Freshly ground white pepper to taste

Several lettuce leaves or thinly sliced cucumbers, for garnish

Restaurant Pic
Anne-Sophie Pic
285, avenue Victor Hugo
26000 Valence
Telephone: 04 75 44 15 32
Fax: 04 75 40 96 03
Web: *www.pic-valence.com*

Wine Suggestion: Do try this with an elegant white wine, one made from either the Viognier or Chardonnay grape. You won't regret it.

I GREW UP WITH a love of open windows, the sun shining in, the afternoon air flowing

through with a gentle breeze. So it was a bit of a shock when I got to Provence and found the homes shuttered during the daylight hours. Was nobody home? And if so, why the darkness? It did not take me too many hot summer days to realize that a shuttered room is a cooler room, with the thick stone walls retaining the cool of the evening. Likewise, in the winter months, a tightly shuttered window helps keep the pesky mistral at bay. There is a lovely, enjoyable French ritual of opening and closing shutters; I especially love opening shutters first thing in the morning, looking out upon the stage of a new day.

A shuttered window in the village of Eygalières

LE GRAND PRE'S SEARED AND ROASTED SALMON WITH SORREL SAUCE

Saumon Rôti, Sauce à l'Oseille Le Grand Pré

One sunny Monday in August, I spent a glorious morning in the kitchen gathering recipes from chef Raoul Reichrath at restaurant Le Grand Pré in the village of Roaix, just outside of Vaison-la-Romaine. He prepared this lovely, simple salmon dish, and when I noticed he was using sorrel for a sauce, I commented that I could have brought a basketful from my garden. He laughed, explaining that he created this dish because he had so much sorrel in his own vegetable garden. We have a gardener in common, Jean-Paul Boyer, who certainly has a way with the tangy green.

1 Preheat the oven to 375 degrees F. Preheat a grill or a ridged grill pan.

2 In a small saucepan, cook the sorrel just until the leaves have softened, 2 to 3 minutes. Add the dried tomato and 1 tablespoon of the vinaigrette, and stir to blend. Season with salt and pepper to taste. Taste for seasoning. Cover, set aside, and keep warm.

EQUIPMENT: A grill or ridged grill pan; an ovenproof pan; a tweezers.

SORREL SAUCE:

8 cups sorrel, loosely packed, stemmed and cut into a *chiffonnade*

1 teaspoon diced sun-dried tomato

2 tablespoons Basil Vinaigrette strained (page 322)

Coarse sea salt to taste

Freshly ground white pepper to taste

2 pounds fresh salmon fillet, skin intact

Le Grand Pré
Flora and Raoul Reichrath
Route de Vaison (D 975)
84110 Roaix
Telephone: 04 90 46 18 12
E-mail: *legrandpre@walka9.com*

3 Run your fingers over the top of the salmon fillet to detect any tiny bones that remain. Use the tweezers to remove the bones. Cut the salmon into four even 8-ounce portions.

4 Place the salmon skin side down on the grill. Grill for about 1 minute. Turn and grill the other side for 1 minute. Transfer the fish to the ovenproof pan. Place the salmon in the oven for 3 minutes.

Wine Suggestion: Raoul's wife, Flora, who is the restaurant's *sommelière*, suggests a rarely seen Laudun blanc from the Domaine Pélaquié, vintage 2000. It is a fragrant, fruity wine that is largely a Roussanne and Viognier blend, two grapes that flatter the richness of salmon.

5 Remove the salmon from the oven. To serve, place a mound of sorrel sauce in the center of a warmed dinner plate. Arrange the salmon skin side up on top of the sorrel sauce. Drizzle with the remaining vinaigrette and serve. Repeat for the remaining three portions.

4 SERVINGS

Fish and Shellfish

ELIANE'S BARBECUED MUSSELS

Les Moules au Barbecue d' Eliane

*E*liane Berenger runs our local fish shop, and I can't remember a day when I did not walk out of the shop with an inspiration, a recipe, a new approach to cooking fish and shellfish. There is almost always a line out the door, and as customers wait in line, everyone talks fish and shellfish. We exchange recipes, or agree or disagree about how something should be cooked, while Eliane adds her few *centimes* with each bit of advice. Like so many before, this recipe was verbally delivered one Saturday in June, at the height of mussel season. I hadn't intended to buy mussels that day, but suddenly they appeared on our dinner menu. Walter is an expert at grilling over grapevine clippings, or *sarments de vigne*. The clippings heat up very quickly, making a fine bed of coals in just a few moments. I love the slightly smoky flavor they give to the mussels.

EQUIPMENT: A 12-inch paella pan or other pan to place over a grill or a barbecue; 4 shallow soup bowls.

2 pounds fresh mussels

2 tablespoons extra-virgin olive oil

2 shallots, peeled and finely minced

2 teaspoons fresh or dried thyme leaves

6 fresh or dried bay leaves

4 tablespoons fresh flat-leaf parsley leaves, minced

Freshly ground black pepper to taste

Poissonnerie des Voconces
Eliane and Aymar Berenger
6, rue Maquis
84110 Vaison-la-Romaine
Telephone: 04 90 36 00 84

ON MEASURING HERBS:

When a recipe calls for herbs to be minced, I find it easier to measure the quantity in whole leaves—such as the parsley in this recipe—then mince the herbs.

A night for mussels and French fries in Saint-Rémy-de-Provence

1 Thoroughly scrub the mussels and rinse with several changes of water. If an open mussel closes when you press on it, then it is good; if it stays open, the mussel should be discarded. Debeard the mussels. (Do not debeard the mussels more than a few minutes in advance or they will die and spoil. Note that in some markets mussels are prepared, in that the small black beard has been clipped off but not entirely removed. These mussels do not need further attention.) Set aside.

2 Heat grill and spread coals out when they are dusted with ash.

3 In the paella pan, combine the oil, shallots, thyme, and bay leaves. Stand the mussels on their ends in the liquid. Place the paella pan over the grill and cook until the mussels open, about 3 minutes. Remove the mussels as they open. Do not overcook. Discard any mussels that do not open.

4 Transfer the mussels and liquid to four warmed shallow soup bowls. Sprinkle each bowlful with parsley and pepper. Serve immediately, with finger bowls or damp towels, as well as plenty of crusty baguette to soak up the memorable sauce.

4 SERVINGS AS A FIRST COURSE, 2 SERVINGS AS A MAIN COURSE

Wine Suggestion: A chilled white or a nice fruity rosé is what I love here. I am particularly fond of the Tavel rosé from the Domaine de la Mordorée, a remarkably complex wine with forward fruits and a nice balance of acidity. With no fewer than six grape varieties—Bourboulenc, Cinsault, Clairette, Grenache, Mourvèdre, and Syrah—this is quite a blockbuster in terms of flavor and finish.

LES VOCONCES

WHEN YOU ARE in northern Provence you will see over and over the word *Voconces*. Since many of us associate *Provence* with *vacation,* I think we assume it is a corruption of one of those favorite times of the year.

Nothing could be further from the truth. The Voconces were in fact a Celtic tribe that occupied Provence before the Roman conquest. They inhabited what is now part of northern Provence, the Drôme Provençale, and the Alpes de Haute-Provence, with the modern-day villages of Vaison-la-Romaine, Die, Gap, and Sisteron forming a rough boundary. From the 1st century B.C. to the 3rd century A.D., the Romans allowed the Voconces self-rule, though they still paid taxes and were part of the military. Our village of Vaison was originally known as *Vasio Vocontorium,* or Vaison of the Voconces.

Two-Minute Steamed Squid with Garlic, Lemon, and Parsley

Calamars Vapeur à l'Ail, au Citron et au Persil

*I*f squid's only attribute were its speed of cooking, that would be enough for me. Add to that its ability to absorb seasoning in a flash and its tender chewy texture, and you have a rare ingredient. This recipe is a snap: the squid are steamed for just a minute or two (any more and they turn into rubber bands), then while they are still warm, they marinate in a mix of lemon juice, lemon zest, and touch of olive oil. Here I like to use a peppery oil, such as one from the Alpes de Haute-Provence. I dress it up with a good hit of freshly cracked black pepper, a bit of garlic, and a touch of parsley. The squid turn a colorful pink when cooked this way, and you end up with a pink, green, and golden affair—just right for the summer table.

1 In a shallow medium bowl, combine the garlic, lemon zest, lemon juice, oil, and parsley. Stir to blend.

EQUIPMENT: A steamer.

1 plump clove garlic, peeled, green germ removed, finely minced

Grated zest of 1 lemon, preferably organic

2 teaspoons freshly squeezed lemon juice

1 tablespoon peppery extra-virgin olive oil

¼ cup parsley leaves, finely minced

1 pound small fresh squid, cleaned and cut into rings (see Note)

Fleur de sel to taste

Freshly ground black pepper to taste

Wine Suggestion: Squid calls out for a young, light white from vineyards close to the sea, such as a Picpoul de Pinet, from the old variety of grape known as Picpoul. The wine has the aromatic air of the seashore encased in the bottle.

2 Bring about 1 quart of water to a simmer in the bottom of a steamer. Place the squid on the steaming rack. Place the rack over the simmering water, cover, and steam until the squid is opaque and tender, just 1 to 2 minutes. (Taste the squid to be sure that it is pleasantly cooked through and very tender.)

3 Drain the squid and immediately transfer it to the bowl, and toss until all of the liquid is absorbed. Season generously with salt and pepper and serve, warm or at room temperature. The salad can also be refrigerated and served chilled the next day.

4 SERVINGS

NOTE: To clean squid, first cut off the tentacles just above the eyes. Then squeeze out and discard the hard little beak just inside the tentacles at the point where they join the head. Use your fingers to pull out the guts and the cuttlebone, or transparent quill, from the body. Discard the guts and cuttlebone. Don't worry about removing the grayish skin, which is edible. Rinse thoroughly in cold water and drain well.

Fish and Shellfish

SQUID STEWED IN TOMATOES AND WHITE WINE

Calamars Mijotés au Vin Blanc et à la Tomate

*T*he saying is that you cook squid 2 minutes or 2 hours, and that's so true. The little critters go through a very rubbery stage after they have been cooked a few minutes, and it can easily take more than an hour to soften them up again. Because it readily absorbs any liquid you cook them in, squid is perfect for this long-simmering stew. We love to eat it hot as well as cold, preferably with brown rice from the Camargue.

1 In the saucepan, combine the oil, onions, and a pinch of salt and stir to blend. Sweat— cook, covered, over low heat until soft but not browned—for about 3 minutes. Add the wine, tomatoes, squid, bouquet garni, and hot pepper. Cover and let simmer gently until the squid is tender, about 2 hours. Remove and discard the bouquet garni.

2 Serve warm with steamed rice or at room temperature or chilled, as a first course or main course.

4 SERVINGS

EQUIPMENT: A large saucepan with a lid.

1 tablespoon extra-virgin olive oil

2 onions, peeled, halved, and thinly sliced

Fine sea salt

2 cups white wine

1 pound ripe tomatoes, cored, peeled, seeded, and chopped

3 pounds squid, cleaned and cut into rings (see Note, page 99)

1 bouquet garni: several parsley stems, celery leaves, and sprigs of thyme, wrapped in the green part of a leek and securely fastened with cotton twine

1 small hot pepper (or hot pepper flakes to taste)

Wine Suggestion: I would use the same wine I used to cook the squid, a local white such as the Côtes-du-Rhône blanc Cairanne la Chèvre d'Or from Domaine Alary Daniel & Denis. The complex wine is made of no less than six grape varieties—with 30 percent Roussanne and 15 percent Viognier—so it has lots of pleasantly fruity notes.

MUSSELS WITH PESTO

Moules au Pistou

I could eat pesto—that appealing purée of fresh basil, olive oil, and salt—with just about anything—swirled into a soup, spread on toast, or in this simple steamed summer preparation. Be sure to have plenty of crusty bread on hand to absorb the flavorful sauce.

1 Place the Light Basil Sauce in a large, shallow bowl. Set aside.

2 Thoroughly scrub the mussels, and rinse with several changes of water. If an open mussel closes when you press on it, then it is good; if it stays open, the mussel should be discarded. Debeard the mussels. (Do not debeard the mussels more than a few minutes in advance or they will die and spoil. Note that in some markets mussels are prepared, in that the small black beard has been clipped off but not entirely removed. These mussels do not need further attention.) Set aside.

EQUIPMENT: A large fine-mesh sieve; dampened cheesecloth.

⅔ cup Light Basil Sauce (page 56)

2 pounds fresh mussels

1 tablespoon extra-virgin olive oil

Fine sea salt

2 onions, peeled, halved, and thinly sliced

1 bottle white wine

Freshly ground black pepper to taste

Wine Suggestion: With this I enjoy a rather complex local white, such as the Castel Mireio from Cairanne. No fewer than eight varieties of grapes go into this wine, one that stands up brilliantly to the sturdy basil sauce.

3 In a large saucepan, combine the oil, onions, and salt and stir to blend. Sweat—cook, covered, over low heat until soft but not browned—for about 3 minutes. Add the wine. Bring to a boil and boil, uncovered, for 5 minutes. Add the mussels, cover, and cook just until the mussels open, about 5 minutes. Do not overcook. Discard any mussels that do not open.

4 Transfer the mussels to a large bowl. Place the sieve over a bowl and line the sieve with several thicknesses of dampened cheesecloth. Carefully strain the liquid through the sieve. Transfer the strained liquid to the bowl with the sauce.

5 Remove the mussels from their shells, discarding the shells. Place the mussels in the bowl with the sauce. Stir to coat the mussels with the sauce. Season generously with black pepper, then serve immediately.

Fish and Shellfish

ON MUSSELS FROM PROVENCE

ONLY ABOUT 10 percent of France's mussel production comes from the Mediterranean, but much of the year that is enough to supply the Provençal table with healthy, sparkling specimens. Remaining mussels come from the Atlantic Coast. Over the past few years the French have expanded their mussel-growing technique, introducing production in the open sea, the products of which are proudly called *moules de pleine mer*. While the more traditional *moules de bouchot* are grown in shallow water, with the mussels attached to wooden sticks, the new method raises the mussels in depths of 200 meters on ropes suspended from a series of long, horizontal ropes. Mussels from the open sea have a stronger, more iodine-rich flavor, a characteristic appreciated by most gourmets.

ON MACKEREL FROM PROVENCE

THE FRENCH CALL mackerel *le poisson bleu* and are staunch defenders of this fish that most people think they love to hate. Until they taste it. Fresh mackerel is deep, dense, rich, and filling, and it marries well with sharp seasoning such as mustard and lively herbs such as oregano. Despite its reputation as a fatty fish, mackerel is actually less fatty than the leanest of meats or chicken, and is filled with the "good" kind of omega-3 fats. I love fresh mackerel because a single fish makes a perfect portion. And mackerel cooks quickly on a grill, in the oven, or even steamed, for a quick, efficient meal. The Greeks and Romans appreciated mackerel, using it as the base of their famed *garum,* a fermented fish sauce used as a seasoning, like salt.

MUSTARD·MARINATED GRILLED MACKEREL

Maquereau Grillé à la Moutarde

This is one of our favorite weekend lunches. I always buy fish on Saturday morning, and much of the year the glistening gray mackerel are there for the asking. Our village fishmonger taught me how to prepare these, and in fact, I have to fight with Eliane Berenger *not* to prepare them for me herself in the fish shop.

EQUIPMENT: A scissors; a barbecue or grill.

6 very fresh mackerel (each about 7 ounces)

Several tablespoons flavored mustard (either coarse·grain or mustard flavored with peppers, spices, herbs, or lemon)

Fine sea salt

Freshly ground black pepper

1 Rinse the mackerel gently under cold running water, gently rubbing the scales off. Gently twist the head off one of the fish, pulling the guts with it. Discard the head and guts. With scissors, gently cut the fish open from the back side, head to tail, pressing the mackerel open like a book. With your fingertips, gently pull the central bone head to tail, being careful not to tear the flesh. With the scissors, gently detach the bone from the flesh, leaving the tail intact. Discard the bone. Open the fish flat, but do not cut it into fillets. Repeat for the remaining fish.

2 Place the fish skin side down on a platter, keeping them open like a book. Slather the flesh with mustard. Season with salt and pepper. Cover securely with plastic wrap and refrigerate for 2 to 4 hours.

3 At serving time, heat a grill and spread the coals out when they are red and dusted with ash. Lightly oil the grill rack and place it about 3 inches above the coals, allowing it to preheat for a few minutes.

4 Place the mackerel on the grill rack skin side down. Grill just until the fish turn white around the edges and remain a delicate pink in the center, 5 to 7 minutes. Grill on one side only; do not turn. With a spatula, carefully transfer the mackerel, still skin side down, to a platter. Season generously with salt and pepper. Serve immediately.

6 SERVINGS

VARIATION: A nice variation on this mustard·marinated version is to season the fish with just a touch of olive oil, lemon juice, salt, pepper, and fresh oregano. The earthy flavor of oregano marries well with mackerel.

Poulet
Roti aux
Herbes de
Provence
5€64/Pièce

Taureau
de Camargue

Agneau
de Provence

Veau
du Gers

Volaille Fermiére
du Gers

Roasted Chicken Stuffed with Rice and Figs

Franck's Roasted Duck Breast with Green Olives

Le Mimosa's Rabbit Stuffed with Pistachios and Sage

Brigitte's Squab Roasted with Honey

Sauteed Quail Marinated with Mustard and Fennel

Guinea Hen Stuffed with Olives, Rosemary, Fennel,
and Olive Leaves

Poultry and Rabbit

Les Volailles et le Lapin

Guinea Hen Braised with Olives and Capers

Fricassee of Chicken with Chorizo and Peppers

Fricassee of Chicken with Garlic
and Sweet Garlic Confit

Fricassee of Chicken with White Wine, Capers,
and Olives

Poulet rôti *sign at a butcher shop in Saint-Rémy-de-Provence*

Roasted Chicken Stuffed with Rice and Figs

Poulet Rôti Farci au Riz et aux Figues

What would Provence be without the ever-present *poulet rôti?* You can't pass a village butcher shop without spying a rotisserie somewhere near the front door, with plump farm chickens turning at a measured pace, changing from pale golden yellow to a deep golden brown. On market days, gigantic trucks pour into the villages, quickly laden with spits roasting all manner of poultry and meat. Our village has one truck that roasts chicken, rabbit, ham hocks, giant pork sausages, spare ribs, and lamb. I never get my fill of chicken, and in the summer months I love to stuff the chicken with rice and fresh purple figs, making for a carefree one-dish meal.

1 Preheat the oven to 425 degrees F.

2 In the skillet, combine the onions, salt, and olive oil. Sweat—cook, covered, over low heat until soft but not browned—for about 3 minutes. Add the rice and figs, and stir to blend. Cook just to blend the flavors, 2 to 3 minutes. Taste for seasoning.

3 Generously season the cavity of the chicken with salt and pepper. Place the giblets in the cavity. Stuff with the rice and fig mixture. Rub the skin of the chicken with the butter. Season all over with salt and pepper.

EQUIPMENT: A large skillet with a lid; a roasting pan just slightly larger than the chicken, fitted with a roasting rack; a fine-mesh sieve.

2 medium onions, peeled, halved, and thinly sliced

Sea salt to taste

1 tablespoon extra-virgin olive oil

3 cups cooked rice

10 small, fresh purple figs, stems trimmed, and quartered lengthwise

1 best-quality farm chicken (about 5 pounds) with giblets cleaned and chopped

Freshly ground white pepper to taste

2 tablespoons unsalted butter, softened

Domaine Santa Duc
Yves Gras
Edmond Gras & Fils
84190 Gigondas
Telephone: 04 90 65 84 49
Fax: 04 90 65 81 63
Tastings by appointment only.
U.S. importer: Robert Kacher Selections, Washington, DC; telephone: (202) 832-9083

4 Place the chicken on its side on the roasting rack. Pour about ½ cup of water into the bottom of the pan to help create a rich and pleasing sauce later on. Place in the center of the oven and roast, uncovered, for 20 minutes. Turn the chicken to the other side, and roast for 20 minutes more. Turn the chicken breast side up, and roast for 20 minutes more, for a total of 1 hour's roasting time. By this time the skin should be a deep golden color. Reduce the heat to 375 degrees F. Turn the chicken breast side down, at an angle if at all possible, with its head down and tail in the air. (This heightens the flavor by allowing the juices to flow down through the breast meat.) Roast until the juices run clear when you pierce a thigh with a skewer, about 15 minutes more.

Wine Suggestion: I would go for a floral white wine here, such as the young, new wine from the outgoing winemaker Yves Gras of the Domaine Santa Duc in Gigondas. His white Côtes-du-Ventoux Santa Duc les Rossignols is a blend of 35 percent Roussanne, 24 percent Grenache Blanc, and 41 percent Clairette, making for a harmonious wine that has a fine balance of fruit and acidity and is made for drinking young.

5 Remove from the oven and season generously with salt and pepper. Transfer the chicken to a platter, and place on an angle against the edge of an overturned plate, with its head down and tail in the air. Cover loosely with foil. Turn off the oven and place the platter in the oven, with the door open. Let rest a minimum of 10 minutes and up to 30 minutes. The chicken will continue to cook during this resting time.

6 Place the roasting pan over moderate heat, scraping up any bits that cling to the bottom. Cook for 2 to 3 minutes, scraping and stirring until the liquid is almost caramelized. Do not let it burn. Spoon off and discard any excess fat. Add several tablespoons cold water to deglaze (hot water will cloud the sauce). Bring to a boil, reduce the heat to low, and simmer until thickened, about 5 minutes.

7 While the sauce is cooking, remove the rice and fig stuffing from the cavity of the chicken. Place it in a serving bowl. Carve the chicken into serving pieces and transfer to a warmed platter. Strain the sauce through the sieve and pour into a sauceboat. Serve immediately.

4 TO 6 SERVINGS

VARIATION: While this *poulet rôti* recipe is ideal for the months when fresh figs are in season, a good winter variation is to replace the figs with a mixture of 4 tablespoons pine nuts and 4 tablespoons golden raisins that have been plumped in warm water for 10 minutes, then drained.

FRANCK'S ROASTED DUCK BREAST WITH GREEN OLIVES

Magret de Canard Rôti aux Olives Vertes

*I*n France, a good corner butcher is someone who knows not only his meat and poultry but also what to do with it and how to attractively display it. Our village butcher, Franck Peyraud, has all of his products—local quail and pigeon, meaty farm chickens, lovely duck breasts, lamb from nearby farms, beef from Burgundy, and wild bull from the Camargue—carefully displayed behind chilled glass cases and in huge refrigerated cases in his front window. For a long time I eyed the duck with olives so artfully arranged in his meat case along with all manner of other poultry and meats. He takes two fatted duck breasts—*magrets de canard*—stuffs them with green olives, then ties them together, meaty side to meaty side, to create a gorgeous roast. It is an easy dish to do at home, and one all duck lovers will devour. I like to add potatoes and additional green olives to the roasting pan, making it a one-dish meal to enjoy with red wine.

Wine Suggestion: Try the "meaty" Château Puech Haut, Tête de Cuvée St. Drézéry 1999.

EQUIPMENT: Cotton twine; a large roasting pan with a lid.

4 fatted duck breasts (each about 1 pound)

2 cups green olives, pitted and halved

Sea salt to taste

Freshly ground black pepper to taste

2 tablespoons extra-virgin olive oil

2 pounds small, yellow-fleshed potatoes, such as Yukon Gold, rinsed and quartered lengthwise (do not peel)

Franck Peyraud
Boucherie la Romane
13, rue de la République
84110 Vaison-la-Romaine
Telephone: 04 90 36 01 25
Fax: 04 90 28 75 11
E-mail: *franck@laromane.com*
Web: *www.laromane.com*

1 Preheat the oven to 500 degrees F.

2 Place two duck breasts—skin side down, meaty side up—on a clean work surface. Arrange a row of green olive halves down the center of the meaty side of the first duck breast. Season the meaty sides generously with salt and pepper. Place the second breast, meaty side down, on top of the first breast, creating a compact roast. With cotton twine, tie the roast at 1-inch intervals six times along the sides. Tie once at the ends. Season generously with salt and pepper. Repeat with the remaining two duck breasts.

3 In the roasting pan, heat the oil over moderately high heat until hot but not smoking. Add the two duck roasts and sear on both sides until golden, about 7 minutes. Remove the duck from the pan, transfer to a platter, and season once again with salt and pepper.

4 Discard the fat in the roasting pan. Place the potatoes in the pan. Season with salt. Place any remaining olives on top of the potatoes. Place the duck roasts on top of the olives. Cover.

5 Place the roasting pan in the center of the oven and cook for 25 minutes for rare duck, 30 minutes for medium, 35 minutes for well done.

6 Remove the duck roasts to a carving board. Cover with foil and let rest for 10 minutes. Test the potatoes for doneness: If they need additional cooking, cover the pan and return to the oven during the resting time.

- Sardines grillées aux épices 12,
- Gigot à la crème d'ail 13,00
- Baron d'agneau aux parfums des alpilles 13,
- Magret de canard 13,00
- Roti de veau à l'ancienne 12,00
- Pavé de rumsteack marchand de vin 16,

A bistrot menu in Saint-Rémy-de-Provence

7 To serve, remove and discard the cotton twine. Slice the duck breasts diagonally into thick slices and arrange on warmed dinner plates. Serve with the potatoes and cooking juices alongside.

8 SERVINGS

Poultry and Rabbit

LE MIMOSA'S RABBIT
STUFFED WITH PISTACHIOS AND SAGE

Râble de Lapin aux Pistaches et Senteurs de Sauge

Chef-owner Bridget Pugh, of restaurant
Le Mimosa in the village of Saint
Guiraud, just north of Montpellier, is
a chef with a light, original, and very
personal touch. I savored this dish one
evening in May, as her husband opened
bottles of new wines from the region for
us to taste. I think that the pistachio-sage
stuffing is brilliant, as is the idea of
brushing the rabbit with soy sauce and
balsamic vinegar for a gorgeous lacquered
hue and a burst of flavor.

Restaurant Le Mimosa
Bridget and David Pugh
34725 St.-Guiraud
Telephone: 04 67 96 67 96
Fax: 04 67 96 61 15

RABBIT SAUCE:

Reserved rabbit bones

1 large onion, halved (do not peel)

2 large carrots, scrubbed and thinly sliced

4 fresh or dried bay leaves

1 cup white wine

1 cup water

THE STUFFING:

3 tablespoons unsalted butter

Reserved rabbit kidneys, chopped

4 small shallots, peeled and minced

4 ounces salted pistachio nuts

4 fresh sage leaves, minced

Coarse sea salt to taste

Freshly ground white pepper to taste

2 tablespoons unsalted butter

4 saddles of rabbit, boned, with belly
flaps intact, kidneys reserved, bones
reserved for stock

Caul fat (optional)

1 tablespoon soy sauce

1 tablespoon balsamic vinegar

1 In a large saucepan, combine the rabbit bones, onion, carrots, bay leaves, white wine, and water. Boil until the liquid is reduced by half. Strain and reserve.

2 Preheat the oven to 400 degrees F.

3 Heat the butter over moderate heat, add the chopped kidneys and the shallots, and cook for 2 to 3 minutes. Add the pistachios and sage, and cook for 3 minutes more. Season generously with salt and pepper. Set aside to cool.

4 Divide the stuffing among the four saddles of rabbit. Roll the belly flaps around to cover and either tie with string or encase in a layer of caul fat. Arrange the rabbit pieces in an ovenproof baking dish. Place in the center of the oven and roast for 12 to 14 minutes. Remove from the oven and let rest at least 5 minutes before serving.

5 To serve, arrange a serving of rabbit on a warmed plate. Drizzle with the sauce. Repeat with remaining rabbit. Serve with rice alongside.

4 SERVINGS

Wine Suggestion: David Pugh suggests a red Collioure Domaine de la Rectorie Col del Bast 1999.

BRIGITTE'S SQUAB ROASTED WITH HONEY

Le Pigeon au Miel de Brigitte

*R*ich, meaty, and gamy, tender Provençal squab is one of the region's veritable treats. As long as we have lived in Provence we've had the good fortune of having access to the ultra-fresh poultry raised by the outgoing Brigitte Celerin on her farm—Le Colombier du Comtat—in nearby Sarrians. She is a fixture at the Tuesday market, with a prized vendor's spot right near the post office, at the very beginning of the main market street. You have to order your squab in advance, or else get to the market by 8:30, or you'll be left high and dry. Brigitte also raises delicious raspberries and fresh farm eggs. She kindly offered this simple and sublime recipe, one ideal for cool weather evenings when I want the oven to help warm the kitchen.

EQUIPMENT: A large cast-iron pot with a lid; trussing string.

4 squabs (each about 1 pound), cleaned, giblets reserved

Fine sea salt to taste

Freshly ground black pepper to taste

8 plump, moist cloves garlic, peeled

8 sprigs of fresh thyme

4 fresh or dried bay leaves

3 tablespoons extra-virgin olive oil

4 tablespoons lavender honey, melted

Wine Suggestion: With this squab preparation I could go two ways: the honey cries out for a companion that sings the same tune, such as a Viognier-based white; but the richness of the meat begs for a hefty Syrah-based wine, such as a pure Hermitage from Gérard Chave. It's your dish, you decide.

1 Pat the squabs dry with paper towels. Generously season the cavities with salt and pepper. Finely chop the giblets and place inside the poultry. Generously season the squabs with salt and pepper. Truss.

2 Preheat the oven to 425 degrees F.

3 Place the squabs breast side up in the cast-iron pot. Scatter the garlic and herbs on top of the poultry. Drizzle with the oil. Cover. Place the pot in the center of the oven and cook, basting from time to time, until the juices run clear when you pierce a thigh with a skewer, about 1 hour.

4 Remove the pot from the oven. Transfer the squabs to a large platter. Drizzle with the honey. Season generously with salt and pepper. Place the squabs at an angle against the edge of the platter, with heads down and tail in the air. (This will help the juices run into the breast meat.) Cover loosely with foil. Let the squabs rest for 10 minutes.

5 Place a squab on its back on a clean cutting board. Remove and discard the trussing string. Spoon out the chopped giblets. With a sharp knife, halve the poultry, cutting down the breastbone and through to the back. Place the two halves of squab on a warmed dinner plate. Spoon the giblets over the squab. Repeat for the remaining squabs. Serve with steamed rice.

4 SERVINGS

Brigitte Celerin, the "squab lady," far right, in the market in Vaison-la-Romaine

"Appetite comes with eating."
—FRANÇOIS RABELAIS, C. 1483–1553

RINSE OR PAT YOUR POULTRY?
The French never rinse their poultry, but prefer to pat the birds dry with a paper towel. I follow their custom: I always ask, what are you going to wash off, anyway?

Sauteed Quail Marinated with Mustard and Fennel

Sauté de Caille Marinée à la Moutarde et au Fenouil

If you love the clean, pure, and dense flavor of poultry as much as I do, then you will love this quick, efficient recipe for sautéed quail. I like to marinate the bird for several hours, then do a quick sauté in a skillet. This is an easy last-minute dish to prepare for a group, and in the summer time it means no lighting the oven and heating up the kitchen!

1 About 8 hours before cooking the quail, place them in a large, shallow dish. Drizzle with 2 tablespoons of the oil and turn the quail to evenly coat with the oil. With a pastry brush, brush the mustard all over the quail. Sprinkle with the coarse salt and fennel seeds and turn again. Cover securely and refrigerate until ready to cook.

2 Heat 2 tablespoons of oil in each of the two skillets over moderately high heat until hot but not smoking. Add the quail to the pans and sauté skin side down until golden brown, 3 to 4 minutes. Turn and sauté until tender and still juicy, another 3 to 4 minutes. Remove the birds to a platter, placing them at an angle, breast down, tail in the air, to allow the juices to flow into the breast meat. Season with fine sea salt. Cover loosely with foil and let rest for 5 minutes. Serve, offering a finger bowl, dampened hand towels, or an extra napkin for each diner.

4 SERVINGS

EQUIPMENT: A pastry brush; 2 large, shallow skillets.

4 large fresh quail (each about 6 ounces), butterflied (see Note)

6 tablespoons extra-virgin olive oil

2 tablespoons imported French mustard

2 teaspoons coarse sea salt

2 teaspoons fennel seeds

Fine sea salt

Wine Suggestion: We last sampled this with a bright young Vacqueyras from Domaine les Armouriers, a fine partner for the tender, meaty bird.

THE PROVENCE COOKBOOK

114

TO BUTTERFLY QUAIL: Place the quail breast side down on a flat surface. With a pair of poultry shears, split the bird lengthwise along the backbone. Open it flat and press down with the heel of your hand to flatten it completely. Turn the quail skin side up and press down once more to flatten. With a sharp knife, make tiny slits in the skin near the top of each drumstick. Tuck the opposite drumstick through the slit to cross the bird's legs. The bird should be as flat as possible to ensure even cooking.

The daily specials at Le Bistrot du Paradou in Le Paradou

115

Guinea Hen Stuffed with Olives, Rosemary, Fennel, and Olive Leaves

Pintade Farcie aux Olives, Romarin, Fenouil et Feuilles d'Olivier

*O*ne sunny day in July, friends and I feasted at the table of Anne-Sophie Pic, a tiny fireball of a chef who had recently taken over the family's restaurant, Pic, in Valence. I had not been to the restaurant in years and was a bit apprehensive, wondering what this thirty-year-old could show us. Fortunately, I had no need to worry: her food was alive, alert, inviting, inventive. That day Anne-Sophie served us a deliciously moist guinea hen, a *pintade* that had been stuffed with fragrant olive leaves, local black olives, rosemary, and wild fennel. This version adds the bed of potatoes, olives, and rosemary, making for an ideal family-style dish. The olive leaves are optional, but make for a marvelously perfumed bird.

1 Preheat the oven to 425 degrees.

2 Generously season the inside of the guinea hen with salt and pepper. Place the giblets, some of the rosemary, and the fennel, olives, and olive leaves inside the guinea hen. Truss. Season all over with salt and pepper.

EQUIPMENT: A roasting pan just slightly larger than the guinea hen.

1 fresh guinea hen (about 3 pounds), giblets reserved

Fine sea salt to taste

Freshly ground black pepper to taste

Several sprigs of fresh rosemary

Several sprigs of fresh wild or domestic fennel

1 cup black olives, preferably from Nyons, pitted

20 fresh olive leaves (optional)

2 pounds yellow-fleshed potatoes, such as Yukon Gold, rinsed and halved lengthwise (do not peel)

2 tablespoons extra-virgin olive oil

Wine Suggestion: At Pic, we sampled the guinea hen with a marvelous red Côtes-du-Rhône from Château d'Hugues. Winemaker Bernard Pradier turns out a marvelously fruity, clean, and intense *grande réserve*, with a combination of Grenache, Syrah, and Carignan grapes from vines more than fifty years old.

3 Layer the potatoes cut side down in the roasting pan. Sprinkle the remaining rosemary over the potatoes. Drizzle with the olive oil. Place the guinea hen breast side up on top of the potatoes. Place in the center of the oven and roast, uncovered, for 20 minutes, basting once. Turn the guinea hen over, breast side down, and roast for 20 minutes more, basting once. Turn the guinea hen breast side up again and roast for 20 minutes more, for a total roasting time of 1 hour, or until the juices run clear when you pierce a thigh with a skewer. Remove the roasting pan from the oven. Generously season the guinea hen with salt and pepper.

4 To serve, carve the guinea hen into serving pieces and place on a platter. Remove the herbs and olives from the cavity. Discard the herbs, but serve the olives with the guinea hen. Arrange the potatoes alongside. Pour the pan juices over all. Serve immediately.

4 TO 6 SERVINGS

Restaurant Pic

Anne-Sophie Pic
285, avenue Victor Hugo
26000 Valence
Telephone: 04 75 44 15 32
Fax: 04 75 40 96 03
Web: *www.pic-valence.com*

Château d'Hugues

Sylviane and Bernard Pradier
84100 Uchaux
Telephone: 04 90 70 06 27
Fax: 04 90 70 10 28
Tastings in summer, Monday to Saturday 8 a.m. to noon and 2 to 7 p.m. Sundays and holidays by appointment only.

GUINEA HEN BRAISED WITH OLIVES AND CAPERS

Pintade aux Olives et aux Câpres

*H*ere we have three of my favorite ingredients: moist golden guinea hen, fennel-scented green olives, and capers. Poultry connoisseurs consider guinea hen—the least fatty of the poultry family—to be the most delicate and delicious. I love the firmness of the flesh, the golden color of the meat, and the almost gamy flavor. I make this often in the summer months and serve it with steamed rice.

EQUIPMENT: A large casserole with a lid; trussing string.

1 fresh guinea hen (about 3 pounds), giblets reserved

Sea salt to taste

Freshly ground black pepper to taste

6 fresh or dried bay leaves

1 cup green olives, pitted

1 cup capers in vinegar, drained

Several branches of wild or domestic fennel

3 tablespoons extra-virgin olive oil

1 quart Homemade Chicken Stock (page 325)

1 Generously season the inside of the guinea hen with salt and pepper. Place the giblets, 2 bay leaves, 12 green olives, 1 tablespoon capers, and several branches of fennel inside the guinea hen. Truss.

2 In the casserole heat the oil until hot but not smoking. Add the guinea hen and brown evenly on all sides. Remove it from the casserole. Discard the fat in the pan. Generously season the guinea hen all over with salt and pepper. Return the guinea hen, breast side up, to the casserole. Pour the chicken stock all around the poultry. Sprinkle with the remaining olives, bay leaves, and capers. Arrange several branches of fennel around the poultry. Cover and braise over low heat, stirring from time to time, until the poultry is cooked through, about 1 hour.

3 To serve, remove and discard the bay leaves, fennel branches, and trussing string. Carve the guinea hen and serve with the sauce, capers, and olives. Serve with steamed rice from the Camargue.

4 TO 6 SERVINGS

Wine Suggestion: This calls for a white wine with youth and a certain boldness. I might consider the white Coudelet de Beaucastel from Château de Beaucastel in Châteauneuf-du-Pape, a wine that can be drunk young but also exudes a certain elegance.

YOU SEE THEM ALL over Provence—round coconut mats in a multitude of colors hanging outside shops known as *drogueries,* similar to a hardware shop. The mats are actually called *scourtins,* for the original beret-like fiber mats that were used as filters in the making of olive oil. Today, by law, the *scourtins* used in the olive oil process are made of synthetic fibers and are used for only one season. But traditionally the coconut mats were used over and over, rinsed with hot water after each use.

At one time there were *scourtin* factories all over Provence, but today only one remains, in the town of Nyons in the Drôme Provençale. Here, in 1882, Ferdinand Feret patented a new *scourtin*-making machine, using tough, sturdy coconut fiber. The business is still alive today, and though the coconut mats are no longer used in the pressing of olive oil, flat *scourtins* can be found in all sizes and colors, without the beret-like flap, and are used regularly in Provence as coasters, table mats, doormats, and even decorative rugs.

Scourtins on sale in Saint-Rémy-de-Provence

La Scourtinerie
36, quartier la Maladrerie
26110 Nyons
Telephone: 04 75 26 33 52
Fax: 04 75 26 20 72

FRICASSEE OF CHICKEN
WITH CHORIZO AND PEPPERS

Fricassée de Poulet au Chorizo et aux Poivrons

*M*y village butcher, Franck Peyraud, has the most delicious chorizo, nice and spicy and not overly fatty. This dish—with a healthy dose of red and green peppers and the deep red sausage—makes me think of trips over the border into Catalan country in Spain.

1 Generously season the chicken on all sides with salt and pepper.

2 In the skillet, combine the butter and oil over moderate heat. When the fats are hot but not smoking, add the chicken skin side down, and brown until the poultry turns an even golden color, about 5 minutes. Using tongs (to avoid piercing the poultry), turn the pieces and brown them on the other side, 5 minutes more. Carefully regulate the heat to avoid scorching the skin. This may have to be done in batches. When all the pieces are browned, transfer them to a platter. Season once again with salt and pepper.

Château Les Palais

11220 Saint-Laurent-de-la-Cabrerisse

Telephone: 04 68 44 01 63

Tastings Monday to Friday, 9 a.m. to noon and 2 to 6 p.m. Saturday and Sunday by appointment only.

EQUIPMENT: A large deep skillet with a lid.

1 fresh farm chicken (3 to 4 pounds), cut into 8 serving pieces, at room temperature

Fine sea salt

Freshly ground black pepper to taste

2 tablespoons unsalted butter

3 tablespoons extra-virgin olive oil

2 onions, peeled, halved lengthwise, and thinly sliced

4 plump cloves garlic, peeled, quartered, green germs removed

2 cups Homemade Chicken Stock (page 325)

2 ripe, red tomatoes, cored, peeled, seeded, and chopped

1 tablespoon tomato paste

2 red bell peppers, trimmed, seeds removed, cut into thin strips

2 green bell peppers, trimmed, seeds removed, cut into thin strips

8 ounces chorizo, cut into bite-size pieces

3 Place the onions and garlic in the fat in the skillet and sweat—cook, covered, over low heat until soft but not browned—for about 3 minutes. Return the chicken and any cooking juices to the pan. Add the stock, tomatoes, and tomato paste. Cover, and cook over low heat, turning the chicken in the sauce once or twice, until the chicken is cooked through and has thoroughly absorbed the sauce, about 20 minutes. Add the peppers and chorizo. Cover and cook over low heat just until the peppers are soft, about 10 minutes more. Taste for seasoning. Serve with rice or fresh pasta.

4 TO 6 SERVINGS

Wine Suggestion: This dish deserves a robust red: I enjoy something from the Languedoc-Roussillon area, such as a Corbières from Château les Palais, a blend of Grenache, Carignan, and Syrah grapes, with overtones of blackberries, jam, and bitter almonds.

Poultry and Rabbit

FRICASSEE OF CHICKEN WITH GARLIC AND SWEET GARLIC CONFIT

Fricassée de Poulet à l'Ail et à l'Ail Confit

A double dose of garlic—what could be better! Beginning in June the Provençal market stalls are laden with long, beautiful braids of plump garlic, as pretty as any arrangement of flowers. That's when I put together three ingredients I love: chicken, garlic, and white wine. I like to make this with a local Viognier white, but any daily drinking white wine you have on hand will do. Serve with Potatoes from the Mas Haut (page 230).

1 Generously season the chicken on all sides with salt and pepper.

EQUIPMENT: A large deep skillet with a lid.

1 fresh farm chicken (3 to 4 pounds), cut into 8 serving pieces, at room temperature

Fine sea salt

Freshly ground black pepper to taste

2 tablespoons unsalted butter

3 tablespoons extra-virgin olive oil

20 plump cloves garlic, peeled, halved, green germs removed

1 recipe Sweet Garlic Confit (page 314)

1½ cups white wine (the same wine to be served with the dish)

Wine Suggestion: I enjoy this with a rich Viognier wine. My very favorite is made by Jean-Pierre Cartier at Domaine les Goubert in Gigondas. His Viognier is a marvel. I have tasted many white wines made from the Viognier grape, and always return to his as my favorite. To me, he extracts the best qualities of the grape, and the result is a wine rich with the flavors of citrus, honey, orange blossom, and white peaches. And it is very chicken-and-garlic friendly! He has just a single hectare of the tricky Viognier grape, which he vinifies in wood for ten months. The wine always offers a rich bouquet, all the while rewarding our palates with freshness and a sense of youth.

2 In the skillet, combine the butter and oil over moderate heat. When the fats are hot but not smoking, add the chicken skin side down, and brown until the poultry turns an even golden color, about 5 minutes. Using tongs (to avoid piercing the poultry), turn the pieces and brown them on the other side, 5 minutes more. Carefully regulate the heat to avoid scorching the skin. This may have to be done in batches. When all the pieces are browned, transfer them to a platter. Season once again with salt and pepper.

3 Add the halved garlic cloves to the fat in the skillet. Reduce the heat to low and return the chicken and any cooking juices to the skillet. Cover and cook over low heat, turning the chicken in the sauce once or twice, until the chicken is cooked through, about 20 minutes. Transfer the chicken and garlic to a large warmed platter. Generously season with salt and pepper. Cover with foil and set aside to keep warm.

4 Discard the fat in the skillet. Return the skillet to the stove over high heat. Add the sweet garlic confit. Once hot, carefully pour the white wine over the garlic and deglaze, scraping up any bits that cling to the bottom of the skillet. Continue to cook, uncovered, over medium-high heat, smashing the garlic to a smooth purée. Spoon the garlic purée over the chicken and serve.

4 TO 6 SERVINGS

Domaine les Goubert
Jean-Pierre Cartier
84190 Gigondas
Telephone: 04 90 65 86 38
Fax: 04 90 65 81 52
E-mail: *jpcartier@terre-net.fr*
Web: *www.terre-net.fr/domaine-les-goubert*
Tastings Monday to Friday, 9 a.m. to noon and 2 to 6 p.m. Saturday by appointment only.
U.S. importers: Chicago Wine Merchants, telephone: (773) 254-9000/ fax: (773) 890-8896; Metrowine Distribution, telephone: (516) 746-4488/fax: (516) 746-4149

What Is It About the Cicada?

SOONER OR LATER in Provence, everyone asks "What *is* it about the cicada?" Cicada—or *cigale*—symbols are everywhere: in china replicas, adorning fabric, decorating tableware, as napkin rings and table weights, decorating T-shirts, and even created in the form of soap bars.

The answer is quite simple: the *cigale* (from the Latin form of two Greek words that mean "the membrane that sings") has been the symbol of the Mediterranean for centuries. To the French it is the sound of Provence. Once the temperature reaches 22 degrees C (71.7 F.), usually around the feast of St. Jean on June 24, the *cigale* begins to sing, a piercing, chirping sound that can be unrelenting as the sun bears down and the heat rises. It takes that degree of heat to put the *cigale's* muscles in action, and the sound is a fine reminder that summer is here and it is vacation time.

In fact, there is not just one *cigale*, but some 4,500 different species, with the famed *cigale noire de Provence* the one we know best. (One can get more detailed, for there is the *cigale* that sings only in the black pines of Mont Ventoux, one that can be heard only in the Dentelles de Montmirail near Gigondas, and another very independent three species that never leave Corsica.) It is only the male that sings, and it is actually a musical instrument—like a pair of cymbals attached to each side of his abdomen—that allows him to make what is really a passionate love call. The *cigale* differs from the cricket *(grillon)* or the grasshopper and locust *(sauterelle)* in that the others sing by rubbing parts of their body together: Only the *cigale* has the cymbals!

But the evolution from a *cigale's* birth to his singing career is a long affair. Eggs are laid in summer, larva forms in fall, and the insect lives and grows underground for a full three to six years. The *cigale* emerges in June and attaches himself to the bark of trees, where he can go almost unnoticed if he is not attacked by such predators as ants, birds, and man in the form of insecticides and forest fires. The singing—calls include nuptial notes and cries of irritation as well as distress—lasts for no more than three weeks, when the *cigale's* career as well as its life are ended. Since the fourth century, man has understood the life of the *cigale*. Then, it was noted, "Happy are the *cigales*, for the female is mute!"

In 1896, the Provençal sculptor and potter Louis Sicard of Menton created the first likeness of the *cigale* in faïence. The rest is history.

FRICASSEE OF CHICKEN WITH
WHITE WINE, CAPERS, AND OLIVES

Fricassée de Poulet au Vin Blanc, Câpres, et Olives

*F*or me, this is comfort food personified. I love the entire process of browning the pieces of chicken, then surrounding them in a big copper pot with all manner of delights, especially my favored trio of tomatoes, olives, and capers. This dish is even better the next day, once the flavors have been allowed to blend. Nothing makes me happy like leftovers!

1 Liberally season the chicken on all sides with salt and pepper.

2 In the skillet, heat the oil over moderate heat until hot but not smoking. Add the chicken pieces and brown until the poultry turns an even golden color, about 5 minutes. Turn the pieces and brown them on the other side, 5 minutes more. Carefully regulate the heat to avoid scorching the skin. This may have to be done in batches. When all the pieces are browned, use tongs—to avoid piercing the meat—to transfer them to a platter.

3 Reduce the heat to low and add the onions and sweat—cook, covered, over low heat until soft but not browned—for about 3 minutes. Return the chicken to the pan. Add the wine,

EQUIPMENT: A deep 12-inch skillet with a lid.

1 fresh farm chicken (3 to 4 pounds), cut into 8 serving pieces, at room temperature

Sea salt

Freshly ground white pepper to taste

3 tablespoons extra-virgin olive oil

2 onions, peeled, halved, and thinly sliced

2 cups white wine

2 pounds ripe tomatoes, peeled, cored, seeded, and chopped

1 cup Picholine green olives, pitted (or substitute pimiento-stuffed olives)

¼ cup capers in vinegar, drained

Wine Suggestion: A truly simple white is nice here. Try the lovely Côtes-du-Rhône from the Châteauneuf-du-Pape vineyard of Le Grand Veneur.

tomatoes, olives, and capers. Cover and simmer over low heat until the chicken is cooked through, about 1 hour. Taste for seasoning. Serve with rice or fresh pasta.

6 SERVINGS

CLOS CHANTEDUC

GROWING UP IN THE Middle West in America, I never even dreamed that one day I would own a vineyard. But when we bought our country home in Provence in 1984, Chanteduc—which means "song of the owl"—came with about five acres of vines. Most of the grapes—a majority of them the red wine grape Grenache, the workhorse of the Rhône Valley wines—were planted in 1956, replacing the olive trees whose trunks died out during successive freezes in the early 1950s. At the time, the grapes were tended by a local farmer and brought to a local wine cooperative, where they were blended with everyone else's grapes. The wine the cooperative produced was less than stellar, and we always felt a little cheated, not being able to see what our little vineyard was capable of producing.

We would sit on the terrace and dream: "What if someday we could sit here, sipping the wine produced from these very grapes." We found a winemaker who agreed to tend the vines and make a wine under our own label. We chose the name Clos Chanteduc, since our property is an authentic *clos*—that is, a self-contained vineyard that is totally surrounded by trees and not adjacent to another vineyard.

Before harvest around the middle of September we would wander through the vineyard tasting grapes from different parcels. The grapes growing on the slope that runs up

"Wine has a mysterious side to its character. Its ability to lift out dark profundities of flavor from the earth is an example of this. No one knows why wines sometimes seem to taste of the soil in which they grow—but they do."

—ANDREW JEFFORD,
EVENING STANDARD, LONDON

from the house were planted in the 1970s, and the soil there is filled with rocks as big as footballs, most of them smooth stones the French call *galets*. This parcel of grapes intrigued me the most, for the slope, the rocky soil, and maybe the wild blackberry bushes that grew nearby gave the grapes a distinctively peppery flavor. Deep, intense, with a bite, they were almost piquant, sharp, and pungent. I hoped that our wine would somehow take on that peppery essence.

We made our first wine in 1991, not one of the Rhône Valley's best years. But once we tasted the wine in the barrel, and later in the bottle, that distinctive peppery flavor was there, and it still is today. Our current winemaker, Ludovic Cornillon, has been making wine for us since the 2001 vintage. He tends the grapes, and replants as old vines die out or need replacing; and we now have a fine vineyard mix of old Grenache (about 60 percent), younger Syrah (about 30 percent), and a smattering of Mourvèdre (about 10 percent). When people ask what percentage of each grape goes into the wine, the local winemakers like to say "the recipe is in the vineyard"—that is, what you grow is what goes into the wine. Ludovic vinifies each grape separately, in traditional concrete vats. The wine is made traditionally, with all the grapes stemmed, and with a fermentation/maceration of 10 to 15 days. After 10 to 12 months of aging in vats, the wines are blended, then bottled. We can count on about 8,000 bottles a year. And there's still that fine peppery note! Yes!

Clos Chanteduc

Ludovic Cornillon
Domaine St.-Luc
26970 La Baume-de-Transit
Telephone: 04 75 98 11 51
Fax: 04 75 98 19 22
Web: *www.dom-saint-luc.com*
U.S. importer: Kermit Lynch Wine Merchant, Berkeley, CA; telephone: (510) 524-1524.

Our winemaker, Ludovic Cornillon, in the Chanteduc vineyards

Franck's Thyme-Marinated Leg of Lamb

Chateau d'Hugues' Red Wine—Marinated Leg of Lamb

Forgotten Red Wine Daube

Robespierre Beef Domaine de la Ponche

MEATS
Les Viandes

White Wine Daube

Moroccan Lamb Meatballs with Cucumber
and Mint Salad

Pork Stew with Sweet and Hot Peppers

Oven-Roasted Suckling Pig

FRANCK'S THYME-MARINATED LEG OF LAMB

Gigot de Franck Mariné au Thym et Rôti

Somewhere along the line, leg of lamb became our ritual Sunday night special. That's when I seem to have more time to heat the wood-fired bread oven to the desired temperature, and generally I cook the entire dinner in the wood oven, keeping the kitchen cool during the intensely hot days of summer. Our butcher, Franck Peyraud, first suggested this method of preparing the lamb several years ago. He bones the lamb, then marinates it in oil and herbs in an airtight plastic bag. Once roasted, the lamb is ever so flavorful and ever so moist. To take advantage of the flavors of the herbs and oil, I like to roast the lamb on a rack, arranging potatoes, carrots, and onions on the bottom of the roasting pan. As the juices drip onto the roasting vegetables, they take on a golden caramelized flavor. I often accompany the roast lamb with the Russian Tomato Gratin (page 189).

EQUIPMENT: A roasting pan with a rack; an instant-read thermometer; a fine-mesh sieve; trussing string.

3 tablespoons extra-virgin olive oil

1 butterflied leg of lamb (4 to 5 pounds), trimmed to an even thickness of 2 to 2½ inches, bone reserved

4 teaspoons fresh or dried thyme

Sea salt to taste

Freshly ground black pepper to taste

6 large potatoes, scrubbed and halved lengthwise but not peeled

6 large onions, halved (do not peel)

6 carrots, peeled and halved

6 large sprigs fresh thyme or 2 teaspoons dried thyme leaves

Franck Peyraud
Boucherie la Romane
13, rue de la République
84110 Vaison-la-Romaine
Telephone: 04 90 36 01 25
Fax: 04 90 28 75 11
e-mail: *franck@laromane.com*
Web: *www.laromane.com*

Lamb on sale in the Velleron market

1 Massage the olive oil into the lamb on all sides. Season the lamb inside and out with the thyme, salt, and pepper. Starting from a longer side, roll the lamb to enclose the herbs. With butcher twine, tie the leg securely at 2-inch intervals to give it a compact cylindrical shape. Reinsert the bone into the leg. (This will help keep the meat moist as it roasts.) The lamb can be roasted immediately, but it will be nicely infused with the thyme if allowed to marinate for 24 hours, covered securely with plastic wrap and refrigerated.

2 Preheat the oven to 450 degrees F.

3 Place the potatoes and onions cut side down on the bottom of the roasting pan, layering if necessary. Add the carrots. Add the thyme sprigs. Add about ½ cup cold water to keep the pan from burning as the lamb roasts, and to begin creating a sauce. Place the lamb on a rack in the roasting pan.

4 Place in the center of the oven and roast, turning the lamb once, until an instant-read thermometer inserted into the thickest part of the meat reads 130 to 135 degrees F., 1½ to 1¾ hours.

5 Remove from the oven and season generously with salt and pepper. Transfer the lamb to a platter, and place on an angle against the edge of an overturned plate. Cover loosely with foil. Turn off the oven and place the platter in the oven with the door open. Let rest a minimum of 10 minutes and up to 30 minutes. The lamb will continue to cook during this resting time. Transfer the vegetables to a platter and cover with foil to keep warm.

6 Meanwhile, prepare the sauce: Place the pan over moderate heat, and with a spatula, scrape up any bits that cling to the bottom. Cook for 2 to 3 minutes, scraping and stirring until the liquid is almost caramelized. Do not let it burn. Spoon off and discard any excess fat. Add several tablespoons cold water to deglaze (hot water will cloud the sauce). Bring to a boil, reduce the heat to low, and simmer until thickened, about 5 minutes.

7 While the sauce is cooking, carve the lamb into ¼- to ½-inch slices and place on the warmed platter with the vegetables.

8 Strain the sauce through the sieve and pour into a sauceboat. Serve immediately, with the lamb.

12 SERVINGS

Meats

CHATEAU D'HUGUES' RED WINE– MARINATED LEG OF LAMB

Le Gigot Mariné au Vin Rouge du Château d'Hugues

A whole leg of lamb, or *gigot*, has been part of our life from our very first year at Chanteduc. Our good friends Rita and Yale Kramer offered the house a gift each year, and the first year we built a wood-fired oven for baking bread and for roasting. It took me a while to master the heating (two full hours at full blast, the oven stuffed with one *International Herald Tribune*, vine clippings, spent vine trunks, and a few chunks of oak), and the cool-down (1 full hour), but after nearly twenty years, the oven is just part of the festive life on the farm. The oven is magical: somehow no matter what you put into it—a roast, a vegetable gratin, even tarts—it knows what to do. The heat is intense but not drying, and the smoky fragrance it imparts is incomparable. This marinated *gigot* recipe was inspired by a small Provençal cookbook, *Les Côtes-du-Rhône du Vignoble à la Table*, illustrated by the talented artist-winemaker Bernard Pradier of Château d'Hugues in the village of Uchaux.

Château d'Hugues

Sylviane and Bernard Pradier

84100 Uchaux

Telephone: 04 90 70 06 27

Fax: 04 90 70 10 28

Tastings in summer, Monday to Saturday 8 a.m. to noon and 2 to 7 p.m. Sundays and holidays by appointment only. U.S. importer: A Jack Siler Selection, Springfield, VA; telephone: (703) 644-5210.

EQUIPMENT: A large fine-mesh sieve; a roasting pan with a rack; an instant-read thermometer.

1 bone-in leg of lamb (7 to 8 pounds), preferably with hip bone removed and excess fat and membrane trimmed and reserved

THE MARINADE:

1½ bottles red wine

1 tablespoon red wine vinegar

1 tablespoon *eau-de-vie*

1 tablespoon extra-virgin olive oil

2 large onions, peeled, halved, and thinly sliced

4 teaspoons fresh or dried thyme leaves

4 fresh or dried bay leaves

1 teaspoon black peppercorns

1 tablespoon extra-virgin olive oil

Fine sea salt to taste

Freshly ground black pepper to taste

1 In a large shallow bowl, combine the lamb and the marinade ingredients. Cover with plastic wrap. Refrigerate for 24 to 48 hours, turning the lamb from time to time. Place a large sieve over a bowl. Pour the meat into the sieve, reserving the marinade ingredients in the bowl. Discard the bay leaves and thyme.

2 Preheat the oven to 450 degrees F.

3 Pat the lamb dry with paper towels. Rub the olive oil all over the lamb. Season generously with salt and pepper. Arrange the reserved bone and trimmings on the bottom of a roasting pan. Place the lamb on a rack in the roasting pan. Add about ½ cup cold water to keep the pan from burning as the lamb roasts and to begin creating a sauce.

4 Place in the center of the oven and roast, turning the lamb once, until an instant-read thermometer inserted into the thickest part of the meat reads 130 to 135 degrees F., about 1½ to 1¾ hours. Baste from time to time with the marinade.

5 Remove from the oven and season generously with salt and pepper. Transfer the lamb to a platter, and place on an angle against the edge of an overturned plate. Cover loosely with foil. Turn off the oven and place the platter and the plate in the oven with the door open. Let rest a minimum of 10 minutes and up to 30 minutes. The lamb will continue to cook during this resting time.

6 Meanwhile, prepare the sauce. Remove and discard the bones and trimmings from the roasting pan. Place the pan over moderate heat, and with a spatula, scrape up any bits that cling to the bottom. Cook for 2 to 3 minutes, scraping and stirring until the liquid is almost caramelized. Do not let it burn. Spoon off and discard any excess fat. Add several tablespoons cold water to deglaze (hot water will cloud the sauce). Bring to a boil, reduce the heat to low, and simmer until thickened, about 5 minutes.

7 While the sauce is cooking, carve the lamb into ½-inch slices and place on a warmed platter.

8 Strain the sauce through a fine-mesh sieve and pour into a sauceboat. Serve immediately, with the lamb.

12 SERVINGS

Wine Suggestion: I am particularly fond of Monsieur Pradier's Côtes-du-Rhône Château d'Hugues Cuvée Sylviane, a blend of 60 percent Grenache, 30 percent Syrah, and 10 percent Mourvèdre, with the flavors of black cherries and currants. I confess that I also love the wine's romantic label of a muscular Provençal woman lifting a basket of grapes in the vineyard.

Meats

Forgotten Red Wine Daube

Daube au Vin Rouge Oublié

Most of us who actively collect wines inevitably end up with bottles that, while totally drinkable, are decidedly less drinkable than others. Sometimes we lose interest in a wine, or we forget about it in the back of the cellar and the wine loses its luster. The reds in this collection are affectionately known as "dead reds." In reality, these wines are far from dead, and cooks can profit from the rich and fruity flavors still inherent in the wines, and use them in cooking. The most traditional use of wine in Provençal cooking is the red wine *daube*, where the color, the fruitiness, and the heartiness of a dense red wine serve to create a thoroughly delicious and memorable sauce for a beef stew. In this recipe, shared with me by our local butcher, Franck Peyraud, the beef is marinated in red wine, oil, herbs, and spices for 24 to 48 hours, then cooked long and slow over very low heat. The resulting meat is meltingly tender, and the stew is set off with the bright, fresh flavors of orange zest and marinated olives. I like to serve this with penne pasta, which nicely absorbs the rich sauce. When I take the time to make this stew, I always make a big batch since any leftovers will freeze nicely.

EQUIPMENT: A large sieve; a large heavy-duty casserole, preferably enameled cast-iron, with a lid; a 6-quart pasta pot fitted with a colander.

6 pounds beef, preferably two or three different cuts, choosing from the top or bottom round, heel of round, shoulder arm or shoulder blade, neck or short ribs of beef, cut into 3-ounce cubes

THE MARINADE:

2 bottles red wine, such as a Gigondas

4 fresh or dried bay leaves

½ teaspoon freshly grated nutmeg

5 whole cloves

Several sprigs fresh thyme

½ cup extra-virgin olive oil

3 tablespoons extra-virgin olive oil

Fine sea salt to taste

Freshly ground black pepper to taste

30 shallots, peeled and trimmed

Grated zest of 4 oranges, preferably organic

2 cups olives from the Chanteduc Rainbow Olive Collection (page 4; or substitute pitted green olives)

3 tablespoons coarse sea salt

1 pound imported Italian penne

1 In a large shallow bowl, combine the meat and the marinade ingredients. Cover with plastic wrap. Refrigerate for 24 to 48 hours, turning the meat from time to time. Place the sieve over a bowl. Pour the meat into the sieve, reserving the marinade ingredients in the bowl. Discard the bay leaves, cloves, and thyme.

Wine Suggestion: A good red, such as a Gigondas or a Vacqueyras.

2 In the heavy-duty casserole, heat the oil over moderately high heat until hot but not smoking. Add several pieces of the meat and brown them over moderate heat, regulating the heat to avoid scorching the meat. Do not crowd the pan and be patient: Good browning is essential for the meat to retain flavor and moistness. Thoroughly brown the meat on all sides in several batches, about 10 minutes per batch. As each batch is browned, use tongs (to avoid piercing the meat) to transfer the beef to a platter. Immediately season generously with salt and pepper.

3 Return all the meat to the casserole. Add the reserved marinade and cover. Bring just to a simmer over moderate heat. Once the liquid has come to a simmer, reduce the heat to low. Cook, covered, maintaining a very gentle simmer, until the meat is very tender, 3 to 4 hours. Stir from time to time to evenly coat the pieces of meat with the liquid. During the last 30 minutes, add the shallots, orange zest, and olives, and stir them into the mixture. The sauce should be glossy and slightly thick. Taste for seasoning. With a slotted spoon, transfer the pieces of meat, shallots, olives, and orange zest to another large covered casserole, leaving the sauce in the pan.

Meats

Barrels outside the château at Château de la Nerthe in Châteauneuf-du-Pape 135

Sylvie Chabran, who conducts expert tastings at Château La Nerthe in Châteauneuf-du-Pape

4 Meanwhile, in the pasta pot, bring about 5 quarts of water to a rolling boil over high heat. Add the coarse sea salt and the pasta, stirring to prevent the pasta from sticking. Cook until tender but firm to the bite, about 11 minutes. Remove the pasta pot from the heat. Remove the colander and drain over a sink, shaking to remove excess water. Immediately transfer the drained pasta to the sauce in the saucepan. Toss to evenly coat the pasta. Cover and let rest for 1 to 2 minutes to allow the pasta to thoroughly absorb the sauce. Taste for seasoning. Transfer to individual warmed shallow soup bowls. Arrange several pieces of meat, shallots, olives, and orange zest on top of the pasta. Serve immediately.

12 SERVINGS

THE MIGHTY MISTRAL — FROM OLIVES TO WINE: In the winter, when the mighty mistral wind blows, Provence can be colder than central or even northern France. In 1956, the mistral blew for three weeks straight, reaching speeds of more than 60 miles an hour, and temperatures plummeted to 15 degrees below zero Fahrenheit. Consequently, most of the olive trees froze; but the grapevines resisted so well that many farmers of the region decided to make vines their major crop.

IN FRANCE, an AOC—which stands for *appellation d'origine contrôlée*—is a standard of quality, in everything from wines to cheese to olives and even hay. For wines, AOC status is granted in recognition of both traditional and everyday practise covering, among other considerations, the soil type, the grape varieties, and the production techniques. A national body known as INAO establishes and monitors these rules, guaranteeing that products bearing the AOC seal meet standards governing maximum yield, vineyard demarcation, grape varieties used, cultivation methods, harvesting techniques, and vinification techniques.

The region of Côtes-du-Rhône was granted its AOC in 1937. Today the region produces some 450 million bottles of wine, known for their rich, spicy quality. It is the second-highest wine-producing appellation after the Bordeaux region, and it lies at 45 degrees latitude north, considered the ideal level for sunshine and rain. There is a hierarchy, with three different categories:

CÔTES-DU-RHÔNE CRUS The Rhône Valley offers thirteen different *crus*, the most prestigious wines of the region, stretching from Vienne in the north to Avignon in the south, with vineyards planted along both banks of the Rhône River. They include:

- Northern *crus*, from Vienne to Valence: red Côte-Rôtie; white Condrieu; white Château Grillet; red and white St.-Joseph; red and white Crozes-Hermitage; red Cornas; and white St.-Péray.

- Southern *crus*, from Montélimar to Avignon: red and rosé Gigondas; red, rosé, and white Vacqueyras; red and white Châteauneuf-du-Pape; red, rosé, and white Lirac; and rosé Tavel.

- *Vins doux naturels*, or sweet wines: white Muscat de Beaumes-de-Venise; and red and white Rasteau

CÔTES-DU-RHÔNE VILLAGES The Côtes-du-Rhône Villages appellation was granted in 1966, and today some ninety-five communes are given the right to label their wines Côtes-du-Rhône Villages. Of these a total of sixteen—because they are considered higher in quality that the generic Côtes-du-Rhône Villages—can also attach the name of their village to the label. These include Beaumes-de-Venise, Cairanne, Chusclan, Laudun, Rasteau, Roaix, Rochegude, Rousset les Vignes, Sablet, Saint-Gervais, Saint-Maurice, Saint Pantaléon les Vignes, Séguret, Valréas, Vinsobres, and Visan. They produce 20 million bottles a year.

CÔTES-DU-RHÔNE Regional Côtes-du-Rhône wines—what we think of as generic Côtes-du-Rhône—make up 80 percent of the entire Rhône Valley's production. They are red, white, and rosé, and are made in some 163 communes. That includes some 10,000 winemakers producing around 300 million bottles a year. Soil and grape varieties are diverse, with the dominant grape being the red Grenache, followed closely by Syrah, Mourvèdre, and Cinsault.

A Look at Three
of My Favorite Crus

MY PERSONAL WINE CELLAR is made up largely of wines from the southern Rhône, with a huge portion of Châteauneuf-du-Pape and a healthy dose of wines from two villages, Gigondas and Vacqueyras. Here is a thumbnail sketch of the three wines:

CHÂTEAUNEUF-DU-PAPE   Châteauneuf-du-Pape is the most prestigious wine of the southern Rhône. The climate is the driest of the Rhône region, dominated by the mistral winds throughout the year. It boasts of some 2,800 hours of sunshine a year and is famed for the giant stones—part of the Rhône riverbed when the river was extremely wide—that cover the soil. The heat stored in the stones by day is released into the soil by night, resulting in an oven effect, making for a dense, powerful wine.

The Châteauneuf story is a dear one. In the 14th century the popes in Avignon chose Châteauneuf as their summer residence, and Pope John XXII built a new castle, thus naming the village Châteauneuf-du-Pape. The popes encouraged the production of wine and developed the vineyards. But once the popes left Avignon—and only one pope, in Rome, was recognized—the wine all but fell into oblivion until the 18th century. Wines of what is now known as La Nerthe were becoming famous, as were those of Domaine de la Solitude. Then came the phylloxera blight, and many winemakers abandoned grape growing in favor of cherries, almonds, apricots, and olives.

Some winemakers continued, among them Baron Le Roy of Châteauneuf-du-Pape's Château Fortia. He felt that the region had the capacity to make truly great wines, and that the region deserved better. The wines of Châteauneuf were in fact traditionally shipped to the better-known wine regions of Bordeaux or Burgundy to give color and strength to those wines. Le Roy felt that if the winemakers of Châteauneuf-du-Pape adhered to higher standards, their wines could stand on their own. Today, Châteauneuf-du-Pape has among the strictest rules of any AOC wine in France, largely due to the fact that they virtually invented the AOC.

Châteauneuf-du-Pape wines are unusually complex, largely because they can be made up of some thirteen different varieties of grapes; yet most winemakers choose to concentrate on Syrah, Grenache, and Mourvèdre. Here is the selection:

Syrah	Muscardin
Grenache	Clairette
Mourvèdre	Picpoul
Cinsault	Picardin
Vaccarese	Bourboulenc
Counoise	Roussanne
Terret Noir	

My favorites are Château du Beaucastel, Château La Nerthe, Domaine de la Mordorée, Le Clos du Caillou, Domaine de la Janasse, and Grand Veneur, and Domaine du Pegaü.

GIGONDAS Much like Châteauneuf-du-Pape, the Gigondas region is blessed with 2,800 hours of sunshine each year and a fine drying effect from the mighty mistral winds. Like most of the vineyards in France, Gigondas was attacked by phylloxera in the 19th century, and farmers replaced the vines with olive trees. When the olive groves were decimated by the frost of 1956, vines once again took over the slopes.

If you hike up above the tiny village of Gigondas—population 656—where carefully marked trails allow you extraordinary vistas of the entire Rhône Valley and a close-up look at terraced vineyards that seem to grow in the middle of nowhere, you will feel that you are on the top of the world. When you drive through the Gigondas vineyards in the summer months, you will see why the wine has such intensity, as the grapes are almost dried to a jamlike *confit* by the sun and the wind.

In the early 1950s Gigondas was awarded its AOC as a Côtes-du-Rhône Village, and in 1971 it was promoted to *cru* status. Wines from Gigondas must include a maximum of Grenache Noir grapes, and a minimum of 15 percent Syrah and Mourvèdre. The wine may also contain up to 10 percent Carignan grapes. Gigondas wines taste like sunshine, with fruity bouquets of plums and kirsch when young, turning musky with age. Gigondas is a winter drinking wine, made for meaty *daubes* and roast lamb.

My favorites are Domaine les Goubert, Domaine du Cayron, Domaine Santa Duc, Château Saint Cosme, Domaine Saint Gayan, Château du Trignon, and Domaine la Bouïssière.

VACQUEYRAS It took Vacqueyras—a village of no more than 1,000 people—until 1990 to achieve *cru* status, but the little village has made great strides in the past twenty years. Its best wines are often compared to Gigondas; some I even prefer over their better-known neighbor. Vacqueyras must contain up to 50 percent Grenache Noir and at least 25 percent of Syrah, Mourvèdre, and Cinsault. The wines of Vacqueyras tend to be a bit more spicy—some say manly—than Gigondas. This is another wintry wine, great for game, roasts, and dense vegetable gratins.

My favorites are Domaine Le Sang des Cailloux, Domaine des Armouriers, La Mornardière, Clos de Cazaux, and La Fourmone.

ROBESPIERRE BEEF DOMAINE DE LA PONCHE

Boeuf à la Robespierre Domaine de la Ponche

*F*ine summer memories include sitting on the terrace of the lovely hotel-restaurant Domaine de la Ponche, situated in the middle of the flat, verdant vineyards just outside the wine village of Vacqueyras. Here, Swiss-born chefs Ruth Spahn and Madeleine Frauenknecht work their special magic with myriad local ingredients. This utterly simple seared steak—embellished with pungent minced garlic and fragrant rosemary—hits the spot, especially when accompanied by one of the meaty, he-man red wines of Vacqueyras. The dish is named after radical French politician Maximilien Robespierre, who was sent to the guillotine on July 28, 1794. Serve these with the crusty Potatoes Domaine de la Ponche (page 225).

EQUIPMENT: A large cast-iron skillet.

4 plump cloves garlic, peeled and finely minced

¼ cup finely minced rosemary leaves

1 tablespoon extra-virgin olive oil

1 pound beef hanger or flank steak, butterflied, about ½-inch thick

Freshly ground black pepper to taste

Fleur de sel or fine sea salt to taste

Wedges of fresh lemon, for garnish (optional)

1 In a small bowl, combine the minced garlic and rosemary. Set aside.

2 Massage the oil into the steak, and lightly season both sides with pepper. If you do not have a skillet large enough to hold the steak, cut it crosswise in half to fit.

3 Heat a large, dry cast-iron skillet over high heat for about 1 minute. When the pan is very hot, sear the steak quickly on both sides, 1 to 2 minutes a side for medium-rare, longer for medium.

4 Remove the steak to a platter. Pour any juices from the pan over the meat. Season generously with salt. Sprinkle with the garlic and rosemary mixture. Cover loosely with foil. Let the meat rest for 5 minutes (to allow the juices to retreat back into the beef) before carving across the grain. Serve immediately, with a few drops of lemon juice, if desired.

4 SERVINGS

Serge L. Ferigoule
Domaine le Sang des Cailloux
Route de Vacqueyras
84260 Sarrians
Telephone: 04 90 65 88 64
Fax: 04 90 65 88 75

Domaine de la Ponche Hotel and Restaurant
Ruth Spahn, Madeleine Frauenknecht, and Jean-Pierre Onimus
84190 Vacqueyras
Telephone: 04 90 65 85 21
Fax: 04 90 65 85 23
E-mail: *domaine.laponche@wanadoo.fr*
Web: *www.hotel.laponche.com*

Wine Suggestion: A favorite Vacqueyras comes from winemaker Serge Ferigoule at Domaine le Sang des Cailloux, which translates as "Blood of the Rocks." I first encountered Serge more than fifteen years ago, when he was just starting out in the wine business. His fame has grown, as has the quality of his wine, traditionally a blend of 70 percent Grenache, 20 percent Syrah, 7 percent Mourvèdre, and 3 percent Cinsault. His vines are from forty to sixty years old and his wine is aged in wood for up to six months, making it an opulent, dense, purple-black nectar.

Braids of purple garlic in an outdoor market

WHITE WINE DAUBE

Daube Avignonnaise

*T*his is a "quick" variation on the traditional Provençal beef *daube,* where the meat is generally marinated in red wine for up to several days. Here, in a traditional beef stew from the city of Avignon, the beef is quickly marinated in white wine for just a few hours. The result is a stew that is ideal for summer, a bit less hearty but just as delicious as its red wine big brother.

1 In a large shallow bowl, combine 2 tablespoons of the olive oil, *eau-de-vie,* beef, salt, and pepper. Cover with plastic wrap. Set aside to marinate at room temperature for 2 hours.

2 Preheat the oven to 325 degrees F.

3 In the casserole, heat the remaining 2 tablespoons of oil over moderately high heat until hot but not smoking. Add the onions, carrots, mushrooms, garlic, orange zest, and salt to taste. Reduce the heat to low, and sweat—cook, covered, over low heat until the onions and garlic are soft but not browned—for about 5 minutes. Add the beef and marinade to the casserole, then add the tomatoes, white wine, bouquet garni, and peppercorns. Cover. Place in the center of the oven and cook until the meat is ultra-tender, 3 to 4 hours. Check from time to time to make sure the liquid is at a very gentle simmer. Do not allow it to boil or the meat will become tough. (There is no need to baste, for the fats and wine will automatically baste the meat.) At serving time, taste for seasoning. Remove and discard the bouquet garni.

EQUIPMENT: A large heavy-duty casserole with a lid; a 6-quart pasta pot fitted with a colander.

4 tablespoons extra-virgin olive oil

2 tablespoons *eau-de-vie* or brandy, such as marc de Châteauneuf-du-Pape or cognac

6 pounds beef, preferably two or three different cuts, choosing from the top or bottom round, heel or round, shoulder arm or shoulder blade, neck or short ribs of beef, cut into 3-ounce pieces

Sea salt to taste

Freshly ground black pepper to taste

2 large onions, peeled, halved, and thinly sliced

4 carrots, peeled and thinly sliced

4 ounces mushrooms, cleaned, trimmed, and thinly sliced

1 plump head garlic, cloves separated, peeled, and halved, green germs removed

4 Meanwhile, in the pasta pot, bring about 5 quarts of water to a rolling boil over high heat. Add the 3 tablespoons coarse sea salt and the pasta, stirring to prevent the pasta from sticking. Cook until tender but firm to the bite, about 11 minutes. Remove the pasta pot from the heat. Remove the colander and drain over a sink, shaking to remove excess water. Place the pasta in a large bowl, sprinkle with the cheese, and toss to evenly coat the pasta. Transfer the pasta to individual warmed shallow soup bowls. Arrange several pieces of meat on top of the pasta, spooning several tablespoons of sauce over the meat. Serve immediately.

6 SERVINGS

Wine Suggestion: Serve this with a white Rhône Valley wine, such as a Châteauneuf-du-Pape. My favorites include offerings from Château de Beaucastel, Grand Veneur, and Domaine de la Janasse.

Grated zest of 1 orange

2 ripe tomatoes, cored, peeled, seeded, and chopped

2 bottles white wine (while a white Châteauneuf-du-Pape is traditional here, any drinkable white without too much oak will work)

1 bouquet garni: large bunch of fresh parsley and several fresh bay leaves, securely fastened with cotton twine or in a wire mesh ball

½ teaspoon black peppercorns

3 tablespoons coarse sea salt

8 ounces imported Italian penne

Several tablespoons freshly grated Parmigiano-Reggiano cheese

Moroccan Lamb Meatballs with Cucumber and Mint Salad

Boulettes Marocaines à la Menthe, Salade de Concombre

A trip to the spice market, a warm summer's evening, and thoughts of a cool, refreshing dinner for four inspired this dish. The markets of Provence are filled with spice merchants and stands selling Moroccan wares, so fresh, fragrant spices are always at hand. These little meatballs hit the spot, with just the right touch of spice and heat to cool one off after a hot August afternoon.

1 In a bowl, combine the cucumber and yogurt and toss to thoroughly coat the cucumbers. (The salad can be prepared several hours in advance.) Cover the bowl securely with plastic wrap and refrigerate until serving time.

2 In a food processor or blender, combine the lamb, onion, cinnamon, cumin, paprika, and chopped mint and process until the mixture is thoroughly blended. Season with salt and pepper. With your hands, roll the mixture into about 24 meatballs the size of a walnut.

3 In a large skillet, heat the oil until hot but not smoking. Add the meatballs and fry until they are deep brown and cooked through to the center, about 5 minutes.

EQUIPMENT: A food processor or blender.

1 large cucumber, peeled and very thinly sliced, salted, and drained (see Note)

2 cups Greek-style plain yogurt

1 pound ground lamb

1 small onion, peeled and finely minced

½ teaspoon ground cinnamon

2 teaspoons ground cumin

2 teaspoons sweet paprika

¼ cup mint leaves, finely chopped

Fine sea salt

Freshly ground black pepper

2 tablespoons extra-virgin olive oil

1 lemon, cut into 4 wedges

2 tablespoons Classic Vinaigrette (page 323)

2 cups fresh mint leaves, tossed with the vinaigrette

Wine Suggestion: A Tavel rosé, from the Domaine de la Mordorée.

4 Place six meatballs and a lemon wedge on one side of each of four dinner plates. Place several spoonfuls of cucumber salad alongside. Place a bouquet of mint salad in the center. Serve.

4 SERVINGS

NOTE: To remove excess water from the cucumbers, place the sliced cucumbers in a bowl, sprinkle with 1 teaspoon fine sea salt, and cover with water. Cover the bowl securely with plastic wrap and refrigerate for 1 hour and up to 4 hours. Drain thoroughly and proceed with the recipe.

Domaine de la Mordorée

Christophe Delorme

30126 Tavel

Telephone: 04 66 50 00 75

Fax: 04 66 50 47 39

Tastings by appointment: 8 a.m. to noon and 1:30 to 6 p.m.

American importer: Kysela Père et Fils, Ltd.; telephone: (540) 722-9228; fax: 540-722-9258.

TAVEL

THE FIRST PLACE MOST French people encounter Tavel rosé is in Chinese restaurants, where the refreshing, almost spicy rosé wine from the village of Tavel on the right bank of the Rhône can always be found. While there is plenty of Tavel that is banal and undistinguished, the one that stands out in my mind comes from the Domaine de la Mordorée. Unlike many Tavels made from a single grape variety, the wine from this estate is an *assemblage* of no fewer than six varieties, including a majority of Grenache, but also Mourvèdre, Syrah, Cinsault, Bourboulenc, and Clairette. Most of the vines are at least forty years old, offering low yields and deep flavor.

Pork Stew with Sweet and Hot Peppers

Daube de Porc aux Poivrons et aux Piments

Our local butcher supplies us with some of the tastiest local pork, the old-fashioned kind of meat that has plenty of flavor. I created this stew, or *daube*, based on one I sampled years ago in the Basque region of France, where the mildly spicy *piment d'Espelette* is grown. It's interesting to see how, over the years, regional lines in France have blurred, and ingredients formerly found only in the region of origin have become popular all over the country. Today in the markets of Provence one finds the Basque Espelette peppers in all forms: fresh in the fall months, powdered for use like a chili powder, in mustards laced with the pepper, and even in vinegars. Like all stews, this one tastes even better the second day, after flavors have had time to mellow.

EQUIPMENT: A 6-quart heavy-duty casserole with a lid.

4 tablespoons extra-virgin olive oil

2 large onions, peeled and thinly sliced

Fine sea salt to taste

3 pounds pork tenderloin, cut into 2-ounce cubes

Freshly ground black pepper to taste

About 2 cups water

1 red bell pepper, rinsed, trimmed, seeds removed, and cut into thin strips

1 green bell pepper, rinsed, trimmed, and cut into thin strips

4 small fresh hot chili peppers, or to taste

1 In the heavy-duty casserole, combine 2 tablespoons of the oil, the onions, and ½ teaspoon of salt and sweat—cook, covered, over low heat without coloring until soft and translucent—for about 5 minutes. Transfer the onions to a bowl.

2 Season the pork all over with salt and pepper. In the same casserole, heat the remaining 2 tablespoons of oil over moderate heat until hot but not smoking. Add the meat and sear well on all sides, about 10 minutes total. This may have to be done in batches. Remove the meat to a platter and season with salt and pepper.

3 Combine the onions and pork in the casserole. Add water—about 2 cups—just to cover the meat. Cover and cook over low heat at a very gentle simmer until the meat is very tender, about 1 hour. (The dish can be prepared ahead of time up to this point.)

4 Once the meat is tender, add the bell peppers and chili peppers and cook until the peppers are soft, about 15 minutes more. Taste for seasoning. Serve immediately, with potatoes or rice.

6 SERVINGS

ON ENTERTAINING IN PROVENCE

LARGE OUTDOOR MEALS are the custom in our house, and more often than not the guests number fifteen to twenty. With that number, careful thought needs to be given to seating. My good friend Devon Fredericks gave me the idea of writing people's names on the small ochre stones from the vineyard. The personalized stones are used instead of traditional place cards. Guests then take the stones home as a souvenir paperweight.

"Seating themselves on the greensward, they eat while the corks fly, and there is talk, laughter and merriment, and perfect freedom, the universe is their drawing room and the sun their lamp. Besides, they have appetite, Nature's special gift, which lends to such a meal a vivacity unknown indoors, however beautiful the surroundings."

—JEAN-ANTHELME BRILLAT-SAVARIN, FRENCH GASTRONOME, 1755–1826

Meats

147

Oven-Roasted Suckling Pig

Cochon de Lait Rôti au Four

*B*irthdays are important feasts in our house, and on those days I always try to cook something I have not cooked before. One birthday—my own—I decided that I wanted to roast a suckling pig. It's quite impressive and quite easy as well. I roasted it ever so simply in the oven, basting it with vinegar, which helps cut the fat and also makes the skin of the pig glisten as it roasts. We were a group of ten, all people who love to cook and eat and drink. We prepared a feast, ending up with my favorite birthday "cake" of all, a homemade *tarte Tatin,* or upside-down apple tart.

EQUIPMENT: A very large roasting pan.

1 suckling pig (12 to 15 pounds)

2 tablespoons extra-virgin olive oil

Fine sea salt to taste

About 2 cups red wine vinegar

Wine Suggestion: On that special birthday we enjoyed a series of wines, including gifts from California, Bordeaux, and Burgundy. Two wines that stood out were Burgundians: a 1978 Pommard les Argillières Domaine Lejeune and a 1979 Pommard Rugiens Domaine Lejeune.

1 Preheat the oven to 400 degrees F.

2 Before roasting, score the skin of the pig so that fat can melt as the meat roasts. With a sharp knife, make a shallow incision along the backbone. Then, without penetrating the flesh, score each side of the pig diagonally at 1-inch intervals from head to tail.

3 Place the pig on its belly in the roasting pan. Rub the oil over it, then rub salt into the skin. Wrap the pig's ears in aluminum foil to protect them from burning.

4 If your oven is deep enough, place the roasting pan with the tail end of the pig to the back of the oven. (This will make for more even roasting, since the tail end is thicker and denser, and the back of the oven is hotter than the front.) If the oven is not deep enough, simply place the pig lengthwise in the oven. Roast the pig at 15 minutes per pound, basting it with the vinegar and turning it every 30 minutes. After about 2 hours, increase the heat to 425 degrees F. for the final 30 minutes of roasting to help deepen the color of the skin and make it crisp. The pig is cooked when the internal temperature reaches 170 degrees F. and the skin has turned a crisp, crackling brown. (A 12- to 15-pound suckling pig should take about 2½ hours of roasting time.)

5 Remove the roasting pan from the oven. Loosely cover the meat with aluminum foil and allow to rest for at least 30 minutes before carving. To serve, carve and place the pieces of meat on a platter. Serve with fall or winter vegetables, such as Herb-Stuffed Mushrooms (page 206), Sheila and Julian's Braised Fennel with Tomatoes (page 203), and a Potato and Celeriac Gratin (page 228).

16 TO 20 SERVINGS

Butcher Franck Peyraud, of Boucherie La Romane in Vaison-la-Romaine, with his son, Jeff

Linguine with Saffron from Provence

Le Mimosa's Spaghettini with Mussels and Baby Clams

Jo's Rigatoni with Lamb Sauce, Tomatoes,
and Fresh Mint

The Maussane Potter's Spaghetti

Tagliatelle with Rosemary and Lemon

Penne with Eggplant and Tomato Sauce

Penne with Basil, Mozzarella, and Pine Nut Oil

PASTA, RICE, BEANS, AND GRAINS
Les Pâtes, Riz, Légumes Secs et Céréales

25th Anniversary Pasta: Penne with Tomatoes,
Rosemary, Olives, and Capers

Spelt Salad with Peppers, Shallots, and Parsley

Lentils with Capers, Walnuts, Walnut Oil, and Mint

Fresh White Beans with Garlic and Light Basil Sauce

White Bean Ragout with Lemongrass

Camargue Rice with Lemon and Pine Nuts

Wicker chairs outside a café in the village of Eygalières

LINGUINE WITH SAFFRON FROM PROVENCE

Linguine au Safran de Provence

I'll try almost anything once. Several years ago I decided to see how difficult it would be to grow saffron crocuses: the idea of my own little saffron crop appealed to me greatly. So I planted dozens of special purple *Crocus sativus* in the garden. I think my entire crop of saffron consisted of about a dozen brilliant orange stigmas, which I delicately steeped in warm stock and used in a soup. And that was the end of that experiment! I have always had saffron in the pantry, but I admit that it was not among my ten most used culinary herbs. That is, until our cheese merchant, Josiane Deal, asked me to sample a new local saffron. This recipe was inspired by one in a small regional cookbook, *Recettes de Provence*. The idea of infusing saffron in milk, then using it as a pasta sauce, was totally intriguing—brilliant, simply brilliant. The deep, bright golden yellow color of the sauce, the fragrance, and the pleasantly sharp, lingering flavor of the dressed pasta make this dish a winner in my house. In the summertime, it's even delicious cold. I often serve this as a side dish to accompany Tuna Fillet with Meyer Lemons and Summer Savory (page 79).

EQUIPMENT: A pasta pot fitted with a colander.

A generous pinch of best-quality saffron threads (about 1 heaping teaspoon, or 0.3 grams)

1⅓ cups whole milk

3 tablespoons coarse sea salt

1 pound imported Italian linguine

1 cup (4 ounces) freshly grated Parmigiano-Reggiano cheese

Fine sea salt to taste

Wine Suggestion: A golden yellow wine that reflects the gorgeous color of the pasta. Try a Viognier wine, or a rich white Châteauneuf-du-Pape, or a younger white Rhône.

1 At least 8 hours (and up to 48 hours) before preparing the pasta, combine the saffron and the milk in a covered container. Shake to blend. Refrigerate until the pasta is prepared.

2 In the pasta pot, bring about 5 quarts of water to a rolling boil over high heat. Add the salt and the pasta, stirring to prevent the pasta from sticking. Cook until tender but firm to the bite, 8 to 10 minutes. Remove the pasta pot from the heat. Remove the colander and drain over a sink, shaking to remove excess water.

3 In a large saucepan, warm the saffron milk over low heat. Add the drained pasta and stir to coat the pasta with the sauce. Add half of the cheese and toss once more. Add salt to taste. Taste for seasoning. Cover and let rest for 2 to 3 minutes to allow the pasta to thoroughly absorb the sauce. Taste for seasoning. Transfer to individual warmed shallow soup bowls. Serve immediately, passing the remaining cheese at the table.

6 SERVINGS AS A MAIN COURSE, 12 SERVINGS AS A SIDE DISH

HOW TO CHOOSE SAFFRON

BECAUSE SAFFRON IS the most expensive and the oldest of cultivated spices, consumers need to be savvy shoppers. There is a great deal of adulteration in the saffron world—unscrupulous saffron dealers have been known to dilute saffron by adding look-alike safflower or marigold petals, or by mixing ground saffron with turmeric, which also has a rich golden color. When buying saffron, select only bright deep red and milder yellow threads, and look for Superior Grade Spanish Mancha saffron or Coupe Grade Spanish Mancha saffron. A single gram of saffron (costing about $6 in the United States) yields about 1 tablespoon of saffron threads, enough to flavor many dishes. A reliable saffron source in the United States is The Spice House, *www.thespicehouse.com.*

A Farmer's Story

MARIE AND FRANÇOIS PILLET were living in Paris, enjoying François's career as an architect.

But the love of city life waned, and they longed for a patch of land of their own. They decided that winemaking was their vocation, so both attained degrees at a winemaking school in France's southeast. They set about to buy a vineyard, but the deal fell through on plot after plot of land. Looking for an agricultural specialty, they found one while researching agriculture history in Provence: it was saffron.

The Phoenicians brought saffron to France, and from Roman times, saffron was an important agricultural crop in the stretch of land that reaches from Orange in the north to Marseille in the south. Up until the 19th century, the towns of Orange and Mazan on Mount Ventoux were known for their quality saffron. In fact, until recent years, every Provençal *potager*—or vegetable garden—had a special plot of land devoted to saffron culture, ensuring that each home would feast on a proper bouillabaisse.

Feeling that the modern world has not sufficiently exploited the culinary potential of saffron, Marie and François found a plot of land in Le Barroux, a tiny village in the Vaucluse known for its monastery, the Monastère Ste.-Madeleine, where the monks bake an exceptional olive bread.

The Pillets planted more than 60,000 purple crocus bulbs on the abandoned land, harvesting their first crop in 2001. Harvest takes place in October when the crocus is in full bloom. Work is laborious and must be done by hand. The flowers are picked, then each stigma (there are only three to a flower) must be removed by hand. The Pillets dry their saffron threads near the fire, often working until 5 in the morning during the week of harvest.

Their product is divine: tiny glass vials filled with slim, long filaments of saffron ready to be used in pasta sauces, rice, desserts, and breads.

Saffron growers Marie and François Pillet at a café in Vaison-la-Romaine

L'Aube Safran

Marie and François Pillet
Chemin du Patifiage
84330 Le Barroux
Telephone: 04 90 62 66 91
Portable: 06 12 17 96 94

THE FLAVOR OF SAFFRON:
Saffron is not an easy flavor to describe, and it resembles no other spice, in either flavor or aroma. Good-quality saffron should have an exotic, almost smoky flavor, a soft bitterness, and something that cannot be mistaken for anything else. Good-quality saffron has a shelf life of about two years.

LE MIMOSA'S SPAGHETTINI WITH MUSSELS AND BABY CLAMS

Spaghettini aux Moules et Tellines

One summer my friend Steven Rothfeld and I toured the Languedoc area in search of great food, great wines, great photos. Our favorite meals were taken at Le Mimosa, the charmingly restored medieval home transformed into a restaurant by owners Bridget and David Pugh. I began my meal that night with this light and refreshing starter. I love the idea of roasting the mussels and clams in a hot oven rather than steaming them open on top of the stove. The flavor is more intense, and almost smoky.

1 Preheat the oven to 500 degrees F.

2 Thoroughly scrub the mussels, and rinse with several changes of water. If an open mussel closes when you press on it, then it is good; if it stays open the mussel should be discarded. Beard the mussels. (Do not beard the mussels more than a few minutes in advance or they will die and spoil. Note that in some markets mussels are prepared, in that the small black beard that hangs from the mussel has been clipped off, but not entirely removed. These mussels do not need further attention.) Set aside.

EQUIPMENT: Cheesecloth; a 6-quart pasta pot fitted with a colander; a large sieve.

2 pounds mussels

8 ounces baby clams

6 tablespoons white wine

6 tablespoons extra-virgin olive oil

2 large cloves garlic, minced

Fine sea salt to taste

12 ounces imported Italian spaghettini

¼ cup finely minced fresh parsley leaves

Grated zest of 1 lemon, preferably organic

Restaurant Le Mimosa
Bridget and David Pugh
34725 Saint-Guiraud
Telephone: 04 67 96 67 96
Fax: 04 67 96 61 15

3 Place the mussels and the clams on separate baking sheets. Place them in the oven until the shells spring open, about 5 minutes. Remove the mussels and clams from their shells and strain the juice through dampened cheesecloth set in a sieve set over a bowl.

4 In a medium saucepan, combine the shellfish liquid, wine, olive oil, and garlic. Boil briskly for 5 minutes.

5 In the pasta pot, bring about 5 quarts of water to a rolling boil over high heat. Add the salt and the pasta, stirring to prevent the pasta from sticking. Cook until tender but firm to the bite, about 6 minutes. Remove the pasta pot from the heat. Remove the colander and drain over a sink, shaking to remove excess water. Immediately transfer the drained pasta to a large serving bowl. Add the shellfish sauce and toss to evenly coat the pasta. Cover and let rest for 1 to 2 minutes to allow the pasta to thoroughly absorb the sauce. Taste for seasoning. Transfer to individual warmed shallow soup bowls. Arrange the mussels and the baby clams in their shells on top of the pasta. Sprinkle with minced parsley and lemon zest. Serve immediately, with finger bowls or dampened hand towels.

Wine Suggestion: David Pugh recommends a Picpoul de Pinet de Saint Martin de la Garrigue 2000.

4 SERVINGS

TELLINES

TELLINES ARE A FRENCH specialty found only in Provence. Tiny clams no bigger than a fingernail, they are beautifully colored from pale pink to a light gray, often striated and shiny. Their habitat is the sandy soil of the Camargue. I like to serve them as an aperitif. After washing, rinsing, and soaking them in salt water for several hours to remove all sand, I drain the *tellines,* toss them into a hot skillet, cook them for just 1 to 2 minutes until they open, then shower them with garlic and parsley. I serve them in little bowls and guests eat the sweet bivalves with their fingers, sucking the meat from the shells.

Pasta, Rice, Beans, and Grains

Jo's Rigatoni with Lamb Sauce, Tomatoes, and Fresh Mint

Rigatoni à la Sauce d'Agneau, Garniture de Tomates-Cerises à la Menthe

*G*eorge Germon and Johanne Killeen—chefs and owners of Al Forno restaurant in Providence, Rhode Island—are neighbors of ours in Provence. When I told them I would help them find a farmhouse to restore, I insisted it could be no more than 20 minutes from ours, so we could spend long family evenings together. And we do, whenever we get the chance. The nice part of having cooks as friends is that when you are not in the mood to cook, they usually are, and vice versa. I was just beginning a week of cooking classes, so the couple kindly invited us for a Sunday night supper at their beautiful restored farm. Johanne created this brilliant dish that evening. With a light lamb sauce, thick rigatoni that cleverly trap the sauce, and the stellar idea of a mint and cherry tomato garnish, this dish is a real winner!

EQUIPMENT: A large frying pan with a lid; a food processor or blender; a 6-quart pasta pot fitted with a colander.

2 onions, peeled and finely diced

5 plump cloves garlic, peeled, halved, green germs removed, finely minced

About 6 tablespoons extra-virgin olive oil

Fine sea salt to taste

1 fresh hot chili pepper (or hot red pepper flakes to taste)

2 carrots, peeled and cut into chunks

1 large rib celery, cut into chunks

A 1-inch piece of peeled fresh ginger

1 pound ground lamb

Wine Suggestion: Red, always red. How about a favorite Vacqueyras, from the cellars of Domaine Le Sang des Cailloux or Domaine la Mornardière, two dependable reds from our region.

Heirloom tomatoes in the Velleron market

1 In a large frying pan, combine the onions, garlic, 4 tablespoons of the oil, and salt, and stir to blend. Sweat—cook, covered, over low heat until soft but not browned—for 3 minutes.

2 In a food processor or blender, chop the hot pepper, carrots, celery, and ginger. Add to the frying pan. Sauté gently until soft, about 5 minutes.

3 Add the lamb and stir until it is no longer pink, about 3 minutes more. Add the parsley, dried mint, and wine. Increase the heat and bring to a boil. Immediately reduce the heat and cook vigorously until most of the wine has evaporated, about 5 minutes more.

¼ cup chopped fresh parsley leaves

2 tablespoons dried mint, crushed with your fingers

2 cups dry white wine

20 ripe cherry tomatoes, halved

40 fresh mint leaves, cut into a *chiffonnade*

3 tablespoons coarse sea salt

1 pound imported Italian rigatoni

Freshly grated Pecorino-Romano cheese, for the table

4 In a bowl, toss the cherry tomatoes, the remaining 2 tablespoons of oil, and the fresh mint. Toss to blend.

5 At serving time, in the pasta pot fitted with a colander, bring about 5 quarts of water to a rolling boil over high heat. Add the coarse sea salt and the pasta, stirring to prevent the pasta from sticking. Cook until tender but firm to the bite, about 11 minutes. Remove the pasta pot from the heat. Remove the colander and drain over a sink, shaking to remove excess water. Immediately transfer the drained pasta to the sauce in the pan. Toss to coat the pasta evenly. Cover and let rest for 1 to 2 minutes to allow the pasta to thoroughly absorb the sauce. Taste for seasoning. Transfer to individual warmed shallow soup bowls. Serve immediately. At the table, garnish with the cheese and with the cherry tomato blend.

4 SERVINGS

THE MAUSSANE POTTER'S SPAGHETTI

Spaghetti à l'Aïoli au Pistou

I have a handy repertoire of simple dishes that take little time, effort, or thought to prepare but pay off big-time with flavor. This spaghetti—with a sauce that combines the pungency of a basil sauce, or *pistou,* and the richness of a golden garlic and egg sauce, or *aïoli*—is one I make often during the summer, when I am in Paris but dreaming of the flavors of Provence. It was dictated to me one summer afternoon by potter friends from the village of Maussane-les-Alpilles.

EQUIPMENT: A food processor or blender; a 6-quart pasta pot fitted with a colander.

4 plump cloves garlic, peeled, halved, green germs removed

2 large egg yolks

½ cup Light Basil Sauce (page 56)

3 tablespoons coarse sea salt

1 pound imported Italian spaghetti

Fine sea salt to taste

Freshly grated Parmigiano-Reggiano cheese, for the table

Wine Suggestion: A simple red Côtes-du-Rhône fits the bill here.

Pottery for sale in Maussane-les-Alpilles

1 In a food processor or blender, combine the garlic and egg yolks and process to blend. Pour the basil sauce through the feed tube, processing to a thick sauce. Transfer the sauce to a large, shallow bowl.

2 In the pasta pot, bring about 5 quarts of water to a rolling boil over high heat. Add the coarse sea salt and the pasta, stirring to prevent the pasta from sticking. Cook until tender but firm to the bite, about 6 minutes. Remove the pasta pot from the heat. Remove the colander and drain over a sink, shaking to remove excess water. Immediately transfer the drained pasta to the sauce in the bowl. Toss to evenly coat the pasta. Cover and let rest for 1 to 2 minutes to allow the pasta to thoroughly absorb the sauce. Add salt to taste. Transfer to individual warmed shallow soup bowls. Serve immediately, passing the cheese at the table.

4 SERVINGS

Robert Del Giudice at his Lis Amélie pottery shop in Maussane-les-Alpilles

Provençal Pottery: Some Personal Favorites

I NEVER NEED AN EXCUSE to purchase another cup, plate, or pottery vessel. There is something special and rewarding about eating off the plates or using the knife rest of the potter you have recently met face-to-face. It's the same way I get a thrill buying fruits and vegetables from the men and women who have toiled the soil to bring them to life.

Pottery in Provence has always been a product of exceptionally good clay soil, making sturdy, long-lived items. Each region of Provence has become known for a different style of pottery with a different use. The pottery of Dieulefit, for instance, has been known since prehistory, when all manner of vessels, from huge storage jars to cookware, were made of clay.

If you've thought that the shapes of some clay objects resemble silver serving pieces, you are right: During the reign of Louis XIV in the 17th century, the Sun King asked the nobility to support the war effort by sacrificing their gold and silver vessels. Before giving them up, though, they had them copied by potters, many of them in the Dieulefit region. Today Dieulefit pottery is mainly functional, and many potters specialize in the bright ochre, green, and traditional red tones.

The area around Uzès—especially the village of St.-Quentin-la-Poterie—has been known for its pottery since Roman times. The region produces a marbled pottery as well as braided baskets.

The vases of Anduze are unique. Inspired by the Medici vases in Italy in the 17th century, they were first used to decorate the gardens of Versailles. While little china is now produced in Marseille, the 17th and 18th centuries saw a prosperous era of elegantly enameled tableware, much of it decorated with flowers, fruits, and fish of the Mediterranean. The glazed pottery of Moustiers was developed at the same time as that of Marseille, and today Moustiers is one of Provence's premiere villages devoted to the craft.

The traditional green, yellow, and honey-toned tableware of Vallauris was popularized by Picasso in 1948, and the soil around the city of Apt boasts of thousands of different colors. It is the Bernard family that today continues a tradition begun in the 14th century.

Here is a list of my favorites in Provence:

AIGUES-VIVES
(SOUTH OF NÎMES)
Richard Estéban
Poterie d'Aigues-Vives
58, rue de l'Abattoir
30670 Aigues-Vives
Telephone: 04 66 35 18 79

My current favorite—everything from tiny dollhouse-like cups to giant pots. Great greens!

APT
Faïence d'Apt
Atelier Bernard
286, avenue de la Libération
84400 Apt
Telephone: 04 90 74 15 31
Fax: 04 90 74 30 51
Web: *www.faiencedapt.com*

Beginning in 1984, I spent hours with Jean Faucon, a sixth-generation potter. I would sit in his *atelier* and watch him form the delicate miniature clump of grapes or tiny olives and olive leaves that adorn his most decorative pieces. My daily tableware is made up of the Faucon collection of fine, brilliantly glazed ochre pieces. Sadly, Jean died in 2002. His brother, Pierre, has taken over the business and it continues to thrive. The shop is like a museum, and you may need to special order. Call before you go!

Atelier Antony Picot
Ponty R.N. 100
84220 Goult
Telephone: 04 90 72 22 79

Monsieur Picot has a lovely *atelier* full of beautiful objects, including bright yellow colanders with stands, small plates in the shape of a leaf, and some astonishing trompe l'oeil masterpieces. Worth a detour!

AUBAGNE
Poterie Ravel
Avenue Goums
13400 Aubagne
Telephone: 04 42 82 42 00
Fax: 04 42 82 42 01
E-mail *poterie.ravel@wanadoo.fr*

Since 1837 Ravel has been known for its ravishing pots. I have a golden *daubière*— for cooking beef stews—that I treasure.

CLIOUSCLAT (NORTH OF MONTÉLIMAR)
La Poterie de Cliousclat
Le Village
26270 Cliousclat
Telephone: 04 75 63 05 69
Fax: 04 75 63 05 13

Very-ancient-style pottery, mostly cookware, lots of good colors and variety. Great ochre colors. Call before you go!

DIEULEFIT (NORTH OF NYONS)
Poterie Mont Rachas
Place Châteauras
26220 Dieulefit
Telephone: 04 75 90 63 25

One day I wandered into the back of this shop, and stood face-to-face with the bowls of my dreams. Sturdy bowls of all sizes, in deep greens, dark ochres, even a deep, dark brown. (Also the factory, Commune aux Terres, Poterie du Mont Rachas, 26160 Poët-Laval; telephone: 04 75 46 46 84; fax: 04 75 46 45 80.)

Poterie Il Etait une Fois
Place de l'Ancien Collège
26220 Dieulefit
Telephone: 04 75 46 87 58

I am in love with the bright celadon color of Provence, and I cherish the set of dishes and soup bowls from this beautiful shop.

Poterie Atelier du Sage
1, Place Châteauras
26220 Dieulefit
Telephone: 04 75 46 35 25

Great tableware, good variety, some too cutesy.

GORDES (NEAR APT)
Pascale Mestre
Nils Descotes-Genon
Poterie du Plan des Amandiers
84220 Gordes
Telephone/Fax: 04 90 72 36 32

Very pure and beautiful porcelain, including gorgeous *santons* (traditional figurines), lovely knife rests, great tableware, and objects.

MAUSSANE-LES-ALPILLES
(NEAR LES BAUX)
Lis Amélie
Dany et Robert Del Giudice
Pont de Monblan
13520 Maussane-les-Alpilles
Telephone: 04 90 54 37 55
Fax: 04 90 54 21 03

A real favorite: everything from giant Anduze pots to works from many potters around Provence. A huge selection of tableware, cookware, gourmet items.

MOUSTIERS (NORTHEAST OF TOULON)
Atelier Soleil
quai Saint-Michel
04360 Moustiers-Sainte-Marie
Telephone: 04 92 74 61 62
Fax: 04 92 74 61 71
E-mail: *franck.scherer@wanadoo.fr*

This shop stands out for its elegance and simplicity: I love my small collection of glazed dinner plates, shiny white with simple pastel-colored borders.

TAGLIATELLE WITH ROSEMARY AND LEMON

Tagliatelle au Romarin et au Citron

One summer this was *the* recipe of the season. I had a guest and we ate this beautifully simple pasta for dinner three nights in a row. I could have gone for a fourth, but we went out to dinner instead. What could possibly be bad about the trio of fresh golden pasta, lemons from the tree, and rosemary from right outside the kitchen door? A touch of Parmesan, a sip of wine, and the celebration has begun!

1 In the pasta pot, bring about 5 quarts of water to a rolling boil over high heat. Add the coarse sea salt and the pasta, stirring to prevent the pasta from sticking. Cook until tender but firm to the bite, 2 to 3 minutes. Remove the pasta pot from the heat. Remove the colander and drain over a sink, shaking to remove excess water, but retain 1 cup of the pasta cooking water.

2 In the skillet, heat the oil and lemon juice just until warm. Add the drained pasta and the pasta cooking water, tablespoon by tablespoon, until the pasta absorbs the liquid. Add the rosemary and toss. Add half of the cheese and toss once more. Cover and let rest for 1 to 2 minutes to allow the pasta to thoroughly absorb the sauce. Taste for seasoning. Transfer to individual warmed shallow soup bowls. Serve immediately, passing the remaining cheese at the table.

4 TO 6 SERVINGS

EQUIPMENT: A 6-quart pasta pot fitted with a colander; a large nonstick skillet with a lid.

3 tablespoons coarse sea salt

1 pound fresh tagliatelle pasta or imported Italian linguine

½ cup extra-virgin olive oil

½ cup freshly squeezed lemon juice

2 cups fresh rosemary leaves, finely minced

2 cups (8 ounces) freshly grated Parmigiano-Reggiano cheese

Fine sea salt to taste

Wine Suggestion: I like a golden white here, one that reflects the lightness as well as the depth of the dish. One evening my friend Steven and I splurged on a bottle of white from the Domaine de la Granges des Pères, a unique white made from the Roussanne grape. This *vin de pays de l'Hérault,* from just north of Montpellier, is velvety, harmonious, and full of fresh fruit and big enough to stand up to the lemony acidity of the pasta as well as the power of rosemary.

Pasta, Rice, Beans, and Grains

PENNE WITH EGGPLANT AND TOMATO SAUCE

Penne aux Aubergines et Sauce Tomate

If I had to name my top ten comfort foods, penne would be on that list. I don't know what it is about this fat, tubular dried pasta that can drag me out of the nastiest of moods, making me sing, smile, or laugh with joy. I sometimes feel that I get into a rut, always cooking the same form of pasta. But then I think again, and I decide that if any food can so easily transform my mood from dark to sunny, why not indulge a bit! I created this dish on the way back from the garden one day. We had a bumper crop of elongated, purple-black eggplant and I decided to use it as simply as possible. This dish brings out the soft texture and haunting flavor of the eggplant but is made with a minimum of fat, so the indulgence is really no indulgence at all!

1 In the large saucepan, combine the oil, onion, garlic, and salt; stir to coat with the oil. Sweat— cook, covered, over low heat until soft but not browned—for 3 minutes. Add the puréed tomatoes, the bouquet garni, and the cubed eggplant. Stir to blend. Cover and simmer over low heat until the eggplant is cooked through and has absorbed the sauce, about 45 minutes. Taste for seasoning. Remove and discard the bouquet garni.

EQUIPMENT: A food processor or blender; a large deep saucepan with a lid; a 6-quart pasta pot fitted with a colander.

2 teaspoons extra-virgin olive oil

1 small onion, peeled, halved, and thinly sliced

2 plump cloves garlic, peeled, green germs removed, minced

Sea salt to taste

One 28-ounce can peeled tomatoes in their juice, tomatoes and juice puréed in a food processor or blender

1 bouquet garni: several parsley stems, celery leaves, and sprigs of thyme, wrapped in the green part of a leek and securely fastened with cotton twine, or in a wire mesh ball

1 pound fresh eggplant, cut into small cubes (do not peel)

3 tablespoons coarse sea salt

8 ounces imported Italian penne

Freshly grated Parmigiano-Reggiano cheese, for the table

2 Meanwhile, in the pasta pot, bring about 5 quarts of water to a rolling boil over high heat. Add the coarse sea salt and the pasta, stirring to prevent the pasta from sticking. Cook until tender but firm to the bite, about 11 minutes. Remove the pasta pot from the heat. Remove the colander and drain over a sink, shaking to remove excess water. Immediately transfer the drained pasta to the sauce in the saucepan. Toss to evenly coat the pasta. Cover and let rest for 1 to 2 minutes to allow the pasta to thoroughly absorb the sauce. Taste for seasoning. Transfer to individual warmed shallow soup bowls, passing the freshly grated Parmesan cheese.

2 SERVINGS

Wine Suggestion: Although my wine cellar in Provence is largely made up of French wines, particularly from the Rhône Valley, there are Italian wines I can't do without. A favorite red comes from the Contini Bonaccossi family, a Tuscan estate just west of Florence, known as Villa Capezzana.

Eggplant in an outdoor market

Penne with Basil, Mozzarella, and Pine Nut Oil

Penne à l'Huile de Pignons de Pin, Basilic, et Mozzarella

*O*nce I realized that the pine trees outside my kitchen window provided pinecones that harbored the prized pine nut—*pignon de pin*—I thought I had a gold mine. Wrong! After spending what seemed like hours prying the nuts from the pine cones, I decided to leave pine nuts to the professionals. Even better than the flavor of pine nuts is pine nut oil, rich with the creamy, nutty flavor of the fresh nut. This recipe comes from my oil supplier, Anne Leblanc, whose family has been pressing precious oils for decades. I prepare this often for family and friends. I have also found that it lends itself to a wealth of variations: in place of pine nut oil and mozzarella, try it with walnut oil, blue cheese, and walnuts; or with goat cheese and mint.

1 At least 2 hours (and up to 6 hours) before serving the pasta, prepare the sauce: In a bowl large enough to hold the pasta later on, combine the olive oil, pine nut oil, basil, Parmesan, and mozzarella. Toss to coat all the ingredients evenly with the oil. Cover with plastic wrap. Set aside to marinate at room temperature, tossing from time to time.

EQUIPMENT: A 6-quart pasta pot fitted with a colander.

2 tablespoons extra-virgin olive oil

2 tablespoons pine nut oil, plus
1 teaspoon for garnish

1 cup fresh basil leaves, cut into
a *chiffonnade*

½ cup (2 ounces) freshly grated Parmigiano-Reggiano cheese

5 ounces buffalo-milk mozzarella, cubed

3 tablespoons coarse sea salt

8 ounces imported Italian penne

Freshly ground black pepper to taste

Fine sea salt

Huilerie J. Leblanc
Anne Leblanc
6, rue Jacob
75006 Paris
Telephone: 01 46 34 61 55

2 At serving time, in the pasta pot, bring about 5 quarts of water to a rolling boil over high heat. Add the coarse sea salt and the pasta, stirring to prevent the pasta from sticking. Cook until tender but firm to the bite, about 11 minutes. Remove the pasta pot from the heat. Remove the colander and drain over a sink, shaking to remove excess water. Immediately transfer the drained pasta to the sauce in the bowl. Toss to evenly coat the pasta. Season generously with freshly ground black pepper, and drizzle with the 1 teaspoon pine nut oil. Cover with plastic wrap and let rest for 1 to 2 minutes to allow the pasta to thoroughly absorb the sauce. Taste for seasoning. Transfer to individual warmed shallow soup bowls. Serve immediately.

4 SERVINGS

Wine Suggestion: Take out your DDR (daily drinking red) for this one!

25TH ANNIVERSARY PASTA: PENNE WITH TOMATOES, ROSEMARY, OLIVES, AND CAPERS

Les Pâtes de Nos Noces d'Argent

When it came time for our twenty-fifth wedding anniversary one September, we debated how to celebrate. A trip to Spain? Champagne? We settled on a busman's holiday to visit the top restaurants in Avignon and spend an evening away from home in a luxury hotel. Not long before we were to leave for the short drive to Avignon, the skies opened and the rains were so forceful we could hardly find our way to the car, much less drive down the road. We cancelled our dinner and then I looked in the cupboard. It was pretty much bare, since we had planned to be away for a few days. The joke was on us! We decided that we would be just as happy with our favorite pasta dish—penne that is flavored with our homemade olive mix and capers from the garden—and a simple bottle of Côtes-du-Rhône. We could leave that special bottle we'd saved for the occasion for another day!

1 In the pasta pot, bring about 5 quarts of water to a rolling boil over high heat. Add the coarse sea salt and the pasta, stirring to prevent the pasta from sticking. Cook until tender but firm to the bite, about 11 minutes.

EQUIPMENT: A 6-quart pasta pot fitted with a colander.

3 tablespoons coarse sea salt

1 pound imported Italian penne

1 cup Spicy Tomato, Fennel and Orange Sauce (page 318)

2 tablespoons salt-cured capers, rinsed and drained

½ teaspoon fennel seeds

1 tablespoon finely chopped fresh rosemary leaves

½ cup olives from the Chanteduc Rainbow Olive Collection (page 4)

Hot red pepper flakes to taste

Freshly grated Parmigiano-Reggiano cheese, for the table

Fine sea salt

Clos Chanteduc

Ludovic Cornillon
Domaine St. Luc
26970 La Baume-de-Transit
Telephone: 04 75 98 11 51
Fax: 04 75 98 19 22
Web: *www.dom-saint-luc.com*
U.S. importer: Kermit Lynch
Wine Merchant, Berkeley, CA;
Telephone: (510) 524-1524

2 Meanwhile, in a saucepan that is large enough to hold the pasta, combine the tomato sauce, capers, fennel, rosemary, olives, and pepper. Cook just until heated through, 2 to 3 minutes.

Wine Suggestion:
Clos Chanteduc, of course!

3 Remove the colander and drain the pasta, shaking to remove excess water. Immediately transfer the drained pasta to the sauce in the saucepan. Toss to evenly coat the pasta. Cover and let rest for 1 to 2 minutes to allow the pasta to thoroughly absorb the sauce. Taste for seasoning. Transfer to individual warmed pasta bowls. Pass the freshly grated cheese.

4 SERVINGS

ON ROSEMARY: Outside my kitchen door I have a creeping rosemary plant—*romarin rampant*—that grows in a stony flowerbed we built in the late 1980s. The perennial is bushy, firm, and beautiful, sprouting tiny mauve-blue flowers in the springtime. Along with basil, thyme, and fennel, rosemary is the herb I reach for most often: when firing up the bread oven or heating up the outdoor grill, I always toss a handful of rosemary branches onto the fire for a burst of festive aromas.

Spelt Salad with Peppers, Shallots, and Parsley

Salade d'Epeautre aux Poivrons, Echalotes et Persil

*I*t is no exaggeration to say that I cook *épeautre*—known as spelt in the United States and *farro* in Italy—about once a week, either like rice, or as this warm-weather side dish that blends the nutty grain with bell pepper, shallots, and parsley. The sweet nuttiness of this Provençal grain means that it can even be served as a main course dish, with a green salad alongside.

In the saucepan, combine the spelt, chicken stock, bay leaves, and ½ teaspoon of the salt. Bring to a boil over high heat. Immediately reduce the heat to low, cover, and cook until the liquid is absorbed and the grains are puffed and tender, about 25 minutes. Let stand, covered, for at least 5 minutes before serving. To serve, remove and discard the bay leaves. Toss with the bell pepper, shallots, and parsley. Taste for seasoning. Serve warm or at room temperature.

6 TO 8 SERVINGS

EQUIPMENT: A 1-quart copper saucepan with lid.

1 cup spelt or *épeautre* (or substitute wheat berries)

2 cups Homemade Chicken Stock (page 325), water, or white wine

2 fresh or dried bay leaves

1 teaspoon fine sea salt

1 green bell pepper, trimmed, seeds removed, finely diced

2 shallots, peeled and minced

1 cup fresh parsley leaves, coarsely chopped

EPEAUTRE, ALSO KNOWN AS SPELT, is an
ancient red wheat that has long been popular in
Europe, favored for its nutty, rich flavor. An ancestor

of modern grains, *épeautre* has been grown since 9000 B.C. and was called the
"wheat of the Gauls." It was the major grain of Europe until Roman times; then
it lost favor, replaced by modern strains of wheat. In France, *epeautre* is enjoying
increased popularity, and it shows up in salads, in soups, and as a stuffing for
vegetables, and is ground for flour. It is grown largely in Provence, at the foot
of Mount Ventoux in the Vaucluse, where it is harvested in late August and has
become known as the "gold cereal" because of its golden brown grain. *Epeautre* is
favored by those who are allergic to standard wheat and is almost always grown
organically. Nutritionally, 3 ounces of the cereal provides enough daily protein
for an average adult. It is low in gluten and rich in minerals, with four times the
magnesium of brown rice; 3 ounces supplies the equivalent of two glasses of milk.

Epeautre is available in health food stores or can be ordered through the
Grain & Salt Society, telephone (800) 867-7258, or via the Internet at
www.celtic-seasalt.com.

THE PERFECT PAN: I have a huge collection of pots and pans in the
country, ranging from copper to stainless, cast iron to Provençal clay. When
time permits, I like to experiment, trying the same recipe in several kinds of
pans. I tried cooking *épeautre* in a rice cooker and it simply would not cook to
the desired consistency. Then I cooked one batch in stainless steel, another in
copper. The batch cooked in copper cooked much more quickly and remained
moist. So, if you have copper on hand, use it for this recipe.

Pasta, Rice, Beans, and Grains

LENTILS WITH CAPERS, WALNUTS, WALNUT OIL, AND MINT

Petit Ragoût de Lentilles aux Câpres, Noix,
Huile de Noix et Menthe

*H*ere is a salad that combines many of my favorite foods. While lentils are generally considered winter fare, they are excellent as a change of pace during the summer months, especially when served with roasted lamb or poultry. Here, the flinty, dense lentil is teamed with the sweet flavor of walnuts, bathed in a walnut oil vinaigrette, and given greater complexity by the addition of capers and fresh mint. While we normally think of lentils as coming from the center of France, in the Auvergne, there is also a thriving lentil culture in the Drôme Provençale. My favorite organically grown, dark green lentils come from the nearby village of Sainte-Jalle, near Nyons.

1 Place the lemon juice and a pinch of salt in the small bottle. Cover and shake to dissolve the salt. Add the oil and shake to blend. Taste for seasoning. Set aside.

EQUIPMENT: A small bottle with a lid; a large fine-mesh sieve; a large heavy saucepan with a lid.

2 tablespoons freshly squeezed lemon juice

Fine sea salt to taste

6 tablespoons best-quality walnut oil

1½ cups (8 ounces) French lentils, preferably *lentilles du Puy*

2 cups Homemade Chicken Stock (page 325)

1 carrot, peeled

1 onion, peeled and stuck with a clove

1 cup freshly cracked walnut pieces, coarsely chopped

½ cup capers in vinegar, drained

1 cup fresh mint leaves, coarsely chopped

Freshly ground white pepper to taste

2 Place the lentils in the sieve and rinse under cold running water. Transfer them to the saucepan, cover with cold water, and bring to a boil over high heat. When the water boils, remove the saucepan from the heat. Transfer the lentils to a fine-mesh sieve and drain over a sink. Rinse the lentils under cold running water. Return the lentils to the saucepan, add the chicken stock, season with salt, and bring just to a boil over high heat. Reduce the heat to a simmer. With a slotted spoon, skim any impurities that rise to the surface. Once the liquid is clear of impurities, add the carrot and onion, and simmer gently, uncovered, over low heat just until cooked yet still firm in the center, about 30 minutes. (Cooking time will vary according to the freshness of the lentils: the fresher they are, the more quickly they will cook.) Remove and discard the onion and carrot.

3 The lentils should have absorbed all of the liquid. If liquid remains at the bottom of the pan, transfer the lentils to a fine-mesh sieve set over a bowl. Drain, discarding the cooking liquid. Transfer the lentils to a large bowl. Add the vinaigrette, the walnuts, capers, pepper, and three-fourths of the mint; and toss to blend. Taste for seasoning. If serving warm, transfer to small warmed plates, garnish with the remaining mint, and serve immediately. If serving at room temperature, taste at serving time for seasoning, and garnish with the remaining mint.

4 TO 6 SERVINGS

FRESH WHITE BEANS WITH GARLIC AND LIGHT BASIL SAUCE

Cocos Blancs à l'Ail et au Pistou

From their sighting early in May and on through to October, fresh white beans known as *cocos blancs* are part of my Provençal diet. I put these creamy beans in soups and eat them bathed in basil sauce, loving the sweet aroma that wafts from the kitchen as they cook away on the stove.

EQUIPMENT: A large heavy-bottomed saucepan

1 tablespoon extra-virgin olive oil

10 plump cloves garlic, peeled, halved, green germs removed

2 pounds fresh small white beans in the pod, shelled (or substitute 1 pound dried white beans)

4 fresh or dried bay leaves

1½ quarts Homemade Chicken Stock (page 325) or cold water

1 teaspoon fine sea salt, or to taste

1 recipe Light Basil Sauce (page 56)

FOR FRESH BEANS: In the saucepan, combine the olive oil and garlic and stir to coat the garlic with the oil. Place over moderate heat and cook until the garlic is fragrant and soft, about 2 minutes. Do not let it brown. Add the beans, stir to coat with the oil, and cook for 1 minute more. Add the bay leaves and the stock and stir. Cover, bring to a simmer over moderate heat, and simmer for 15 minutes. Season with salt. Continue cooking at a gentle simmer until the beans are tender, about 15 minutes more. Stir from time to time to make sure the beans are not sticking to the bottom of the pan. Add additional stock or water if necessary. Taste for seasoning. Remove and discard the bay leaves.

FOR DRIED BEANS: Rinse the beans, picking them over to remove any pebbles. Place the beans in a large bowl, add boiling water to cover, and set aside for 1 hour. Drain the beans, discarding the water. In the heavy saucepan, combine the olive oil and garlic, and stir to coat the garlic with the oil. Cook over moderate heat until the garlic is fragrant and soft, about 2 minutes. Do not let it brown. Add the beans, stir to coat with the oil, and cook for 1 minute more. Add the bay leaves. Add the stock and stir. Cover, bring to a simmer over moderate heat, and simmer for 30 minutes. Season with salt. Continue cooking at a gentle simmer until the beans are tender, about 30 minutes more. Stir from time to time to make sure the beans are not sticking to the bottom of the pan. Add additional stock or water if necessary. (Cooking time will vary according to the freshness of the beans.) Taste for seasoning. Remove and discard the bay leaves.

To serve, stir the basil sauce into the beans, taste for seasoning, and serve.

6 SERVINGS

A blackboard outside a shop in Vallabrègues

WHITE BEAN RAGOUT WITH LEMONGRASS

Ragoût de Haricots Blancs à la Citronnelle

*T*his unusual and highly successful combination of white beans and fresh lemongrass, flavored with a touch of celeriac purée, is a most welcome addition to my ever-growing repertoire of bean recipes. The house is deliciously fragrant as the beans simmer away on the stove, and the gentle hint of lemon turns what might be an ordinary plate of beans into a veritable feast. Lemongrass grows easily in my vegetable garden, so I am always looking for French ways to use this delightful herb.

1 Place the beans in the pot and cover with cold water. Bring to a boil over high heat, reduce the heat to a simmer, and blanch for 2 minutes. Drain the beans through the sieve, discarding the liquid.

2 Return the beans to the pot. Add the carrot, onion, bouquet garni, lemongrass, and 1 teaspoon of salt. Add the stock and cover. Simmer gently over low heat until the beans are very tender, about 1½ hours. Remove and discard the carrot, onion, bouquet garni, and lemongrass.

3 Drain the beans and stir in the celery root purée. Stir in the butter. Taste for seasoning. Add salt and pepper to taste. At serving time, garnish with the mint.

4 SERVINGS

EQUIPMENT: A large pot with a lid; a fine-mesh sieve.

3 cups (about 12 ounces) dried white beans

1 carrot, peeled

1 onion, peeled but left whole

1 bouquet garni: several parsley stems, bay leaves, and sprigs of thyme, wrapped in the green part of a leek and securely fastened with cotton twine or in a wire mesh ball

3 stalks fresh lemongrass

Sea salt to taste

2 quarts Homemade Chicken Stock (page 325) or water

½ cup Celeriac Purée (page 214)

1 tablespoon unsalted butter

Freshly ground black pepper to taste

1 cup fresh mint leaves, finely minced

Wine Suggestion: Any wine from my repertoire of Rhône whites would be great here. My three favorite white wine grapes—Viognier, Roussanne, and Marsanne—show up often at my table. Try a young Viognier *vin de pays* from Châteauneuf-du-Pape producer Domaine de la Janasse, or my all-time favorite, Domaine les Goubert.

Camargue Rice with Lemon and Pine Nuts

Riz de Camargue au Citron et Pignons de Pin

We are certified grain nuts in our house. I am not sure which I love more, the fragrance that wafts through the kitchen as the rice cooks, the act of eating the tender grains, or knowing that there is some rice left over to turn into a festive salad at lunchtime. My pantry always includes many varieties of rice from the Camargue, including white and brown rice.

Combine the stock, rice, salt, olive oil, and bay leaves in a rice cooker and cook for 16 minutes or until the liquid has evaporated and the rice is cooked through but still fairly firm. Do not stir. Turn off the heat. Cover and keep warm for up to 20 minutes. Remove the bay leaves. At serving time, stir in the lemon zest, lemon juice, and toasted pine nuts. Serve.

6 CUPS; 8 SERVINGS

EQUIPMENT: A rice cooker.

2 cups Homemade Chicken Stock (page 325), white wine, or water

1½ cups brown Camargue rice (or other top-quality rice)

1 teaspoon salt

1 tablespoon olive oil

4 fresh or dried bay leaves

Zest of 2 lemons, grated

3 to 5 tablespoons freshly squeezed lemon juice

½ cup pine nuts, toasted

Pasta, Rice, Beans, and Grains

179

LE MIMOSA'S ARTICHOKES, GRILLED ALMONDS,
LEMON ZEST, AND HONEY

MY VEGETABLE MAN'S ASPARAGUS FLAN

ASPARAGUS WITH GOAT CHEESE AND SALMON EGGS

JOHANNES' OLIVADES: TOMATOES, OLIVES, CAPERS, MINT, AND BASIL

RUSSIAN TOMATO GRATIN

ROASTED CHERRY TOMATOES

DOMAINE ST. LUC'S GREEN BEANS WITH BASIL

QUICK SAUTEED GREEN PEPPERS

MIREILLE'S EGGPLANT

L'OUSTALET'S EGGPLANT AMBROSIA

SWISS CHARD TWO WAYS

ZUCCHINI BLOSSOMS STUFFED WITH MINT-INFUSED FRESH CHEESE

VEGETABLES

Les Légumes

ELIANE'S CHUNKY ZUCCHINI GRATIN

GOLDEN ZUCCHINI GALETTE

SHEILA AND JULIAN'S BRAISED FENNEL WITH TOMATOES

WILD MUSHROOM AND WALNUT TARTE TATIN

HERB-STUFFED MUSHROOMS

OVEN-ROASTED SHALLOTS WITH ROSEMARY AND BALSAMIC VINAIGRETTE

CAULIFLOWER GRATIN

JOHANNES' ANCHOVY DIP WITH STEAMED WHOLE CAULIFLOWER

PROVENÇAL CARROT OSSO BUCO

BEETS IN PISTACHIO OIL

CELERIAC PUREE

Alain Betti outside his shop, Coin Gourmand, in Vaison-la-Romaine

Le Mimosa's Artichokes, Grilled Almonds, Lemon Zest, and Honey

Artichauts, Amandes Grillées,
Zeste de Citron Confit au Miel Le Mimosa

"*W*hat great balance!" is what I said the first time I sampled this dish at Le Mimosa, the lovely country restaurant not far from Montpellier run by Bridget and David Pugh. There is everything to love about this dish, for it combines so many of my favorite Provençal ingredients. The lemon confit can be reserved for other uses, as in couscous salads or in preparing a chicken or rabbit fricassee.

1 Halve and juice the lemons, reserving the juice and lemons separately. In the bowl of a food processor or blender, combine the lemon juice, honey, and olive oil. Blend until creamy. Stir in ¼ cup of the thyme leaves. Set aside.

2 Place the halved lemons in a large pot, cover with about 1 quart of water, and add the ½ cup coarse sea salt. Bring to a boil over high heat and cook until the lemons can easily be pierced with a knife, about 10 minutes. Drain, cool, and cut each piece into four small wedges. Scrape away and discard the white pith. Place the lemon zest wedges in a small jar. Cover with half of the marinade. Cover securely. (The confit may be stored, refrigerated, for up to 1 week.)

EQUIPMENT: A food processor or blender.

THE MARINADE:

4 lemons, preferably organic, scrubbed

¼ cup thyme honey

1 cup extra-virgin olive oil

⅓ cup fresh thyme leaves

½ cup plus 3 tablespoons coarse sea salt

1 cup whole unblanched almonds

3 tablespoons distilled white vinegar

8 large or 16 small artichokes

1 teaspoon fresh thyme flowers or leaves

Restaurant Le Mimosa
Bridget and David Pugh
34725 Saint-Guiraud
Telephone: 04 67 96 67 96
Fax: 04 67 96 61 15

3 Place the almonds in a large, dry skillet over moderate heat. Toast, stirring or shaking the pan frequently to prevent burning, until they are evenly toasted and beginning to release their fragrance, about 4 minutes. Transfer the nuts to a bowl and while warm, toss with just enough of the remaining marinade to coat lightly. Set aside.

4 Bring a large pot of water to a boil over high heat. Add the 3 tablespoons coarse sea salt and the vinegar. Add the artichokes and boil, uncovered, until the central leaves pull away with little resistance, about 20 minutes. Strip away the outer leaves, trim the stalks to about 1 inch, and remove any strings or fiber. Cut each artichoke in half and cut away the choke.

5 To serve, place four large or eight small artichoke halves on each of four salad plates. Spoon a generous amount of the remaining marinade over the artichoke hearts and garnish with the lemon confit, almonds, and thyme flowers or leaves.

4 SERVINGS

Wine Suggestion: To bring out the flavor of the artichoke and marry well with the sweet thyme honey, David Pugh recommends a white wine from the Languedoc, a youthful Mas Jullien, where superstar winemaker Olivier Jullien's white is made largely from the Viognier grape, offering fruity notes of peaches and apricots.

LES SAINTS DE GLACE: THE ICE SAINTS

IN PROVENCE, THERE are three critical dates in May when temperatures can drop dramatically and there can be frosts, ruining the budding and flowering fruits. The days are May 11 (the Catholic feast day of Saint Mamert), May 12 (Saint Pancrace), and May 13 (Saint Servais), and these saints are traditionally known as the Ice Saints. Tradition also suggests that when planting your vegetable garden, you always wait for the feast days of the Ice Saints to pass, so tender vegetables do not risk a sudden freeze.

My Vegetable Man's Asparagus Flan

Le Flan d'Asperges de Mon Marchand de Légumes

*I*t's funny how merchants in the market generally resemble their produce. The farmer selling gnarled old carrots and turnips always sports hands that advertise his long hard labor in the sun. The lady offering pristine little rounds of goat cheese manages to reflect a prim, proper, tidy life. Raymond Chapuis, who supplies me with first-of-season asparagus, tender peas, firm and shiny zucchini, and gorgeous fava beans, is always trim, neatly dressed, and sporting a well-kept beard and a hearty smile. I see him at the Tuesday market in Vasion-la-Romaine, then again on Wednesdays in Saint-Rémy. His wife, Simone, kindly shared this favored asparagus flan. Note that for this recipe you need only the tender tips, which in Provence are sold separately. The stems can be steamed, puréed, and blended with chicken stock to prepare a soup.

EQUIPMENT: A 10½-inch round porcelain gratin dish; a vegetable steamer.

1 pound thin green asparagus tips (about 2 cups)

4 ounces smoked slab bacon, rind removed, cut into cubes (1 cup)

1 cup light cream

4 large eggs, lightly beaten

Fine sea salt to taste

Freshly ground white pepper to taste

Wine Suggestion: This delicate spring flan calls for a floral white, perhaps one with a Viognier base. Try the *vin de pays* from the reputable Châteauneuf-du-Pape vineyard Domaine de la Janasse.

1 Preheat the oven to 425 degrees. Butter the gratin dish and set aside.

2 Bring about 3 cups of water to a simmer in the bottom of a vegetable steamer. Place the asparagus tips on the steaming rack. Place the rack over the simmering water, cover, and steam until they are cooked through, 3 to 5 minutes. Drain. Set aside.

3 Place the bacon in a large skillet and cook, stirring frequently, over medium-high heat just until it begins to give off its fat and starts to brown, 4 to 5 minutes. Drain. Set aside.

4 In a large bowl, combine the cream and eggs. Whisk to blend.

5 Pour half of the cream and egg mixture into the gratin dish. Scatter the bacon over the mixture. Layer the asparagus tips on top of the bacon. Season with salt and pepper. Cover with the remaining cream and egg mixture.

6 Place the baking dish in the center of the oven. Bake until the mixture is set and the top is golden, 30 to 35 minutes. Remove from the oven and let cool for 10 minutes. Serve in wedges as a first course, or as a main luncheon dish with a tossed salad alongside.

8 SERVINGS AS A FIRST COURSE

Raymond Chapuis at the Tuesday market in Vaison-la-Romaine

Vegetables

ASPARAGUS WITH GOAT CHEESE AND SALMON EGGS

Asperges Vertes, Chèvre Frais et Oeufs de Saumon

When asparagus are in season, I could eat them every day, and just about do. Here, the vegetable is treated as simply as possible, embellished only by a touch of balsamic vinaigrette, which adds a welcome note of sweetness. The creamy richness of the goat cheese and the saltiness of the salmon eggs serve as proper, and elegant, partners.

1 Trim the asparagus, discarding the tips of the woody ends. Trim the tender stalks to about 7 inches.

2 Prepare a large bowl of ice water.

3 Fill the pasta pot with about 5 quarts of water and bring to a boil over high heat. Add the coarse salt and the asparagus. Boil, uncovered, until the stalks are crisp-tender, 3 to 4 minutes. (Cooking time will vary according to the size of the asparagus.) Immediately drain the asparagus and plunge them into the ice water so they cool down as quickly as possible and retain their crispness and bright green color. (The asparagus will cool in 1 to 2 minutes. After that, they will soften and begin to lose crispness and flavor.) Transfer the asparagus to a colander, drain, and wrap in a thick towel to dry.

EQUIPMENT: A food processor or blender; a 6-quart pasta pot fitted with a colander.

2 pounds fresh green asparagus

3 tablespoons coarse sea salt

About 7 ounces soft fresh goat cheese

2 to 3 tablespoons whole milk

¼ cup salmon eggs

Fine sea salt to taste

Freshly ground black pepper to taste

Balsamic Vinaigrette (page 323)

Wine Suggestion: A white from the Rhône, of course: one of my current favorites is the white Côtes-du-Rhône Domaine du Clos du Caillou, Bouquet des Garrigues, a rich blend that includes plenty of Viognier, offering beautiful floral tones that do not fight with asparagus.

4 In a food processor or blender, combine the goat cheese and milk, and blend until the mixture is light and fluffy. Transfer the mixture to a bowl and stir in the salmon eggs, distributing them evenly through the goat cheese. Season to taste.

5 Arrange the asparagus in a fan shape on four large dinner plates. Place a dollop of the goat cheese mixture at the bottom of each fan. Drizzle the asparagus with the vinaigrette. Serve.

4 SERVINGS

On Blanching

ONE OF THE MOST CLASSIC techniques of French cooking is blanching and refreshing, a technique that not only helps preserve the vegetable's bright color but also minimizes any loss of nutrients. To blanch, bring a very large pot of water to a boil, add salt (some French chefs say the water should be so salty you can barely stand to taste it), then plunge the vegetable into the rapidly boiling water. The golden rule is, *do not cover* the pot. Leaving the pot uncovered allows the volatile acids that would dim the bright color of the vegetables to escape. To retain the bright color, do not cook the vegetable more than 7 minutes. As soon the vegetable is cooked to desired tenderness, immediately drain it and plunge it into a bowl of ice water, a technique called refreshing or shocking, which stops the cooking, firms up the vegetable, and again helps it maintain that bright color. As soon as the vegetable is cooled, drain it thoroughly. Many vegetables can be cooked several hours ahead in this manner and then reheated at serving time, usually with a quick sauté in olive oil.

Johannes' Olivades: Tomatoes, Olives, Capers, Mint, and Basil

Olivades: Tomates, Olives, Câpres, Menthe et Basilic

Marlies and Johannes Sailer run one of our favorite neighborhood restaurants, L'Oustalet, in the village of Gigondas. There are few greater summer pleasures than settling into one of their tables on the terrace, under the canopy of mature sycamore trees, as the sun is setting. Order up a bit of local white Viognier, and you are on your way to a heavenly evening! One summer's night Johannes served this wonderful vegetable condiment as a side to one of his simple grilled or roasted fish dishes. I love the combination of colors, textures, and flavors—the multicolored olives, vibrant red tomatoes, deep green capers, a hit of garlic, and just a suggestion of hot pepper, all offset by the bright green herbs and the surprise of fresh grains of coriander.

In a large bowl, combine all the ingredients and toss to blend. Serve as a condiment to poultry, fish, or meats.

6 SERVINGS

5 ripe tomatoes, cored, peeled, seeded, and chopped

1 cup Chanteduc Rainbow Olive Collection (page 4)

2 tablespoon salt-cured capers, rinsed and drained

5 plump cloves garlic, peeled and thinly sliced

½ teaspoon hot red pepper flakes

1 cup fresh mint leaves

1 cup fresh basil leaves

2 teaspoons fresh or dried coriander seeds (optional)

Fine sea salt to taste

L'Oustalet
Marlies and Johannes Sailer
Place de la Mairie
84190 Gigondas
Telephone/Fax: 04 90 65 85 30

RUSSIAN TOMATO GRATIN

Gratin de Tomates Russes

Some years ago, the most extraordinary tomatoes began appearing in the summer farmers' market: giant bright red tomatoes simply labeled "Russes." I began inquiring as to whether this was a new variety. No, the farmers responded, they always grew them for themselves but didn't think they were commercially viable. How wrong they were! I now have at least twenty plants—known officially as Russian #117—in my tomato garden, and they are my very favorite heirloom variety. Their flavor is gargantuan, with hearty flesh, bright red juice, and sweet, intense bursts of fresh tomato taste. Each plant is super-productive, and a single tomato can grow as big as 2 pounds. Sliced, a 1-pound tomato can fill a platter. We have been known to eat this gratin twice a day for days on end when the tomato harvest is exceptionally abundant.

This recipe has seen many permutations. It began as a huge pie, with the tomatoes cut into thick slices. But the results were too soupy. I then moved to preparing individual gratins, and after several different versions—those in which I drained the tomatoes for an hour and those in which I used bread crumbs to soak up the liquid—I decided this was the one I liked the best. Thin slices of toast at the bottom of the ramekins help soak up the delicious tomato juice. By baking the gratins individually, you need only bake for 12 to 15 minute, resulting in a fresh tomato flavor. I do like to make the egg, cheese, and herb mixture a few hours in advance. The herbs beautifully infuse the mixture, making for a grand summer dish.

Tomatoes "plein champs," or grown in an open field, in the farmers' market in Maussane-les-Alpilles

1 Preheat the oven to 375 degrees F.

2 In a small bowl, combine the eggs, fresh cheese, Parmigiano-Reggiano, and summer savory. Season lightly with salt and whisk to blend. Set aside. (The mixture can be made up to 2 hours in advance, covered, and refrigerated until baking.)

3 Core and peel the tomatoes. Chop coarsely. Place the chopped tomatoes in the sieve set over a large bowl to drain slightly.

4 Arrange the ramekins side-by-side on a baking sheet. Using the cookie cutter, cut the toast into 2½-inch rounds. Place a round of toast on the bottom of each of the ramekins. Spoon the chopped tomatoes on top of the toast. Pour the batter over the tomatoes.

5 Place the baking sheet in the center of the oven and bake until the batter is set and the gratins are golden and bubbling, 12 to 15 minutes. Serve warm or at room temperature, as a first course or as a side vegetable course.

8 SERVINGS

EQUIPMENT: Eight ½-cup porcelain ramekins; a fine-mesh sieve; a 2½-inch round cookie cutter.

3 large eggs, lightly beaten

½ cup Fresh Homemade Cheese (page 236) or ricotta cheese

½ cup (2 ounces) freshly grated Parmigiano-Reggiano cheese

2 teaspoons fresh summer savory leaves or rosemary leaves, very finely chopped

Fine sea salt

2 pounds firm, ripe tomatoes

About 4 thin slices white bread, or *pain de mie,* toasted

Wine Suggestion: Any good drinking red is right here. My preference is a young Côtes-du-Rhône.

VARIATIONS: A tiny bit of cooked bacon or chopped ham sprinkled on top of the bread before adding the tomatoes makes for a pleasant, heartier gratin. This can also be cooked in a single 10½-inch (6-cup) round porcelain baking dish. Proceed with the recipe through step 3. Arrange the toast on the bottom of the baking dish, trimming it to form a single layer, add the chopped tomatoes, and pour the batter over the tomatoes. Bake until set, about 15 minutes.

"What was paradise, but a garden full of vegetables and herbs and pleasures. Nothing there but delights."
—WILLIAM LAWSON

ROASTED CHERRY TOMATOES

Tomates-Cerises au Four

When the welcome bumper crop of cherry tomatoes arrives, I seem to serve them at every meal. One Friday lunch I was looking for one more dish to squeeze into the wood-fired bread oven, which had been fired up to roast a guinea hen with assorted vegetables. While in the vegetable garden in search of herbs and greens, I gathered all the cherry tomatoes that were ripe, layered them in a gratin dish with herbs and vinaigrette, and, *voilà*, we had one more dish for our luncheon buffet.

EQUIPMENT: A shallow ovenproof casserole.

1 pound whole cherry tomatoes

2 teaspoons fresh lemon-thyme leaves (or use traditional thyme leaves)

2 tablespoons Balsamic Vinaigrette (page 323)

1 teaspoon coarse sea salt

1 Preheat the oven to 450 degrees.

2 In the casserole, arrange the tomatoes in a single layer. Sprinkle with the thyme. Drizzle with the vinaigrette and the salt. Place in the center of the oven and roast until the tomatoes are warmed through and the skins are slightly split, about 10 minutes. Remove from the oven and serve warm as a vegetable accompaniment.

Tomatoes at the Sunday morning farmers' market in Coustellet

6 TO 8 SERVINGS

DOMAINE ST. LUC'S GREEN BEANS WITH BASIL

Haricots Verts au Basilic Domaine St. Luc

Young, tender green beans and basil are a Provençal marriage made in heaven. The vibrant herb serves as a perfect foil for the herbal sweetness of fresh green beans. Serve this as a side vegetable dish or as a first course. It should be offered warm to best enhance the pungency of the herb. I have often enjoyed this energizing vegetable-herb dish at the hands of Eliane Cornillon, our winemaker's wife, in the village of La Beaume-de-Transit in the Drôme Provençale.

EQUIPMENT: A 6-quart pasta pot fitted with a colander.

¼ cup coarse sea salt

1 pound green beans, trimmed at both ends

1 cup fresh basil leaves, tightly packed, cut into a *chiffonnade*

1 tablespoon extra-virgin olive oil

Fine sea salt

Freshly ground black pepper

Domaine St. Luc
Eliane and Ludovic Cornillon
26970 La Baume-de-Transit
Telephone: 04 75 98 11 51
Fax: 04 75 98 19 22
Web: *www.dom-saint-luc.com*

Green beans for sale at the Tuesday market in Vaison-la-Romaine

1 Prepare a large bowl of ice water.

2 Fill the pasta pot with about 5 quarts of water and bring to a boil over high heat. Add the coarse sea salt and the beans, and cook until crisp-tender, about 5 minutes. (Cooking time will vary, according to the size and tenderness of the beans.) Immediately remove the colander from the water, allow the water to drain from the beans, and plunge the colander with the beans into the ice water so they cool down as quickly as possible. (The beans will cool in 1 to 2 minutes. If you leave them longer, they will become soggy and begin to lose flavor.) Drain the beans and wrap them in a thick towel to dry. (The beans can be cooked up to 4 hours in advance. Keep them wrapped in the towel and refrigerate, if desired.)

3 At serving time, place the beans in a large frying pan over medium heat. Add the basil and the oil. Warm the mixture, tossing to coat the beans, 1 to 2 minutes. Season to taste. Serve warm.

8 SERVINGS

WHEN WE PURCHASED Chanteduc, many furnishings—including pots and pans and dishes—came with the house. Among my favorites are the collection of thin, long-handled tin skillets that are well seasoned and blackened with age. There are certain dishes I make in nothing else, including the pepper recipe on page 194. Somehow, no matter what I do in that pan, things turn out beautifully. Would that life were like that with everything we touched every day!

ARE YOU ATTACHED
TO CERTAIN PANS?

Quick Sauteed Green Peppers

Sauté Rapide de Poivrons Verts

*E*ach year we plant a row of peppers—Petit Marseillais—that grow not much bigger than 3 or 4 inches long and weigh less than an ounce each. The peppers burst out a deep green, and if you leave them long enough, they turn a bright egg-yolk yellow. I also plant a row of spicy Sucette de Provence, peppers that are not searingly hot but have a nice bite. Come August, I seem to crave the flavors of this quick sauté of peppers, a vegetable dish that I prepare for dinner, making sure there is enough for leftovers for lunch the next day. This recipe works for any kind of young pepper—sweet, hot, or otherwise!

1 pound tiny green, yellow, or red peppers, a mix of sweet and hot

2 tablespoons extra-virgin olive oil

Fleur de sel to taste

1 Rinse the peppers. Cut off and discard the stem ends. Run cold water into the peppers and reach in with your fingers to pull out the seeds and any large pieces of white pulp. Discard the seeds and white pulp. Drain the peppers in a colander.

2 In a large skillet, heat the oil over moderately high heat until hot but not smoking. Add the peppers and sauté—being careful that you are not burned by the splatter of oil—until the skins are slightly browned but the peppers are still firm and crunchy, no more than 2 minutes.

3 With a large slotted spoon, transfer the peppers to a platter covered with a double thickness of paper towels to absorb the oil. Generously season the peppers with *fleur de sel*. To serve, flip the peppers onto the platter, discarding the paper towels.

6 SERVINGS

MIREILLE'S EGGPLANT

Les Aubergines de Mireille

During the summer months, this delicious golden eggplant preparation is almost always on the menu at Le Bistrot du Paradou in Le Paradou. Slender slices of the freshest eggplant are fried in olive oil and accompanied by a brilliant red homemade tomato sauce. Most weeks it is followed by Mireille Pons's delectable roasted rabbit with whole roasted garlic and a rich potato purée enriched with the local olive oil.

2 small eggplants (about 1 pound total), stem ends trimmed

⅔ cup extra-virgin olive oil

Fine sea salt to taste

2 cups Mireille's Two-Tomato Sauce (page 317)

Le Bistrot du Paradou
Jean-Louis and Mireille Pons
13125 Le Paradou
Telephone: 04 90 54 32 70

1 Cut each eggplant lengthwise into four even slices. Set aside.

2 Line a platter with several thicknesses of paper towel. Set aside.

3 In a large frying pan, heat ⅓ cup of the oil over moderate heat until hot but not smoking. Add half the eggplant and cook until golden and brown on one side, about 45 seconds. Turn and brown the other side, about 45 seconds more. Transfer the eggplant slices to the platter lined with paper towels. Repeat with the remaining oil and eggplant.

4 To serve, place two slices of drained eggplant on each of four dinner plates. Spoon a dollop of tomato sauce alongside. Serve as a first course or as part of a buffet.

4 SERVINGS

Jean-Louis Pons behind the bar at Le Bistrot du Paradou in Le Paradou

L'Oustalet's Eggplant Ambrosia

Gâteau d'Aubergines L'Oustalet

*S*itting in the shade of the giant sycamore trees in the village square in Gigondas, our group of diners declared L'Oustalet chef Johannes Sailer's eggplant *gâteau* pure ambrosia. The dish had just the right balance of sweetness, richness, and smoky eggplant essence, and we downed this first-course Provençal specialty with pure joy.

1 Preheat the oven to 400 degrees F. Butter the ramekins and set aside.

2 Slice each eggplant in half lengthwise. With a sharp knife, make several crisscross slits in each half of the eggplant pulp without cutting through the skin. Place the eggplant halves side-by-side, cut side up, on a baking sheet. Drizzle with the oil and salt. Place in the center of the oven and bake until soft, about 20 minutes.

3 Remove the eggplant from the oven. Reduce the oven heat to 275 degrees F.

4 With a large spoon, scoop out the eggplant pulp. Place it in the bowl of a food processor or blender along with the egg, egg yolk, and light cream. Blend to a smooth purée. Season to taste.

EQUIPMENT: Eight ½-cup ramekins; a food processor or blender.

4 small eggplants (about 2 pounds total)

1 tablespoon extra-virgin olive oil

Fine sea salt to taste

1 whole egg

1 egg yolk

1½ cups light cream

Fine sea salt to taste

Freshly ground black pepper to taste

2 cups Spicy Tomato, Fennel, and Orange Sauce (page 318)

L'Oustalet

Marlies and Johannes Sailer
Place de la Mairie
84190 Gigondas
Telephone/Fax: 04 90 65 85 30

5 Divide the eggplant mixture evenly among the ramekins, filling each about half full. Place the ramekins in a baking pan large enough to hold them generously. Add enough hot tap water to the baking dish to reach about halfway up the ramekins. Cover the pan loosely with aluminum foil to prevent a skin from forming. Place in the center of the oven and bake until the mixture is just set around the edges but still trembling in the center, about 20 minutes.

Wine Suggestion: Since this recipe comes from Gigondas, I'd recommend a youthful Gigondas from one of the village's better winemakers and the one that supplies the "house" wine at L'Oustalet, the Château du Trignon.

6 Remove the pan from the oven and carefully remove the ramekins from the water. Let sit until firm, about 5 minutes. Serve the eggplant warm or at room temperature, unmolded, with a spoonful of the tomato sauce alongside.

8 SERVINGS

VARIATION: This can also be cooked in a single buttered 10½-inch (6-cup) round porcelain baking dish. Proceed with the recipe through step 4. Pour the mixture into the large baking dish and bake as instructed in step 5, baking until set, about 40 minutes. Serve directly from the dish, passing the tomato sauce.

Yves Gras of the Domaine Santa Duc vineyard in Gigondas with chef Johannes Sailer of restaurant L'Oustalet in Gigondas, on a picnic at the belvédère above Gigondas

Vegetables

Swiss Chard Two Ways

Blettes en Deux Façons

The gardens of Provence are plentiful with all manner of Swiss chard, with names like *Bondissima di Trieste* and brilliant red-ribbed Rhubarb Chard, and yellow-ribbed Bright Yellow, and even those with every rib color in the rainbow, called Bright Lights. While most recipes call for just the ribs or just the leaves, this one makes use of the entire vegetable and is a fine summer side dish.

EQUIPMENT: A 6-quart pasta pot fitted with a colander.

2 pounds Swiss chard (ribs and leaves), thoroughly washed and drained

3 tablespoons coarse sea salt

Extra-virgin olive oil

3 shallots, finely minced

About 2 tablespoons freshly squeezed lemon juice, or to taste

Fine sea salt to taste

1 Carefully separate the ribs from the Swiss chard leaves. Cut the leaves into a fine *chiffonnade*. Set aside.

2 Trim and remove any large, fibrous strings from the ribs. Cut the ribs crosswise (against the grain of the rib) into 4-inch lengths. Cut each 4-inch length lengthwise (with the grain of the rib) into matchstick-size pieces. Set aside.

3 In the pasta pot, bring about 5 quarts of water to a boil over high heat. Add the coarse sea salt and the Swiss chard ribs, and cook until just tender, 1 to 2 minutes. Drain, rinse under cold running water until cooled, and drain again. Set aside.

4 In a large skillet, heat the oil over moderately high heat until hot but not smoking. Add the *chiffonnade* of Swiss chard leaves and cook just until wilted, about 1 minute. Add the cooked Swiss chard ribs and toss to heat and thoroughly coat with the oil. Add the shallots and toss to blend. Season to taste with with the lemon juice and salt. Serve immediately.

4 TO 6 SERVINGS

EVERYTHING IN PROVENCE seems to be ruled by the moon. When we planted our first vegetable garden, we

WE ARE ALL *LUNATIQUES*

soon learned in which moon to plant root vegetables, when was a good time to seed, when to harvest. We then found out that moonlight could ruin furniture, so we learned to close our shutters during the full moon to protect the ancient armoires and oak dressers. I even once purchased fabric for outdoor furniture that was labeled waterproof, mildew-proof, sun-proof, and moon-proof!

The moon laws don't just apply to the garden and the home but to our bodies as well. To best benefit from the lunar cycle, here are some Provençal directives:

- Cut your hair in the full moon, and it will grow faster and more vigorously.

- Cut your nails in the waxing moon, and they will be stronger.

- Begin a diet during the last quarter of the moon—when it is in the form of a C—and your body will more readily eliminate toxins.

- Never begin a diet in the first quarter—when the moon is in the form of a D—for the body will be stocking those calories.

ZUCCHINI BLOSSOMS STUFFED WITH MINT-INFUSED FRESH CHEESE

Fleurs de Courgettes Farcies au Fromage à la Menthe

*F*ew ingredients say summer and Provence like zucchini blossoms, the bright golden, tender, and fragile flowers that grow from both the male and female infant zucchini. While the female of the plant goes on to produce fruit, the male produces just the blossoms. In the markets—especially at farmers' markets like those in Velleron each evening at 6 p.m. from Monday to Saturday—one usually finds them sold by the dozen, and often merchants distinguish between the male and female, selling the female blossoms with two to three inches of tender fruit attached. This is now my favorite way of preparing the blossoms: They are stuffed with a mix of the young fresh goat or sheep's milk cheese known as *brousse* and fresh garden mint. I then drizzle the blossoms with a good olive oil, cover with foil and bake them. The result is sweet, fragrant, and ever appealing.

EQUIPMENT: A 10½-inch round baking dish.

12 zucchini blossoms

1 recipe Mint-Infused Fresh Cheese (page 257)

Fine sea salt to taste

Freshly ground white pepper to taste

1 tablespoon extra-virgin olive oil

Stuffed zucchini blossoms, ready for baking

1 Preheat the oven to 425 degrees F.

2 With a sharp knife, carefully cut through one side of each zucchini blossom to slightly open it up. With a tiny spoon—such as a demitasse spoon—spoon the cheese into the blossom. Carefully close the blossom and arrange them like spokes on a wheel in the baking dish. Season with salt and pepper. Drizzle with the oil. Cover with foil.

3 Place in the center of the oven and bake until golden, 15 to 20 minutes. Serve immediately.

4 TO 6 SERVINGS

ELIANE'S CHUNKY ZUCCHINI GRATIN

Le Gratin de Courgettes d'Eliane

*E*liane Cornillon, at the Domaine St. Luc in La Beaume-de-Transit, never stops amazing us with her simple, sublime preparations. This chunky zucchini gratin can be put together in minutes and is perfect light summer fare.

1 Preheat the broiler.

2 In a large skillet, heat the oil over moderate heat until hot but not smoking. Add the garlic and zucchini, and brown the zucchini for about 5 minutes. Reduce the heat to low, cover, and cook until soft, about 10 minutes more.

3 With a slotted spoon, transfer the zucchini to the gratin dish. Drizzle the light cream all over. Season to taste with salt and freshly ground black pepper. Sprinkle with the cheese. Place under the broiler and broil until the cheese is melted and golden, 2 to 3 minutes.

4 SERVINGS

EQUIPMENT: A 1-quart gratin dish.

2 tablespoons extra-virgin olive oil

4 plump cloves garlic, peeled and halved

1 pound zucchini (about 4), trimmed and cut into chunks

¼ cup light cream

Sea salt

Freshly ground black pepper

¼ cup (1 ounce) freshly grated French Gruyère cheese

Domaine St. Luc
Eliane and Ludovic Cornillon
26970 La Beaume-de-Transit
Telephone: 04 75 98 11 51
Fax: 04 75 98 19 22
Web: *www.dom-saint-luc.com*

Wine Suggestion: Here, winemaker Ludovic Cornillon's Viognier-based white—Domaine St. Luc—would be ideal.

GOLDEN ZUCCHINI GALETTE

Galette Dorée de Courgettes

*T*his is a favorite luncheon dish in our house, served with a nice arugula salad.

1 Preheat the oven to 425 degrees F.

2 Using the coarse grating blade of a food processor, coarsely grate the zucchini. Transfer to a colander, sprinkle with 1 teaspoon of the salt, and let sit to drain for 30 minutes. Rinse the zucchini under cold running water, spread it out in an absorbent dish towel, and press to remove as much liquid as possible.

3 Place the eggs in a large bowl and beat lightly with a fork. Add the bread crumbs, cheese, curry powder, and final teaspoon of salt. Add the zucchini and stir to thoroughly coat the zucchini with the batter. Place in the baking dish and even out the top with the back of a spatula.

4 Place in the center of the oven and bake until golden, 15 to 20 minutes. Serve with a fresh tomato sauce, if desired.

4 SERVINGS

EQUIPMENT: A food processor; a 10½-inch round baking dish.

1 pound zucchini (4 medium), trimmed

2 teaspoons fine sea salt

2 large eggs

¼ cup fresh bread crumbs

½ cup (2 ounces) freshly grated Parmigiano-Reggiano cheese

1 teaspoon Homemade Curry Powder (page 326)

Fresh tomato sauce (optional)

Male and female zucchini blossoms for sale at the Constellet market

SHEILA AND JULIAN'S BRAISED FENNEL WITH TOMATOES

Fenouils à la Tomate

Sheila and Julian More are two of our best friends and neighbors in Provence. We always have a grand time dining outdoors on their terrace beneath the grape arbors or indoors near a roaring fire. I always look forward to being guests at their table, for both the company and the always surprising, always different fare. One winter they served this deliciously simple dish as a first course, and agreed to share it with me.

¼ cup extra-virgin olive oil

2 large onions, peeled and quartered lengthwise

Fine sea salt to taste

2 pounds fennel bulbs, trimmed and quartered lengthwise

6 plump cloves garlic, peeled, halved lengthwise, green germs removed

½ cup white wine

One 28-ounce can peeled Italian plum tomatoes in their juice

1 In a large skillet, combine the oil, onions, and salt. Sweat—cook, covered, over low heat until soft but not browned—for about 5 minutes.

2 Add the fennel, cover, and cook for 10 minutes. Add the garlic and wine, and cook, uncovered, over moderate heat until the liquid is reduced by half, about 5 minutes. Add the tomatoes with their juice and crush to break them up. Simmer, uncovered, until the fennel is soft, about 30 minutes. Taste for seasoning. Serve warm or at room temperature.

8 SERVINGS

WILD MUSHROOM AND WALNUT TARTE TATIN

Tarte Tatin aux Cèpes et Cerneaux de Noix

I was in a particularly inspired mood one weekday evening in September, and this upside-down mushroom tart seemed to create itself as I went along. There were gorgeous wild *cèpe* mushrooms at Les Gourmandines, my local vegetable merchant, as well as first-of-the-season walnuts from the Ardèche region, just a bit north of Vaison-la-Romaine. I had some of Anne Leblanc's exquisite walnut oil and a plump, rosy braid of garlic. As the tart came from the oven, Walter smiled, I glowed: what a feast we had! This has been a family favorite ever since. I generally prepare this in a traditional *tarte Tatin* mold, but in a pinch I have prepared a huge version in a large nonstick frying pan, to excellent results. I am just sorry that I never took a photo of the one we made one exceptionally warm, blue-skied Friday in November, when Walter, myself, and students from my Wine Week lunched outdoors beneath the oak tree.

EQUIPMENT: A 9-inch *tarte Tatin* pan or a nonstick frying pan with an ovenproof handle.

2 teaspoons goose fat (or substitute olive oil)

2 pounds large *cèpe* or porcini mushrooms (or substitute *chanterelles* or *girolles*, cremini, portobello, or standard cultivated mushrooms), cleaned, trimmed, and cut into thick slices

Fine sea salt to taste

1 teaspoon fresh or dried thyme leaves

3 plump cloves garlic, green germs removed, minced

3 tablespoons minced fresh parsley

½ cup freshly cracked walnut pieces

Freshly ground black pepper to taste

½ recipe Light Flaky Pastry (page 285), rolled into a 9-inch round, placed on a baking sheet, and refrigerated

WALNUT OIL VINAIGRETTE:

1 tablespoon freshly squeezed lemon juice

Fine sea salt to taste

¼ cup best-quality walnut oil

Fleur de sel for garnish

1 Preheat the oven to 425 degrees F. Place a rack in the center of the oven.

2 Heat the goose fat in a large nonstick frying pan over moderate heat until hot but not smoking. Add the mushrooms, season lightly with salt, and sauté just until the mushrooms begin to give up their juices, about 5 minutes. Reduce the heat and add the thyme, garlic, half the parsley, and half the walnuts. Cook, stirring regularly, for about 1 minute more. Season generously with salt and pepper.

Wine Suggestion: That day in November we sampled this with a stunning chilled white 1998 Châteauneuf-du-Pape, Château Rayas. The wine's touch of golden nuttiness enhanced even more the pleasures of the warm, steaming tart. Another great choice is a Côtes du Jura, Domaine Berthet-Bondet, 1997, made from the Savagnin grape. The wine has the aroma and the flavors of fresh walnuts and totally complements this mushroom tart.

3 Transfer the mixture to a *tarte Tatin* pan or the frying pan. Place the pan on a baking sheet. Remove the pastry from the refrigerator and place it on top of the mushroom mixture, gently pushing the edges of the pastry down around the edge of the pan. Place the baking sheet in the oven and bake until the pastry is golden, 20 to 25 minutes.

4 Meanwhile, in a small jar, combine the lemon juice and salt. Cover and shake to dissolve the salt. Add the walnut oil, cover, and shake again. Taste for seasoning.

5 Remove the baking sheet from the oven. Immediately invert a serving platter with a lip over the *tarte* pan. Quickly but carefully unmold the tart onto the serving platter so the mushrooms are on top and the pastry is on the bottom. Remove any mushrooms sticking to the bottom of the pan, and place them back onto the tart. Sprinkle the mushrooms with the remaining parsley and walnuts. Season with freshly ground black pepper. Drizzle with the vinaigrette, sprinkle with *fleur de sel,* and serve warm, cut into wedges.

8 SERVINGS

Vegetables

205

HERB-STUFFED MUSHROOMS

Petits Champignons Farcis aux Herbes

While our woods in Provence are filled with all manner of wild mushrooms, I am equally thrilled at the sight of common cultivated mushrooms. These small stuffed vegetables reward you with the intense and woodsy flavor of mushrooms, and serve as classic vegetable finger food. I like to play around with the stuffing, sometimes adding chopped hazelnuts, or using hazelnut oil in the place of cream or butter. And in the winter, minced truffles are always an option.

Wine Suggestion: One of my favorite local white wines in the world is Christophe Delorme's white Lirac, Cuvée de la Reine des Bois from Domaine de la Mordorée, a complex white that is an assembly of seven distinct grape varieties, including Grenache Blanc, Viognier, Roussanne, Marsanne, Picpoul, Clairette, and Bourboulenc. The wine is perfumed with the aromas of peaches, apricots, pears, and violets. Very round and with a very long finish, it is a top example of a Lirac white, and seems at home in the company of mushrooms.

EQUIPMENT: A 6-quart pasta pot fitted with a colander.

1 pound fresh mushrooms, cleaned, stems trimmed and separated from caps

3 tablespoons coarse sea salt

4 tablespoons unsalted butter

1 small shallot, peeled and finely minced

Fine sea salt

⅓ cup heavy cream

2 teaspoons freshly squeezed lemon juice

3 tablespoons finely minced fresh chives (or substitute 3 tablespoons minced fresh black truffles)

Domaine de la Mordorée
Christophe Delorme
30126 Tavel
Telephone: 04 66 50 00 75
Fax: 04 66 50 47 39
Tastings by appointment: 8 a.m. to noon and 1:30 to 6 p.m.
American importer: Kysela Père et Fils, Ltd., Winchester, VA; telephone: (540) 722-9228; fax: (540) 722-9258
Web: *www.kysela.com*

1 Finely chop the mushroom stems. Set aside.

2 Fill the pasta pot with about 5 quarts of water and bring to a boil over high heat. Add the coarse salt and the mushroom caps. Boil, uncovered, until crisp/tender, 3 to 4 minutes. Immediately drain the mushrooms.

3 In a small frying pan, combine the butter, minced shallot, and a pinch of salt and sweat—cook, covered, over low heat until soft but not browned—for about 2 minutes. Add the chopped mushroom stems, the cream, and the lemon juice. Cover and cook for 5 minutes. Remove from the heat and set aside.

4 With a small spoon, stuff the mushroom caps with the chopped mushroom mixture. Garnish with the minced chives (or truffles) and serve warm or at room temperature.

8 TO 12 SERVINGS

WHY A PASTA POT WITH A COLANDER? Many of my recipes—for vegetables as well as pasta—call for using a pasta pot fitted with a colander. I find that whenever I am blanching a vegetable, the use of the colander makes draining easier and more efficient than a simple pot without a liner.

Vegetables

Oven-Roasted Shallots with Rosemary and Balsamic Vinaigrette

Echalotes Rôties au Romarin et à la Vinaigrette Balsamique

Shallots tend to be forgotten in the vegetable world, often edged out by garden-variety onions or the more powerful garlic. Whenever I serve this, guests dive in, for the tender shallot serves as a soothing accompaniment to a simple roast chicken, guinea hen, or leg of lamb.

1 Preheat the oven to 450 degrees F.

2 In the casserole, layer the rosemary and shallots. Sprinkle with the salt. Drizzle with the vinaigrette. Place in the center of the oven and roast until tender, about 35 minutes. Remove from the oven, and serve warm as a vegetable accompaniment.

6 TO 8 SERVINGS

EQUIPMENT: A shallow ovenproof casserole.

4 large sprigs fresh rosemary

1 pound shallots (about 30), peeled

1 teaspoon coarse sea salt

2 tablespoons Balsamic Vinaigrette (page 323)

Braids of shallots at a Provençal farmers' market

CAULIFLOWER GRATIN

Gratin de Chou-Fleur

*L*ike velvety, pure white pillows, this ethereal gratin is a dream. It makes me think of holiday feasts, where no fewer than half a dozen vegetables may hold court alongside a giant roasted turkey or goose.

1 Preheat the broiler.

2 Bring about 3 cups of water to a simmer in the bottom of a vegetable steamer. Place the florets of cauliflower on the steaming rack. Place the rack over the simmering water, cover, and steam until the cauliflower is soft, 15 to 20 minutes. Drain thoroughly.

3 Transfer the cauliflower to the bowl of a food processor or a blender. Purée. Add the fresh cheese and the cream, and purée until very smooth. Season to taste with nutmeg and salt.

EQUIPMENT: A vegetable steamer; a food processor or blender; a 10½-inch (6-cup) round baking dish.

1 whole cauliflower (about 2 pounds), trimmed and broken into florets

6 tablespoons Fresh Homemade Cheese (page 236) or ricotta cheese

½ cup light cream

Freshly grated nutmeg

Fine sea salt

½ cup (2 ounces) freshly grated Parmigiano-Reggiano cheese

4 Transfer the mixture to the baking dish, smoothing it out with the back of a spatula. Sprinkle with the Parmigiano-Reggiano cheese. Place the baking dish about 5 inches from the broiler. Broil until golden, about 3 minutes. Serve warm.

6 TO 8 SERVINGS

JOHANNES' ANCHOVY DIP
WITH STEAMED WHOLE CAULIFLOWER

L'Anchoïade de Johannes, Chou-Fleur à la Vapeur

*A*s a special treat during my cooking classes in Provence, we often have a catered picnic lunch under the pine trees near the *belvédère* above the village of Gigondas. It is chef Johannes Sailer and his staff who drive up the hill (we often hike) and deliver a sumptuous picnic of fresh foods, usually including a giant platter of vegetables to accompany this exquisite anchovy dip, a typical Provençal sauce made up of salt-cured anchovies, olive oil, vinegar, and garlic. I like to serve this dip with freshly steamed whole cauliflower showered with a touch of fresh parsley from the garden.

1 At least 5 hours (and up to 24 hours) before preparing the anchovy dip, soak the anchovies: Rinse them, cover with cold water, and refrigerate until ready to prepare the dip.

EQUIPMENT: A food processor or blender; a vegetable steamer.

THE ANCHOVY DIP:

About 8 plump, salt-cured whole anchovies

2 plump cloves garlic, peeled

2 teaspoons best-quality red wine vinegar

1 cup extra-virgin olive oil

Fine sea salt

Freshly ground black pepper

1 whole cauliflower (about 2 pounds)

3 tablespoons fresh parsley, finely minced

2 Remove the anchovies from the water, drain, and separate into fillets, pulling them apart and removing the central bones. Rinse and drain.

3 In the bowl of a food processor or blender, combine the drained anchovies, garlic, and vinegar. Process to blend. With the machine running, slowly pour the oil through the tube and process again. Season to taste. Stir again before serving.

4 Bring about 3 cups of water to a simmer in the bottom of a vegetable steamer. Place the whole cauliflower on the steaming rack. Place the rack over the simmering water, cover, and steam until the cauliflower is soft, 15 to 20 minutes.

5 Drain the cauliflower and place in a bowl just large enough to hold it comfortably. Drizzle with a bit of the anchovy dip and sprinkle with the minced parsley. Serve immediately, passing the remaining anchovy dip.

4 TO 6 SERVINGS

VARIATIONS: You can also serve the anchovy dip as an appetizer or first course with a selection of sliced raw vegetables, including carrots, celery, cauliflower, broccoli, and radishes. A wonderful place for sampling this *panier de légumes* is at Le Saint Hubert.

Le Saint Hubert
84340 Entrechaux
Telephone: 04 90 46 00 05
Fax: 04 90 46 00 06

Provençal Carrot Osso Buco

Carottes Provençales Façon Osso Buco

*T*his dish—introduced to me by Parisian chef Guy Martin of Le Grand Véfour—is typical of the creativity one can apply to vegetables. Not content to stick with the standards, here he transforms a favorite Italian specialty—braised veal shanks with a lemon and parsley garnish—making carrots the star of the day. I love this dish hot as well as cold, and particularly love it in wintertime, with a nice warming roast.

1 In a large skillet, heat the oil over moderate heat until hot but not smoking. Add the carrots, season lightly with salt, and cook, uncovered, until evenly browned, about 20 minutes. Roll the carrots in the oil from time to time so they brown evenly. Remove the carrots and set aside.

2 Place the onion in the skillet with the oil and sweat—cook, covered, over low heat until soft but not browned—for about 5 minutes. Add the tomatoes, celery, garlic, bouquet garni, orange, and salt and pepper. Place the carrots on top of the tomato mixture. Cover and cook over low heat until meltingly tender, about 1 hour. Roll the carrots around in the sauce from time to time so they absorb the sauce. Taste for seasoning. At serving time, garnish with parsley and serve.

4 SERVINGS

1 tablespoon extra-virgin olive oil

1 pound carrots, peeled and trimmed

Sea salt

1 medium onion, peeled, halved, and thinly sliced

4 large tomatoes, peeled, cored, seeded, and chopped (or one 15-ounce can peeled tomatoes in their juice, drained and chopped)

1 rib celery, finely chopped

1 plump clove garlic, peeled, halved, green germ removed

1 bouquet garni: several parsley stems, celery leaves, and sprigs of thyme, wrapped in the green part of a leek and securely fastened with cotton twine, or in a wire mesh ball

1 orange, minced (rind included)

Freshly ground black pepper to taste

Minced fresh parsley, for garnish

BEETS IN PISTACHIO OIL

Betteraves à l'Huile de Pistache

*M*y husband, Walter, is a bona fide beet addict. Even in the days when he was too busy to do any of the fruit and vegetable shopping, whenever I was away for a few days, beets would mysteriously appear in our refrigerator. I got the message! I love this beet preparation, rich with the nutty flavor of pistachio oil. I serve these antipasto-style, with a series of salads at lunchtime.

In a small bowl, combine the shallots, salt and pepper to taste, cider vinegar, pistachio oil, and grapeseed oil. Stir to blend. Let infuse for 1 hour at room temperature to allow the flavors to blend and to soften the flavor of the shallots. At serving time, toss with the beets.

4 SERVINGS

2 shallots, peeled and finely minced

Sea salt

Freshly ground black pepper

1 tablespoon cider vinegar

1 tablespoon pistachio oil
(or substitute another nut oil
or extra-virgin olive oil)

1 tablespoon grapeseed oil

1 pound beets, cooked and
cut into matchsticks (julienne)

TO STEAM BEETS: Bring a quart of water to a simmer in the bottom of a vegetable steamer. Place the beets on the steaming rack. Place the rack over the simmering water. Cover, and steam until the beets can be pierced with a paring knife, about 20 minutes for baby beets, up to 1 hour for larger beets. (You may have to add water from time to time to keep the steamer from running dry.) Drain, and let cool just long enough so you can handle them. Most of the peel will just slip off, but stubborn patches can be peeled off with a paring knife. Cut off the root end.

Vegetables

CELERIAC PUREE

Purée de Céleri-Rave

To my mind, celeriac, or celery root, is one of the most welcoming and refreshing of winter vegetables. I love its bright flavor and tang, and the smooth and creamy texture it takes on when puréed. This can be served alone as a side dish or used to flavor the White Bean Ragout with Lemongrass (page 178).

EQUIPMENT: A food processor or blender.

1 pound celeriac, quartered, peeled, and cubed

2 tablespoons freshly squeezed lemon juice

Sea salt

In a large pot, combine the cubed celeriac, lemon juice, and a pinch of salt. Cover with cold water. Simmer gently until the celery root is very soft, about 20 minutes. Drain and transfer to the food processor or blender and purée, adding, if necessary, some cooking liquid to thin out the mixture. Taste for seasoning and serve.

4 SERVINGS

MARKETS OF PROVENCE

THE TRADITIONAL MARKETS of Provence date back to the beginning of the 1st century, when the Roman culture thrived and weekly markets for purchasing everything from soaps to fruits and vegetables were instituted. Today I always say that you can find everything from tractors to panty hose, with all sundry manner of fruits, vegetables, meats, poultry, and plants in between. That's not to mention pottery, snake oil salesmen selling handy choppers, sure-bet polishing cream, pizzas from the pizza truck, and even a touch of flea market. Fashions change not by the season but by the week, and what to many of us might seem sleazy and cheap somehow becomes cute and chic. (I treasure some of my 5 euro T-shirts as much as an Armani suit and probably get more wear out of them!)

Our village of Vaison-la-Romaine has its designated market day on Tuesday, and that means rain or shine, Christmas or New Year's, you'll find hundreds of merchants there each week, lining the streets and filling the parking lots with their wares. The regulars can be found in their normal spots, while newcomers are assigned to the end of the street or faraway corners until they work their way up the pecking order by showing up with certain regularity.

Markets generally open at around 8:30 in the morning, though by 8 you will see people lining up at the fish truck to get the best and the freshest fish and shellfish. Come noon, the market begins to wind down and by 1 p.m. the merchants have packed up and left, and the village garbage trucks pass through to clear the streets and sidewalks. At each village market you will find plenty of precooked fare—pizzas and paella, couscous and *tajines*, rotisserie-roasted poultry, cakes and tarts—since the homemaker will spend her morning at the market, leaving no time to prepare lunch.

Here is a list of some of the best markets, day by day, *département* by *département*. Each *département* in France is numbered according to alphabetical order (i.e., the Vaucluse *département* is 84, the Bouches-du-Rhône is 13), and you can tell the department number by both automobile license plates and zip codes. The liveliest markets are marked with an asterisk.

Monday

Vaucluse (84) Bedarrides, Bédoin, Cadenet, Cavaillon, Lauris, Mazan, Piolenc, St.-Didier, St.-Saturnin-les-Avignon

Bouches-du-Rhône (13) Fontvielle

Gard (30) Alès, *Nîmes

Alpes-de-Haute-Provence (04) *Forcalquier

Tuesday

Vaucluse (84) *Avignon, Beaumes-de-Venise, Caderousse, Caromb, Cucuron, Fontaine-de-Vaucluse, Gordes, Lacoste, Lapalud, La Tour d'Aigues, Mondragon, Montfavet, Mormoiron, St.-Saturnin-les-Apt, Vedène, *Vaison-la-Romaine

Bouches-du-Rhône (13) *Aix-en-Provence, Cabannes, Eyguières, Rognonas, Tarascon

Gard (30) *Nîmes, Roquemaure

WEDNESDAY

Vaucluse (84) *Avignon, Châteauneuf-du-Gadagne, Entraigues-sur-Sorgues, Gargas, Le Thor, Malaucène, Malemort du Comtat, Merindol, Mouriès, Puymeras (5:30 p.m. to 8 p.m.), Rustrel (summer only), Sault, Serignan-du-Comtat, *Valréas, Velleron, Villes-sur-Auzon, Violès

Bouches-du-Rhône (13) *Arles, Mouriès, Salon-de-Provence, *St.-Rémy-de-Provence

Gard (30) Bagnols-sur-Cèze, *Nîmes

Alpes de Haute-Provence (04) Digne-les-Bains, Riez

Hautes-Alpes (05) Gap

THURSDAY

Vaucluse (84) *Avignon, Cairanne, Caumont sur Durance, Fontaine-de-Vaucluse, *L'Isle-sur-la-Sorgue, Le Pontet, Les Beaumettes, Malemort-du-Comtat, Mirabeau, *Orange, Robion, Roussillon, St.-Christol-d'Albion, Vacqueyras, Villelaure

Bouches-du-Rhône (13) *Aix-en-Provence, La Roque d'Anthéron. Maussane-les-Alpilles, Senas

Gard (30) Beaucaire, Pujaut, St.-Gilles, Villeneuve-lès-Avignon

Alpes de Haute-Provence (04) Cèreste, Reillane

Drôme (26) *Nyons

FRIDAY

Vaucluse (84) *Avignon, *Bonnieux, *Carpentras, *Cavaillon, Châteauneuf-du-Pape, Courthézon, Lagnes, Lourmarin, Pertuis, Velleron, Visan

Bouches-du-Rhône (13) Barbentane, Eyragues, Fontvieille, Lambesc, Mallemort, St.-Andiol, St.-Martin-de-Crau, Salon-de-Provence

Gard (30) *Nîmes, Remoulins

Drôme (26) Pierrelatte, Mirabel-aux-Baronnies

SATURDAY

Vaucluse (84) *Apt, Aubignan, *Avignon, Beaument-de-Pertuis, Cheval Blanc, Grillon, Le Barroux, Le Thor, Mallemort-du-Comtat, Mornas, Oppède, *Pernes-les-Fontaines, Puymeras (5:30 p.m. to 7 p.m.), *Ste.-Cécile-les-Vignes

THE PROVENCE COOKBOOK

216

Bouches-du-Rhône (13) *Aix-en-Provence, *Arles, Barbentane

Gard (30) Pont St-Esprit, *Uzès (8 a.m. to 7 p.m.), Villeneuve-lès-Avignon

Alpes de Haute-Provence (04) Digne-les-Bains, Riez, Manosque, *Sisteron

Hautes-Alpes (05) Gap

Drôme (26) Donzère, Mollans-sur-Ouvèze

SUNDAY

Vaucluse (84) *Avignon, Camaret-sur-Aigues, *Coustellet (May to December), *l'Isle-sur-la-Sorgue, *Jonquières, Maubec, Mirabeau, Monteux, Sarrians, Sivergues, Sorgues, Villars (summer only)

Bouches-du-Rhône (13) Châteaurenard, Meyrargues, Pélissanne

Gard (30) Beaucaire, Rochefort-du-Gard, St-Gilles

Drôme (26) Séderon

For more information:
Comité Permanent Promotion des Marchés, Telephone: 04 90 39 00 42 Fax: 04 90 39 00 43

A SPECIAL MARKET

While most markets take place in the morning, one of Provence's liveliest markets takes place at the end of the day. In the village of Velleron—near l'Isle-sur-la-Sorge—farmers set up shop at the end of the day. From the first Monday in April to September 30, the market takes place Monday through Saturday from 6 p.m. to 7 p.m. From the first Tuesday in October to the last Saturday in March, it is held on Tuesday, Friday, and Saturday from 4:30 p.m. to 6 p.m.

BRAISED BABY POTATOES WITH GARLIC, SHALLOTS,
AND SPRING ONIONS

JEAN-LOUIS MARTIN'S POTATOES WITH OLIVES,
HERBS, AND BACON

POTATO SALAD WITH ROSEMARY AND CAPERS

BAY-SCENTED ROASTED POTATOES

POTATOES DOMAINE DE LA PONCHE

POTATOES
Les Pommes de Terre

RAGOUT OF NEW POTATOES, ARTICHOKES,
GARLIC, PARSLEY, AND MINT

POTATO AND CELERIAC GRATIN

POTATOES GRILLED WITH ROSEMARY BRANCHES

POTATOES FROM THE MAS HAUT

MIREILLE'S SUMMER POTATO GRATIN

WARM POTATO, CHIVE, AND BLOOD SAUSAGE SALAD

Baby potatoes with garlic, shallots,
and spring onions, ready for braising

BRAISED BABY POTATOES WITH GARLIC, SHALLOTS, AND SPRING ONIONS

Petites Pommes de Terre Cuites à l'Etouffée,
à l'Ail, Echalotes et Cébettes

I first sampled a version of this lovely summer potato dish at the charming Camargue restaurant La Chassagnette. With its beautiful raised organic vegetable garden and a spacious dining room complete with wood-fired oven and open rotisserie, this is a dream of a spot. I make this dish often in warm months since everything is cooked on top the stove, not in the oven.

Place all the ingredients in a large pot and stir to coat with the oil. Cover and cook over the lowest possible heat, turning from time to time, until the potatoes are tender when pierced with a fork and are browned in patches, and the other vegetables are soft, about 45 minutes. (Cooking time will vary according to the size and freshness of the potatoes.) Remove and discard the bay leaves and the sprigs of thyme. Using a slotted spoon, transfer the ingredients to a serving bowl.

8 SERVINGS

2 pounds baby potatoes (fingerlings or small Yukon Gold), scrubbed but not peeled

1 plump head garlic cloves, separated and peeled

12 scallions or spring onions *(cébettes)*, trimmed

6 shallots, peeled

5 fresh or dried bay leaves

1 teaspoon coarse sea salt

¼ cup extra-virgin olive oil

2 tablespoons cold water

Several sprigs fresh thyme

La Chassagnette
Route de Sambuc
13200 Arles
Telephone: 04 90 97 26 96
E-mail: *restaurantchassa@aol.com*

ON CEBETTES: *Cébettes* are typical Provençal spring onions—larger than our scallions—that are used in all sorts of dishes, most often braised in combination with potatoes, served alone as a single braised vegetable, or served raw in very thin slices as a garnish for tomatoes or other vegetables. When a recipe calls for *cébettes*, you can substitute spring onions.

JEAN-LOUIS MARTIN'S POTATOES WITH OLIVES, HERBS, AND BACON

Les Pommes de Terre de Jean-Louis Martin aux Olives,
aux Herbes et au Lard

Only the potato-loving French would think of turning potatoes into a stew. This recipe comes from one of my best friends in Provence, Jean-Louis Martin, of olive fame. At his shop in Maussane-les-Alpilles I always buy fresh green olives in the fall, as well as his well-made tapenades and varied sauces year-round.

1 In a large frying pan, combine the bacon, olive oil, onions, and a pinch of salt. Brown the bacon and onions over moderate heat, about 5 minutes.

2 Add the garlic, potatoes, thyme, bay leaves, and olives. Cover with the chicken stock, cover the pan, and simmer until the potatoes are tender, about 30 minutes. There should still be some liquid remaining. Taste for seasoning, adding black pepper to taste. Serve warm, as an accompaniment to roast meat or poultry.

8 SERVINGS

4 ounces smoked slab bacon, rind removed, cut into cubes (1 cup)

1½ tablespoons extra-virgin olive oil

2 onions, peeled and thinly sliced

Fine sea salt

2 plump cloves garlic, peeled, halved, green germs removed

2 pounds small yellow-fleshed potatoes (such as Yukon Gold), peeled and very thinly sliced

1 teaspoon fresh or dried thyme leaves

4 fresh or dried bay leaves

1 cup olives from the Chanteduc Rainbow Olive Collection (page 4)

2 cups Homemade Chicken Stock (page 325) or water

Freshly ground black pepper

Boutique Jean Martin

Jean-Louis Martin
Rue Charloun Rieu
13520 Maussane-les-Alpilles
Telephone: 04 90 54 30 04
Fax: 04 90 54 40 79
Web: *www.jeanmartin.fr*
Open 9:30 a.m. to noon and 2:30 to 6 p.m.;
closed Sunday, and Monday morning.

The sign outside Jean-Louis Martin's shop in Maussane-les-Alpilles

POTATO SALAD WITH ROSEMARY AND CAPERS

Salade de Pommes de Terre aux Câpres et au Romarin

*I*n my childhood, potatoes were served baked, mashed, in a gratin (we called them scalloped potatoes), or as a potato salad. Almost every Sunday my father grilled bratwurst sausages on the outdoor grill, and potato salad was a frequent accompaniment. I have never gotten over my love for potato salad, and I created this one as a memory of childhood, adding some of my favorite Provençal ingredients, such as bay leaves, olive oil, capers, and rosemary. It's a great dish any time of year, and always welcome as part of a summer buffet.

2 pounds small yellow-fleshed potatoes (such as Yukon Gold), scrubbed but not peeled

1 fresh or dried bay leaf

1 teaspoon coarse sea salt

1 teaspoon extra-virgin olive oil

THE DRESSING:

4 tablespoons extra-virgin olive oil

1 onion, peeled, halved lengthwise, and very thinly sliced

Fine sea salt

2 tablespoons best-quality sherry vinegar (or substitute balsamic vinegar)

2 tablespoons capers in vinegar, drained

3 tablespoons finely chopped fresh rosemary leaves

1 Place the potatoes in a large pot. Add the bay leaf, sea salt, oil, and several tablespoons of cold water. Cover and cook over the lowest possible heat, turning from time to time, until the potatoes are tender when pierced with a fork and browned in patches, about 25 minutes. (Cooking time will vary according to the size and freshness of the potatoes.)

2 While the potatoes are cooking, prepare the dressing: In a small saucepan, combine 1 tablespoon of the olive oil, the onion, and a pinch of salt, and sweat—cook, covered, over low heat until soft but not browned—for about 3 minutes. Transfer to a large mixing bowl. Add the remaining oil, the vinegar, capers, and 2 tablespoons of the rosemary. Toss to blend.

3 Once the potatoes are cooked, drain them. As soon as they are cool enough to handle, peel them and cut into thin slices, tossing each slice directly into the warm dressing. Toss to thoroughly coat the potatoes with the dressing. Add the remaining tablespoon of rosemary and toss again. Taste for seasoning. Serve warm or at room temperature.

8 SERVINGS

Potatoes

BAY-SCENTED ROASTED POTATOES

Pommes de Terre Rôties au Laurier

If one can be addicted to an herb, then I am addicted to fresh bay leaves. I had never seen bay leaves grow in such profusion before I moved to Provence. There were several prolific bay leaf trees—known as *laurier sauce*—already on our property at Chanteduc when we arrived in 1984. But I wanted more, and soon potted two huge bay laurel trees outside my kitchen door, part of what I call my "dinner garden"—the herb garden I visit when it is raining or dark outside.

This dish is a family favorite. What is amazing and also pleasant is the way the sweet aroma of the fragrant bay leaves—almost intoxicating, I would say—invades the kitchen. And it's not just the aroma! Their fresh green flavor truly infuses the potatoes, turning an already appealing vegetable into one that is irresistible.

EQUIPMENT: A baking dish.

2 pounds (about 16) small yellow-fleshed potatoes (such as Yukon Gold), scrubbed but not peeled

About 16 fresh or dried bay leaves

2 teaspoons extra-virgin olive oil

Several tablespoons Homemade Chicken Stock (page 325)

Fine sea salt

Freshly ground black pepper

New potatoes for sale at the farmers' market in Maussane-les-Alpilles

1 Preheat the oven to 425 degrees F.

2 Starting at one end of each potato, make a slit lengthwise, cutting about halfway through the potato. Pinch the potato at both ends to keep the slit open, and stick a bay leaf in the slit. Place the potatoes in a baking dish. Drizzle with the oil and then the stock. Season lightly with salt.

3 Place the baking dish in the oven and bake, uncovered, until the potatoes are tender and brown and most of the cooking liquid has evaporated, 45 minutes to 1 hour. Remove from the oven, remove and discard the bay leaves, season to taste with pepper, and serve.

4 TO 6 SERVINGS

POTATOES DOMAINE DE LA PONCHE

Pommes de Terre Domaine de la Ponche

I have lost count of the number of times I have devoured these golden potatoes at the lovely country restaurant Domaine de la Ponche. There, the potatoes are always served with the rosemary and garlic–showered Robespierre Beef Domaine de la Ponche (page 140), a custom I have continued at my own table.

EQUIPMENT: A vegetable steamer.

1 pound large yellow-fleshed potatoes (such as Yukon Gold), scrubbed but not peeled

1 tablespoon extra-virgin olive oil

1 teaspoon fine sea salt

Freshly ground black pepper

1 Bring about 1 quart of water to a simmer in the bottom of a vegetable steamer. Place the potatoes on the steaming rack. Place the rack over simmering water, cover, and steam until the potatoes can easily be pierced with a paring knife, about 20 minutes for small potatoes, longer for large potatoes. Drain. Slice lengthwise in half.

2 In a large skillet, heat the olive oil over moderately high heat until hot but not smoking. Add the potatoes side-by-side, cut side down, and sear until golden, about 5 minutes. This may have to be done in batches. Transfer to a large bowl and season with salt and pepper. Serve immediately.

4 SERVINGS

RAGOUT OF NEW POTATOES, ARTICHOKES, GARLIC, PARSLEY, AND MINT

Ragoût de Pommes de Terre Nouvelles, Artichauts,
Ail, Persil et Menthe

*A*rtichokes and new potatoes seem to have a natural affinity for one another. They share a similar texture, and yet when paired, each shines in its own way. When the first-of-season potatoes come into the market, they sit side-by-side with artichokes and fresh garlic at the farmers' market, creating a natural inspiration. I love adding the touch of hot pepper for a bright flavor, and the parsley and mint for color and contrast.

Juice of 1 lemon, plus 1 lemon, cut in half

8 globe artichokes or 16 baby artichokes

1 cup loosely packed fresh flat-leaf parsley leaves

1 cup loosely packed mint leaves

8 plump cloves garlic, peeled

½ teaspoon hot red pepper flakes, or to taste

Sea salt

2 cups Homemade Chicken Stock (page 325)

16 small new potatoes (such as Yukon Gold), scrubbed but not peeled

1 tablespoon walnut oil (or substitute extra-virgin olive oil)

Fleur de sel

1 Prepare a large bowl of cold water, adding the lemon juice and the lemon halves to the water. Rinse the artichokes under cold running water. Using a stainless steel knife to minimize discoloration, trim the stem of each artichoke to about 1½ inches from the base. Carefully trim and discard the stem's fibrous exterior. Bend back the tough outer green leaves, one at a time, and snap them off at the base. Continue snapping off leaves until only the central cone of yellow leaves with pale green tips remains. Lightly trim the top cone of leaves to just below the green tips. Trim any dark green areas from the base. Halve the artichokes lengthwise. With a small spoon, scrape out and discard the hairy choke. Cut each trimmed artichoke half lengthwise into eight even slices. Place the slices in the acidulated water. Set aside.

2 With a large chef's knife, finely chop together the parsley, mint, garlic, red pepper flakes, and salt to taste. Transfer to a heavy-duty saucepan and add the chicken stock. Thoroughly drain the artichoke slices and add to the saucepan. Add the potatoes, cover, and bring just to a simmer over moderate heat. Reduce the heat to low and simmer very gently until the artichokes and potatoes are soft and offer no resistance when pierced with a knife, about 45 minutes. They should still be bathed in liquid.

3 With a slotted spoon, transfer the artichokes and potatoes to warmed shallow soup bowls, then carefully spoon a bit of the sauce over them. Drizzle with the walnut oil and season with *fleur de sel*. Serve as a first course or vegetable side dish. Pass plenty of crusty bread for sopping up the delicious sauce.

4 TO 6 SERVINGS

Potatoes

POTATO AND CELERIAC GRATIN

Gratin de Pommes de Terre et Céleri-Rave

*C*ome winter, potatoes and celeriac are firmly entrenched in our cold-weather diet. The play of flavors calls out for pairing with a touch of cream, a hint of garlic, and a healthy dose of freshly grated cheese. I could make a meal of this lovely, fragrant gratin, one that should be on the table at every winter holiday feast.

1 Preheat the oven to 375 degrees F.

2 Place the potatoes and the celeriac in a large saucepan and cover with the milk and cold water. Add the garlic, salt, bay leaves, and bunch of thyme. Bring to a simmer over medium-high heat, stirring occasionally to prevent the vegetables from sticking to the bottom of the pan. Reduce the heat to medium and cook, stirring from time to time, until the vegetables are tender but not falling apart, about 10 minutes.

3 Using a slotted spoon, transfer half of the vegetables to the gratin dish. Discard the milk and water mixture and the thyme. Season to taste with nutmeg and pepper, and cover with half of the cream and half of the cheese. Cover with a final layer of vegetables, cream, and cheese. Season again with nutmeg and pepper. Sprinkle with the thyme leaves.

4 Place in the center of the oven and bake until crisp and golden on top, 1 to 1½ hours. Serve immediately.

8 SERVINGS

EQUIPMENT: A 2-quart gratin dish.

1½ pounds large Yukon Gold or russet potatoes, peeled and very thinly sliced

1½ pounds celeriac (celery root), peeled and very thinly sliced

2 cups whole milk

2 cups cold water

3 plump cloves garlic, peeled, halved, green germs removed, minced

¾ teaspoon fine sea salt

3 bay leaves, preferably fresh

A bunch of fresh thyme, tied with cotton twine or secured in a wire mesh ball

Freshly grated nutmeg

Freshly ground black pepper

1 cup heavy cream

2 cups (about 8 ounces) freshly grated imported French or Swiss Gruyère cheese

1 tablespoon fresh thyme leaves

POTATOES GRILLED WITH ROSEMARY BRANCHES

Pommes Grenailles en Brochette de Romarin

Pommes grenailles are tiny, first-of-season potatoes that weigh no more than an ounce. They are firm, moist, and full of fresh flavor. I find many uses for those little gems. In this version, I precook the potatoes so the inside is creamy and tender, then skewer them on firm stems of rosemary and grill them for a crispy crust. Enjoy them with a tossed salad, or as an accompaniment to grilled or roasted meat, poultry, or fish.

1 Place the potatoes in a large pot. Add the bay leaf, sea salt, oil, and several tablespoons of cold water. Cover and cook over the lowest possible heat, turning from time to time, until the potatoes are tender when pierced with a fork and browned in patches, about 25 minutes. (Cooking time will vary according to the size and freshness of the potatoes.)

EQUIPMENT: A pastry brush.

24 baby potatoes (fingerlings or small Yukon Gold), scrubbed but not peeled (about 1½ pounds)

1 bay leaf, preferably fresh

1 teaspoon coarse sea salt

1 teaspoon extra-virgin olive oil

6 thick branches of fresh rosemary, leaves removed and finely chopped for garnish, branches removed

Several teaspoons extra-virgin olive oil

Fleur de sel to taste

Freshly ground white pepper to taste

2 Build a medium-size fire in a barbecue. When the coals are deep red and dusted with ash, place the grill rack on the barbecue. Let it heat up for 5 minutes. (Alternatively, preheat an oven broiler.)

3 Drain the potatoes, discarding the bay leaf. As soon as they are cool enough to handle, skewer them on the rosemary branches, threading four potatoes lengthwise on each branch. With a pastry brush, brush the skewered potatoes with olive oil. Place on the grill (or under the broiler), turning to brown them evenly, about 5 minutes. Season with salt and pepper. Serve each guest the potatoes on the skewer, garnished with chopped rosemary.

6 SERVINGS

Potatoes

POTATOES FROM THE MAS HAUT

Les Pommes de Terre du Mas Haut

*O*ne stormy evening in December, a local winemaker and his wife invited us to a dinner of freshly caught game birds—tiny *grives,* or thrush—grilled in their kitchen fireplace. You need to be a brave eater, for the tiny birds are consumed whole, innards and all, leaving just the beak behind on your plate. They are moist, gamey, rich, and delicious, especially when downed with the substantial local red wine. The second course of the evening was this marvelous potato dish: simply halved, tossed in a bit of extra-virgin olive oil, then roasted in the oven cut side down. The yellow-fleshed potatoes—I use the French variety known as Charlotte—emerge from the oven golden, puffy, and fragrant. Simplicity at its finest.

EQUIPMENT: A nonstick baking sheet.

1 pound large yellow-fleshed potatoes (such as Yukon Gold), scrubbed and halved but not peeled

1 teaspoon fine sea salt

1 tablespoon extra-virgin olive oil

1 Preheat the oven to 425 degrees F.

2 In a large bowl, combine the potatoes, salt, and olive oil. Place the potatoes cut side down on the baking sheet. Roast until the potatoes are golden, puffy, and tender when pierced with a fork, about 40 minutes. Remove from the oven and serve immediately.

4 SERVINGS

MIREILLE'S SUMMER POTATO GRATIN

Le Gratin de Pommes de Terre Estival de Mireille

*M*any a Wednesday lunch I can be found feasting at the hands of Mireille Pons, chef-owner of Le Bistrot du Paradou, not far from Saint-Rémy. This light summer gratin—made without the traditional cream or butter—is great for those sizzling days of July and August. She uses the reserved juices from roasting meats and poultry to moisten the potatoes. A good homemade chicken stock, reduced to a syrup, is a worthy substitute.

1 Preheat the oven to 375 degrees F.

2 In a large skillet, combine the onions, olive oil, bacon, garlic, and salt. Over moderate heat, cook to lightly brown the bacon and onions, about 5 minutes.

3 Layer the potatoes in the gratin dish. Cover with the onion, bacon, and garlic mixture. Pour the juices or reduced stock over the mixture. Season generously with freshly ground black pepper. Place the gratin dish in the center of the oven and bake until the potatoes are cooked through, 1 to 1½ hours. Serve immediately.

6 SERVINGS

EQUIPMENT: A 2-quart gratin dish.

2 large onions, peeled, halved lengthwise, and finely sliced

2 tablespoons extra-virgin olive oil

4 ounces smoked slab bacon, rind removed, cut into cubes (1 cup)

20 plump cloves garlic, peeled, halved, green germs removed

Fine sea salt to taste

2 pounds large Yukon Gold potatoes, peeled and very thinly sliced

1 cup reserved juices from roasting meats or poultry; or 1 cup Homemade Chicken Stock (page 325), reduced to a syrup

Freshly ground black pepper

Le Bistrot du Paradou
Jean-Louis and Mireille Pons
13125 Le Paradou
Telephone: 04 90 54 32 70

WARM POTATO, CHIVE, AND BLOOD SAUSAGE SALAD

Salade de Pommes de Terre, Ciboulette et Boudin Noir

*T*his is a Saturday lunch special if there ever was one! In the cooler months, my butcher, Franck Peyraud, makes the most delicious *boudin*, or rich pork-blood sausage, that pairs perfectly with yellow-fleshed Charlotte potatoes. Along with a tossed green salad, this makes a meal.

1 Bring about 1 quart of water to a simmer in the bottom of a vegetable steamer. Place the potatoes on the steaming rack. Place the rack over simmering water, cover, and steam until the potatoes can easily be pierced with a paring knife, about 20 minutes for small potatoes, longer for large potatoes.

2 Meanwhile, in a large salad bowl, combine 5 tablespoons of the olive oil, the vinegar, and the mustard, and whisk to blend. Season to taste with salt and pepper. Set aside.

3 Once the potatoes are cooked, drain them. As soon as they are cool enough to handle, peel and thinly slice them, dropping them into the vinaigrette in the salad bowl. Toss to evenly coat the potatoes with the dressing.

EQUIPMENT: A vegetable steamer.

1 pound small yellow-fleshed potatoes (such as Yukon Gold), scrubbed but not peeled

6 tablespoons extra-virgin olive oil

2 tablespoons best-quality sherry wine vinegar

1 tablespoon imported French mustard

Fine sea salt

Freshly ground black pepper

8 ounces blood sausage (or substitute good-quality pork sausage), sliced

¼ cup finely chopped fresh chives

Wine Suggestion: A nice chilled red is perfect here, such as a young Côtes-du-Rhône, a Côtes-du-Roussillon-Villages, or a Brouilly from Beaujolais.

4 In a large skillet, heat the remaining tablespoon of olive oil over moderately high heat until hot but not smoking. Place the slices of sausage side-by-side in the pan, cooking them until browned on each side, about 2 minutes per side. (This may have to be done in batches.) Toss them with the potatoes and dressing as they are cooked. Add the chives and toss. Season with freshly ground black pepper and serve immediately.

2 SERVINGS AS A MAIN COURSE

YOU'LL FIND MORE than twenty-five varieties of potatoes in the French markets, depending upon the season. They come, as ever, with fetching names like Charlotte and Franceline, Manon and Mona Lisa, Amandine and Bleue d'Auvergne. Here are some notes on my favorite varieties:

A BRIEF FRENCH POTATO GLOSSARY

FINGERLINGS Of the French fingerling potatoes, the most prized is the Ratte, a tapered and elongated potato actually popularized by chef Joël Robuchon in the 1980s. The skin is pale, satiny, and golden; the interior is yellow and finely textured. The flavor is almost sweet and very creamy. They are great for purées or cooked with the skins on, on top of the stove in a covered cooking vessel.

GOLDEN TO TAN-SKINNED The most popular and versatile potatoes in this category include the Charlotte, Mona Lisa, and Bintje, which can easily be substituted for the American Yellow Finn or Yukon Gold. They are beautiful in that they have a firm and golden flesh, are good keepers, and have great taste. I love to use them in potato salads or, when small, for cooking whole, skins and all.

RED-SKINNED The most common red-skinned, yellow-fleshed potato is the Roseval, a fairly common potato similar to our Red Bliss. They are not always high on flavor, but they hold together well for gratins and keep well.

Potatoes

233

FRESH HOMEMADE CHEESE

JOSIANE'S FRESH GOAT CHEESE WITH PROVENÇAL HERBS

FRESH GOAT CHEESE WITH FRESHLY CRACKED
BLACK PEPPERCORNS

GOAT CHEESE WITH OLIVE PUREE FROM NYONS

TRUFFLED SAINT-MARCELLIN

EGGS AND CHEESE
Les Oeufs et les Fromages

BAKED ARUGULA OMELET

POACHED EGGS WITH RED WINE SAUCE

GOAT CHEESE SOUFFLE

MINT-INFUSED FRESH CHEESE

FRESH HOMEMADE CHEESE

Fromage Frais Maison

*O*nce you've made homemade fresh cheese, you'll never bother with store-bought again. I adore making this cheese, for when I prepare it I feel as though I'm in contact with the clearest, simplest processes of food creation. The fresh lactic aroma that fills the kitchen and the clean lactic flavor that fills your mouth in sampling are rewards enough. I have been making this cheese for years and have long lost track of its origins. I try to prepare it with whole, raw cow's milk, when I can find it. The cheese is also delicious prepared with fresh homogenized milk. All that's required is a bit of patience, for you can't hurry the cheese-making process. And if you have the prized French sea salt—*fleur de sel*—on hand, use it to season this light, delectable fresh cheese. The cheese can also be seasoned with fresh chives or mixed herbs (or even prepared with a bunch of thyme added to the milk at the beginning), though I prefer my fresh cheese "neat," savoring it warm with fresh tomatoes and basil; at breakfast, with a touch of honey or cherry preserves; or tossed into thick rounds of rigatoni for a quick Sunday-night supper.

EQUIPMENT: A thermometer; a large fine-mesh sieve or colander; cheesecloth.

2 quarts whole milk

3 tablespoons distilled white vinegar

⅛ teaspoon fine sea salt, or to taste

"Age doesn't matter.
Unless you are a cheese."

1 In a 3-quart stainless steel or enameled pan, combine the milk and vinegar. Over the lowest possible heat, warm the mixture to 205°F. This will take 20 to 25 minutes on the lowest setting of a gas stove, up to 1 hour and 35 minutes on the lowest setting of an electric burner. During this time, stir the mixture only three or four times during the first few minutes to keep the curds small and delicate. You will see the milk bubble up and eventually separate into white curds and thin, milky whey.

2 Turn off the heat and allow the mixture to stand, undisturbed, for 10 minutes. The resting period allows the curds to cool down and firm up, making them easier to separate from the whey.

3 Meanwhile, line a large fine-mesh sieve or colander with a double thickness of cheesecloth and place it over a large bowl. Pour boiling water through the cheesecloth to dampen and sterilize it. Discard the water. With a large slotted spoon, carefully transfer the large white curds—spoonful by spoonful—to the cheesecloth-lined colander set over the bowl. Note that there will always be some solids that are difficult to strain out by hand. When most have been strained out, pass the whey through another fine-mesh sieve set over a large bowl to collect any last bits. Add these solids to those draining in the cheesecloth. (The whey can be saved to use in cooking—rice, in soups—or can be discarded.) Sprinkle the cheese with the salt and let rest, undisturbed, until it has thoroughly drained, 2 to 3 minutes. At this point the mixture should resemble very dry cottage cheese. Using a spatula or a knife, break up the cheese to distribute the salt. Serve warm, or spoon into molds and refrigerate for 2 to 3 days to use in recipes calling for fresh cheese such as drained yogurt (yogurt cheese), drained *fromage blanc, brousse, brocciu,* or ricotta.

ABOUT 1 POUND

ON PRECISION IN THE KITCHEN: There are times in the kitchen when precision makes all the difference in the world. And cheese making is one of them. Don't even attempt this recipe without an accurate thermometer. I often cook with a stopwatch around my neck—not because I'm crazed, but because accuracy to the second is important in writing a recipe that will work for everyone. You will have great success at cheese making as long as you keep your utensils spotlessly clean, make the cheese in a noncorrosible pot (either glass or stainless steel—no aluminum please, because it will react with the vinegar), and begin with the freshest whole milk you can find.

On Bread, Cheese, Wine, and Pairing

I HAVE HAD MORE food epiphanies over bread, cheese, and wine than over any other combination. As the late French baker Lionel Poilâne once pointed out to me, "Bread, cheese, and wine are all fermented foods. Bread is nothing more than flour and water and natural yeast. Cheese is nothing more than fermented milk. Wine is nothing more than fermented grapes. And each becomes what it is through the intervention of man." I guess that I care deeply about the enjoyment of all three ingredients, and so always pay special attention to them in my daily life.

Such an epiphany occurred one summer evening while I was reading and also eating a slice of Fourme d'Ambert. I rather absentmindedly took a bite of cheese, a sip of a red Côtes-du-Ventoux, and suddenly my mouth exploded with the wintry sensation of fresh black truffles! I paused, was stunned and amazed, inhaled, and felt certain that there was a truffle in my midst. It was, of course, the earthiness of the blue cheese in combination with the truffle-like essence of the wine that triggered the sensation. And I did not want it to fade. I savored the seconds of unanticipated pleasure and only wished they could be turned into hours. Alas, it was elusive, for a second morsel of cheese and another few drops of wine were pleasurable, but no greater than the sum of the parts.

A few weeks later, Fourme d'Ambert came into play again, at the very end of an extraordinary meal. But this time the first taste, the second, and on to the last built like a crescendo. The creamy Fourme d'Ambert was teamed with a rich, rosy, fragrant, buttery toasted brioche laced with sweet cherries and spice, and moistened with a glass of rich but not overly sweet ruby Port wine. The trio was as good as a whole meal to me, perfection multiplied like a symphony of colors and textures on the palate. The cheese was just slightly chilled and its buttery coolness melted into the warm toast, with its hint of spice and sweet and the smoothness of the cherries, then the rounding out of the alcohol on the tongue supplied by the choice of the Rozès Vintage 1985 Porto. Today much ado is made of food and wine pairing, which is both a science and an art. As my two experiences suggest, pleasure explosions can be accidental or planned, but when the pairing works, it is hard to find more satisfactory gastronomic pleasure.

The best pairings are neither complicated nor complex, nor are they traditional. Try it yourself. Look for notes in a wine—whether it's one of fresh or dried fruit, of toasted nuts, of wood or the woods; of iodine or black cherries, of herbs of the scrubland *garrigue* of Provence (fennel, thyme, bay leaf); whether it has a touch of curry, butter, and vanilla; or hints of wet leaves from the woods and mushrooms, honey, or a confit of oranges. So when you find these elements in wines, why not just match them up with the real thing?

When pairing foods you already know you love, what do you have to lose in trying to embellish and expand their own horizons? I can easily make a meal of a tiny plate of firm goat's milk cheese, a few Provençal crackers, black olives and almonds, and a few dried figs that have been stuffed with fennel and walnuts. The Basque have always served cherry jam with their firm aged sheep's milk cheese, and so I follow suit, offering a tray of four or five different French sheep's milk cheeses ranging from the Basque Oussau Iraty to my favorite artisanal Roquefort from the Carles brothers, and on to the adorable Corsican Brin d'Amour, scattered with all the wonderful wild herbs of the *garrigue*. When cherries are in season, they go on the platter too, as I find the slight acidity cuts the fat of the cheese and leaves a fine, mingling aftertaste on the palate.

In the winter months, when fresh black truffles are in season, I dream up all sorts of ways to work them and cheese into a meal. I make "reverse Oreos" by slicing disks of a small goat cheese and layering slices of truffles between the slices of cheese. One year I bought a whole Chaource—the soft-rinded cow's milk cheese from Champagne that weighs about a pound—and cut it into three even slices like a layer cake. I put a layer of truffle slices between the layers, reconstructed the Chaource, then wrapped it tightly in plastic and let it mature for a good week in the refrigerator, with stupendous results. It was cheese merchant Philippe Alléosse from Paris who convinced me that vintage Champagne and Chaource were a marriage made in heaven. I took it one step further with toasted walnut bread and *Chaource aux truffes* as the highlight of a New Year's Eve feast.

Conditioned to an avalanche of flavors and sensations in a single meal, we rarely have time to pause and reflect, to stop and pay attention. When a single wine and a single dish seem to merge as one, we *are* forced to pause, stop, listen, taste, and reflect upon our reactions to the interplay of wine and food.

Josiane's Fresh Goat Cheese with Provençal Herbs

Le Chèvre Frais aux Herbes de Provence de Josiane

*J*osiane Deal has been my local cheese supplier for more than a decade. Along with her husband, Christian, she runs the fragrant village cheese shop Lou Canestéou. Their tidy, welcoming shop is certainly one of the ten best in France, with more than 100 varieties of cheese, all beautifully aged. They specialize in local goat and sheep's milk cheeses, and they have a creative flair for flavoring these fresh, tangy cheeses. Josiane seasons the rounds of very fresh goat's milk cheese known as Valréas, or of fresh Banon, a mix of goat and sheep's milk, with her highly perfumed home blend of *herbes de Provence.* The cheese is welcome on any cheese platter, but I also love to make a meal out of it, teamed with a tossed green salad, roasted potatoes, and a glass of red wine.

Scatter the dried herbs in an even layer on a dessert plate. Roll the cheese in the herbs, completely coating all sides. With your fingertips, press any remaining herbs into the cheese. Set the cheese on a plate or a platter. Serve immediately. Or cover delicately with plastic wrap and refrigerate for up to 3 days.

2 SERVINGS

2 teaspoons Provençal Herb Blend (page 313)

1 fresh round goat cheese (about 6 ounces)

Lou Canestéou

Josiane and Christian Deal
10, rue Raspail
84110 Vaison-la-Romaine
Telephone: 04 90 36 31 30
Fax: 04 90 28 79 33

Wine Suggestion: I have to suggest our wine—Clos Chanteduc, a fruity young Côtes-du-Rhône that is a blend of Grenache, Syrah, and Mourvèdre grapes.

HERE'S A LOOK at some of my favorite cheeses and the cheese tray that has become the trademark of Chanteduc.

LE RÔVE This tiny, pristine white cheese is the size of a golf ball. It takes its name from a breed of goat known as *Rôve*. The cheese is made in the department of the Hérault, north of Montpellier, and is sold when it is only two or three days old. Historians believe that the *Rôve* is the original breed of goat brought to France by the Greeks more than 2,000 years ago. The *Rôve* is prized for the rich quality of its milk and its density. While other breeds give up to 750 quarts of milk a year, the *Rôve* gives only 400, meaning it offers a milk that is concentrated and full of the flavors of the *garrigue*—wild herbs and flowers.

This is a cheese that is great with a fruity rosé, such as the Tavel from Domaine de la Mordorée.

BANON Banon, the tidy little goat's milk cheese wrapped in four to five dried brown chestnut leaves and tied with raffia, has existed since Gallo-Romain times. Today this tiny disk—weighing just over 3 ounces—is made of raw goat's milk and aged for at least fifteen days. The cheese takes its name from the village of Banon, a small spot that is enveloped in lavender fields along the slopes of Mount Ventoux.

When you cut the raffia ties of a Banon, you enter a secret world. The cheese itself is allowed to breathe and exhale its personality. A finely aged Banon will run like a volcanic landslide, its ivory-hued crust holding it back only so long. The imprint of the chestnut leaves remains, as does their pleasantly musty aroma, almost that of a forest after the rain. What's more, the chestnut leaves impart of bit of tannin to the cheese, making it one goat cheese that is truly red wine friendly. The cheese itself exudes a fresh lactic odor, and on the mouth it is fresh, supple, and faintly acidic. The goats roam through the *garrigue* amid the lavender, wild thyme, wild summer savory *(sarriette)*, Scotch broom *(genêt)*, and hawthorn *(aubépine)*, so it is no surprise that hints of all of these treasures find their way into the prized cheese.

Young reds can easily accompany a Banon, especially those with a bit of acidity, such as a young Côtes-du-Rhône, a Coteaux d'Aix-en-Provence, a Côtes-de-Provence, or a wine from Les Baux-de-Provence. The best white wines include anything made with a percentage of the Roussanne or Marsanne grapes, either alone or in combination with other grapes. A real winner from my cellar is Château La Nerthe's classic white, with 25 percent Roussanne, and the prized Clos de Beauvenir, with 60 percent Roussanne. Another favorite is the white Châteauneuf-du-Pape from Château de Beaucastel (a killer would be their 100 percent Roussanne Vieilles Vignes) or from Domaine Grand Veneur, with 33 percent Roussanne in their regular *cuvée* and 100 percent in the *cuvée* La Fontaine.

BRIN D'AMOUR This square, squat cheese made from raw sheep's milk can make me swoon. It's one cheese I can never get enough of, and when there are cheeses left over, this is the one that gets consumed first. There are many versions and many qualities of the cheese that translates as "brindle of love." The very-fine-textured ivory-colored cheese is coated with *fleurs de maquis,* the wild herbs found in the scrubby Corsican landscape, including rosemary, summer savory, and juniper berries. Sometimes the cheese is flavored with tiny red peppers known in Provence as *pili-pili.* As the cheese ages and dries, the intense flavors of the herbs penetrate the cheese, making for a strong, slightly sour taste—certainly one that cannot be ignored. Made artisanally, the cheese is usually aged one month before it is shipped from the cheese maker to market. Younger, smaller versions of the cheese are simply called Fleur de Maquis. I find this cheese quite ambidextrous as to wine: a good solid white or a powerful red marries beautifully here. A dream would be an aged white Châteauneuf-du-Pape from either Château du Beaucastel, Château La Nerthe, or Grand Veneur's 100 percent Roussanne, Domaine La Fontaine.

FOURME D'AMBERT Fourme d'Ambert is not a Provençal cheese but one from the Auvergne region, in the center of France. This mild blue cheese appears on our tray because it is my husband, Walter's, favorite. I have also come to share an affinity for its creamy texture, its golden color, and its ability to transform one's palate and pick up the flavors of black truffles, as it did one summer's evening. The cheese takes its name from the Latin word *forma,* for form or shape, and the town in which it is made, Ambert. I particularly love this cheese with a chilled *vin doux naturel,* especially the pure Grenache version from the winemaker at Domaine la Soumade in Rasteau.

PICODON This raw goat's milk cheese can be found in many forms and under many names, including Picodon de l'Ardèche, Picodon de la Drôme, Picodon de Crest, and Picodon de Dieulefit. They range in age from the young Picodon de l'Ardèche (aged fourteen days) to the well-matured version, Picodon de Dieulefit, which every twelve days for three months is washed, brushed, and dried until it is hard, brittle, beautifully ripened, and has shrunk to little more than 3 ounces. I love Picodon in its many stages, according to my mood. For lunch with sliced fresh tomatoes from the garden, I opt for the creamy young cheese no more than two days old. In the winter months with a nice glass of red wine, I choose the aged version from Dieulefit or one that is just slightly younger, when the cheese is covered with a pale blue-gray mold.

SAINT-MARCELLIN This small (less than 3 ounces when young, less than 2 ounces once aged up to six weeks), mild, acidic, and salty cheese was one of my first introductions to life in Provence. Although it is made north of Provence, in the area known as the Dauphiné, it has pretty much been accepted as a Provençal cheese because of its southern accent. By that I mean that even though it is made with cow's milk, it has that small, round, disk form of a Provençal goat cheese. I find that the best Saint-Marcellins are aged just over two weeks, when they take on a golden, bloomy crust, are a bit runny, and have a nice level of acidity. I am not afraid to put it up against many of the better reds in my cellar, including Jean-Pierre Cartier's Gigondas from Domaine les Goubert.

SAINT-FÉLICIEN AND TENTATION I always refer to Saint-Félicien as Saint-Marcellin's older, fatter brother, since it is made with extra cream, for a cheese that is 60 percent fat as opposed to one made with whole milk at 45 percent fat. An even richer version, with even more cream and served in a small wicker mold, is known as Tentation. Northern Rhône wines, such as a St.-Joseph red, are ideal here.

BRIQUE DE BREBIS I always call this cheese "ugly but delicious." The name, of course, comes from the fact that it is shaped like a brick, and *brebis* is French for "ewe." This raw sheep's milk cheese that comes from the Rhône Alps is elegant, pungent, creamy, and just sensational on the palate. I enjoy it with a light red, such as a Beaujolais or a light St.-Joseph or St.-Péray.

CHÈVRE FRAIS Fresh goat cheese, or *chèvre frais,* is simply made with milk that is curdled, molded, and aged for no more than one or two days. It can be eaten as is; sprinkled with herbs, spices, or pepper; or eaten as a dessert when paired with sugar and/or honey. On my cheese tray, I serve it as is, or flavor it with herbs or crushed black peppercorns; or I slice and spread it with a black olive purée.

Le Rôve, Banon, Saint-Félicien,
Saint-Marcellin, Chèvre Frais, Brique de Brebis

Fresh Goat Cheese with Freshly Cracked Black Peppercorns

Fromage de Chèvre Frais à la Mignonnette

The Betti family runs Le Coin Gourmand—a multipurpose *épicerie*—in our village of Vaison-la-Romaine. They supply our kitchen with everything from fresh fruit and vegetables to a great assortment of cheeses and on to wines and spirits. One holiday weekend I purchased a version of this flavored cheese, a large round of goat cheese coated with coarsely ground peppercorns. I have added this variation to my cheese tray, along with other cheeses that can easily be flavored at home. I always use the finest black peppercorns—the clean, pungent, and aromatic Tellicherry from India.

1 teaspoon black peppercorns

1 round fresh goat cheese
(about 6 ounces)

Le Coin Gourmand

Danielle and Alain Betti
14, rue Maquis
84110 Vaison-la-Romaine
Telephone: 04 90 36 30 04

Cave de Cairanne

84290 Cairanne
Telephone: 04 90 30 82 05
Fax: 04 90 30 74 03
E-mail: *inof@cave_cairannne.fr*
Web: *www.Cave_Cairanne.com*
Open Monday to Friday,
8 a.m. to 7 p.m. Saturday and Sunday
from 8 a.m. to noon and 2 to 6 p.m.

Blackboard outside a shop in Vallabrègues

On a clean work surface, crush the peppercorns with a heavy mallet or by using a swipe-and-crush motion with the bottom of a heavy skillet. Alternatively, crush the peppercorns in a mortar with a pestle. Place the crushed peppercorns on a dish. Press just the top of the cheese into the peppercorns to evenly coat it. Using your fingertips, press any remaining peppercorns into the top of cheese. Set on a plate or platter and serve immediately. Or cover delicately with plastic wrap and refrigerate for up to 3 days.

2 SERVINGS

Wine Suggestion: Why not a peppery red? The exemplary wine from the Cave de Cairanne is a blend of Grenache, Syrah, and Mourvèdre. Their special *cuvée,* Réserve des Voconces Rouge, is rich with hints of black pepper, plums, raspberry, and spice.

AN EXEMPLARY *CAVE COOPERATIVE*: There was a time, say twenty years ago, when no self-respecting wine drinker in Provence would buy wine from a *cave coopérative,* a wine-making operation that groups many different growers from a specific area. *Coopérative* wines were known to be thin, boring, often undrinkable. However, many *coopératives* have made special efforts to produce exemplary wines, and the operation in the village of Cairanne, a *coopérative* created in 1929, is a good example. Their special *cuvée* Réserve des Voconces comes from vines located in the village of Cairanne, facing the Dentelles de Montmirail and Mount Ventoux. The vines are planted in clay and limestone hillsides covered with small pebbles. The slopes are gentle and well exposed to the sun. The grapes are all hand-harvested. Some of the grapes are not destemmed, in order to preserve the character of the *terroir.* After twelve days of vatting, the oenologist proceeds with the blending.

Goat Cheese with Olive Puree from Nyons

Fromage de Chèvre à la Crème d'Olives Noires de Nyons

*P*rovençal markets offer all sorts of tricks and ideas for embellishing simple products, such as the ever-present fresh goat cheese. When visiting the daily village markets, you will see up to a dozen varied artisanal goat cheese makers, all selling their fragrant, delicate cheeses at many stages of development. The most popular is *chèvre frais,* or small disks of cheese that are soft, moist, and aged for just a week. This is the cheese I like to use for this delicious, colorful flavored cheese dish. Unlike many other flavored cheeses that seem to profit from several days' aging, this one tastes best the day it is made.

With unflavored dental floss or a very sharp knife, carefully cut the cheese in half crosswise. Carefully spread the Olive Purée on top of the bottom half of the cheese. Replace the top half of the cheese. Arrange the 4 olive halves like petals of a flower on top of the cheese. Serve immediately. (Alternatively, wrap securely with plastic wrap. Refrigerate for up to 6 hours.)

Wine Suggestion: A youthful red is good here. Try the Domaine de Gramenon Côtes-du-Rhône, a pure Grenache.

1 round fresh goat cheese (about 6 ounces)

1 tablespoon Olive Purée from Nyons (page 311)

2 best-quality French brine-cured black olives, pitted and halved

Domaine Gramenon
26770 Montbrison-sur-Lez
About 15 minutes north of the village of Nyons.
Telephone: 04 75 53 57 08
Fax: 04 75 53 68 92
Tastings by appointment only.
U.S. importer: Robert Kacher Selections, Washington, DC; telephone: (202) 832-9083.

YEARS AGO, I ASKED Joël Robuchon—still considered the very best chef of his generation— how it felt to wake up every morning knowing that everyone considered you *the best*. His response was simple: "You do the very best work you can every day, day in and day out. Then you look around you and see that your colleagues are not doing the very best they can day in and day out. Quite logically, you become the best."

I think of that uncomplicated and surprising response often, especially when I spend time with some of the most stimulating people in the world: winemakers. One of my longtime favorite winemakers is Michèle Laurent, and her Côtes-du-Rhône from Domaine Gramenon I consider to be in the best-of-class category.

Michèle and her late husband, Philippe, began quietly in 1979, he the son of a vegetable farmer and winemaker, she a trained nurse. Their newly purchased property—in the dry, mountainous region of northern Provence known as the Drôme Provençale—had beautiful old vines, with some Grenache nearly 100 years old. From the beginning their wines stood out from all the other Côtes-du-Rhônes. Together they created a collection of wines made from extremely ripe fruit, from vines tended without chemicals, wine that was fermented with indigenous yeasts and bottled without filtering or fining, giving birth to flavors that were pure, rustic, and uncomplicated.

To my mind, you cannot be the best in any class if you do not first have a passion, a specific philosophy of life, and a lifestyle that carries a well-defined road map. The Laurents evoked all three. When I asked Michèle what the best compliment was she had ever received for their wines, she said: "People always say the wine smells of grapes!" Although that may seem redundant, it is not. Think of all the other aromas we pick up by sniffing a glass of wine: truffles, cherries, blackberries, leather, but rarely do we respond "Grapes!"

While some winemakers work to achieve celebrity and produce wines that are big and complex, with colors and flavors that all but hit you over the head, the Laurent goal for Domaine Gramenon was to be known for a wine and a lifestyle that was close to the land and to nature, not dispersed. It was one that respected the grape varieties for what they were, so that the pure Grenache or the pure Syrah tasted like the finest examples of pure Grenache or pure Syrah in the world.

In late 1999, when Philippe died tragically in a hunting accident, Michèle's world was turned upside down. But there was never a question of her continuing. I, for one, would say that the wines under her sole direction have even more finesse—a femininity and directness—all the while losing none of their purity or sense of purpose. With her passions intact, her brilliant blue eyes gleaming, and a gamine-like grin, the forty-three-year-old winemaker knows that she has a good deal to prove. And she proves it, bottle after bottle.

Truffled Saint-Marcellin

Saint-Marcellin aux Truffes

I first sampled this marvelously simple and sublime cheese preparation some twenty years ago at La Beaugravière, one of our favorite restaurants in Provence. There, Tina and Guy Julien run a most exquisite restaurant, specializing in truffles during the season from late November to late March. I can't count— but can remember in rich detail—all the feasts we have enjoyed under the Juliens' care: birthdays, Sunday lunches, summer weeknight dinners on the terrace, special meals during our annual truffle workshop. In season, this preparation is always on our table at Chanteduc.

1 Using unflavored dental floss or a very sharp knife, carefully cut the cheese in half horizontally, like a layer cake. Layer the truffle slices on top of the bottom half of the cheese. Replace the top half of the cheese. Wrap securely with plastic wrap. Refrigerate for 24 to 48 hours to flavor the cheese with the truffles.

1 firm Saint-Marcellin cow's milk cheese, chilled

4 thick slices fresh black truffle

Château du Beaucastel

Jean-Pierre and François Perrin
Chemin de Beaucastel
84350 Courthézon
Telephone: 04 90 70 41 00
Fax: 04 90 70 41 19
Web: *www.beaucastel.com*
Tastings by appointment only:
9 a.m. to noon and 2 to 5 p.m.

La Beaugravière

Tina and Guy Julien
Route N 7
Quai Pont Neuf
84430 Mondragon
Telephone: 04 90 40 82 54
Fax: 04 90 40 91 01
Web: *www.beaugraviere.com*

2 At serving time, preheat the broiler.

3 Transfer the disk of Saint-Marcellin to a baking sheet. Place the baking sheet about 5 inches from the broiler. As soon as the cheese begins to melt—about 1 minute—removed the baking sheet from the oven. With a spatula, cut in wedges and carefully transfer the cheese to small individual salad plates. Serve immediately, with plenty of crusty sourdough bread.

2 SERVINGS

Wine Suggestion: With this special cheese I suggest a real splurge, a nicely chilled white Châteauneuf-du-Pape Château du Beaucastel special *cuvée* Vieilles Vignes. The Perrin family's exquisite and rare white is made from 100 percent Roussanne grapes—grapes that are fragrant, flowery, and offer a memorable depth of flavor. Not to mention immense pleasure!

Josiane and Christian Deal at Lou Canestéou cheese shop in Vaison-la-Romaine

Eggs and Cheese

249

On Cleaning Truffles

I REMEMBER AS THOUGH it was yesterday the first time I saw a freshly unearthed truffle. It was the day before Thanksgiving in 1984, and we had just acquired Chanteduc. It seemed fitting that our first family meal would include some of our best friends, Americans who either lived in France or were passing through.

Just months before we had got to know Yves Reynaud, who lived at Chanteduc as a child and hunted our thirteen acres of woods and vineyard as though they were still his own. We could always hear him coming, since there were seven yappy dogs trailing behind him. Regularly, he brought us wild rabbits, a handful of mushrooms, and now fresh black truffles.

That November day I was waiting for the remainder of our guests to arrive, and there was Yves, digging with a friend's dog, a sweet little pup named Pamela. (As Yves later explained, his dogs were great for hunting game, but they were worthless as truffle hounds.) He came up from the vineyard and presented me with what seemed like a wealth of truffles, about a dozen tiny, gnarled things that looked like coal thickly covered with moist packed dirt. I had no idea what to do with the truffles, but I figured the dirt had to go. I always save the toothbrushes from the amenities kit on airplanes to scrub wild mushrooms, and I figured they could serve double duty for truffles. I scrubbed and scrubbed under cold running water, and since no one was looking, I popped the first one into my mouth as soon as it was clean. Bingo! Bursts of flavor, perfume, texture, heaven!

I don't even remember how we ate the remaining truffles that night. All I remember is sneaking that first tiny truffle. The variety of truffle that grows in our vineyard is not the regal *Tuber melanosporum*, but the smaller, firmer, almost musky truffle known as *Tuber brumale*. I didn't know it then—even now, I would hardly eschew the *Tuber brumale*, which in some ways has an earthier, sharper flavor. I also like to say that given the choice, I would take a *brumale* truffle over a carrot any day.

"Truffles are to the soil as stars are to the sky."
—HENRI-FRÉDÉRIC BLANC, FRENCH CARTOONIST

During the truffle season from November to March, I buy most of my truffles from truffle purveyor Hervé Poron. Hervé soaks his truffles in cold water overnight to help remove the dirt, then brushes them in an old-fashioned truffle washer with cold running water. The truffles are sorted and sold, clean as a whistle. But I'm not about to give up my toothbrush collection! I still wait for Yves to come up from time to time to share the winter bounty.

BAKED ARUGULA OMELET

Omelette à la Roquette

A few years ago my gardener surprised me by planting an entire row of wild arugula, a perennial that grows and grows, offering a potentially endless supply of fragrant, spicy greens for salads. But within hours of the first planting, a female wild boar and two infant boars decided they also loved arugula, and they chomped the tender new greens down to the roots. We put up a fence, replanted, and now hoard the greens as if they were gold! I love arugula's brilliant green color and tangy flavor, a lovely foil for the delicate flavor of fresh farm eggs. This baked omelet can be served as a first course, as part of a buffet meal, or all on its own as a filling luncheon dish.

1 Preheat the oven to 425 degrees F. Butter the springform pan and set it aside.

EQUIPMENT: A 9-inch springform pan.

1 tablespoon extra-virgin olive oil

2 onions, peeled, halved, and very thinly sliced

½ teaspoon fine sea salt

About 4 cups (4 ounces) loosely packed fresh arugula, stemmed

8 extra-fresh large farm eggs

About 2 cups Mireille's Two-Tomato Sauce (page 317)

Wine Suggestion: With the tomato sauce, a young red would shine here: any good and youthful Côtes-du-Rhône would be fine.

2 In a large skillet, combine the oil, onions, and salt. Cover and sweat—cook, covered, over low heat until soft but not browned—for about 5 minutes. Add the arugula; cook just until wilted, about 1 minute, and remove from the heat. Set aside.

3 In a large bowl, gently beat the eggs with a fork. Add the onion-arugula mixture and mix to blend. Pour the mixture into the pan. Place the pan in the center of the oven and bake until firm and golden, 35 to 40 minutes.

4 Remove the omelet from the oven. Transfer the pan to a rack and allow to cool for 10 minutes. Then run a knife around the sides of the pan; release and remove the springform side, leaving the omelet on the pan base. Serve at room temperature, cut into wedges, accompanied by a spoonful of tomato sauce.

8 SERVINGS

An egg display at the farmers' market in Coustellet

POACHED EGGS WITH RED WINE SAUCE

Oeufs en Meurette à la Provençale

*T*here is always an open bottle of red wine in the house (from tastings, from cooking, leftovers from the night before), and there are always eggs, so no matter how bare the cupboard, I can whip this dish together in no time flat. Poached eggs in red wine is one of the most classic of French home-style dishes, a way to dress up simple poached eggs and turn them into a one-dish meal. For this dish use a sturdy red wine—such as a daily drinking Côtes-du-Rhône—and the freshest eggs possible. The red wine sauce, by the way, can be used in other dishes, such as a sauce for a nice grilled steak.

Wine Suggestion: Serve the same wine as used to prepare the sauce, such as a nice and hearty young Côtes-du-Rhône.

EQUIPMENT: A fine-mesh sieve; 2 large, shallow pans, each at least 10 inches in diameter, with lids.

THE RED WINE SAUCE:

1 carrot, peeled and cut into thin rounds

2 shallots, peeled and quartered lengthwise

2 plump cloves garlic, peeled and quartered lengthwise

1 sprig rosemary

2 cups red wine, such as a Côtes-du-Rhône

1 tablespoon unsalted butter, softened

1 tablespoon all-purpose flour

2 tablespoons distilled white vinegar

8 large eggs, at room temperature

8 slices sourdough bread

Sea salt

Freshly ground black pepper

2 teaspoons Provençal Herb Blend (page 313)

1 In a large stainless steel pot, combine the carrot, shallots, garlic, rosemary, and wine. Bring to a boil over high heat and boil until reduced by about half, about 6 minutes. Strain the wine through the sieve into a bowl. Return the liquid to the pot; discard the vegetables and herbs. On a plate, mash the butter and flour together to form a well-blended paste *(beurre manié)*. Bring the reduced wine back to a simmer. Carefully whisk in the butter and flour paste a little at a time, whisking until the sauce is lightly thickened and glassy. Remove from the heat and keep warm.

2 In the two shallow pans, bring about 3 inches of water to a boil. Add 1 tablespoon of the vinegar to each pan. Turn off the heat and immediately break 4 eggs directly into the water of each pan, carefully opening the shells as close to the water's surface as possible so that the eggs slip into the water in one piece. Immediately cover the pans with a lid to retain the heat. Allow the eggs to cook for 3 minutes before lifting the lids. The eggs are ready when the whites are opaque and the yolks are covered with a thick, translucent layer of white.

3 While the eggs cook, toast the bread. Place two pieces of toast on each of four warmed dinner plates. Using a flat slotted spoon, carefully lift the eggs from the water, drain, and place on top of the toast. Spoon the wine sauce all around. Season to taste with salt, pepper, and the herbs. Serve immediately.

4 SERVINGS

GOAT CHEESE SOUFFLE

Soufflé au Fromage de Chèvre

My favorite recipes are those that create themselves. During cooking class one Friday—when I allow myself to experiment and play a bit—I opened the refrigerator to see what I might create to add to our traditional buffet lunch. I took all the leftover bits of cheese—an assortment of Roquefort, varied fresh goat cheeses, and fresh sheep's milk cheese—put them in the food processor with five whole eggs, poured the mixture into a small gratin dish, and baked it. I had no idea what I might come up with, but I had a hunch it would be good. It puffed up beautifully—very soufflé-like—with a golden crust. I had planned to add herbs halfway through but forgot. Once it was baked, it looked too good to embellish, so the planned herbs ended up in the day's green salad. But as I made the soufflé again and again, herbs did often creep in, so make this according to your mood of the day. I do not add salt to this dish, since the cheese adds enough.

EQUIPMENT: A food processor or blender; an 8-inch gratin dish.

About 8 ounces mixed soft cheeses (such as Roquefort, fresh goat's milk cheese, fresh cow's milk cheese, or fresh sheep's milk cheese)

5 large eggs

Herbs to taste: chopped tarragon, chives, rosemary, thyme (optional)

Wine Suggestion: While Sancerre is a traditional match for goat cheese, a lovely rosé such as the Tavel from Domaine de la Mordorée would be a welcome accompaniment.

1 Preheat the oven to 425 degrees F.

2 In the bowl of a food processor or a blender, combine the cheese, eggs, and herbs (if using) and blend until the mixture is smooth and frothy. Pour into the gratin dish. Place in the center of the oven and bake until firm, puffy, and golden brown on top, 30 to 40 minutes. Remove from the oven and let cool about 5 minutes before serving. Serve with a large serving spoon, allowing guests to serve themselves.

6 TO 8 SERVINGS

MINT-INFUSED FRESH CHEESE

Fromage Frais à la Menthe

One Sunday at a café in L'Isle-sur-la-Sorgue
I sampled a welcoming version of this
combination of fresh local goat cheese curds—
or *brousse*—mixed with fresh mint, making for a

1 cup Fresh Homemade Cheese
(page 236) or ricotta cheese

1 cup mint leaves, finely minced

combination of a lactic and tangy taste with the sweetness of the herb. Since then I have
found many other uses, including spreading it on toast to accompany a mixed salad or
using it as a stuffing for delicate fresh zucchini blossoms. One batch is sufficient for at
least twelve toasts and for stuffing twelve zucchini blossoms.

Place the cheese on a large, flat plate. Sprinkle with the minced mint and mash with a
fork until evenly blended. Store, refrigerated, in a covered container for up to 2 days.

1 CUP

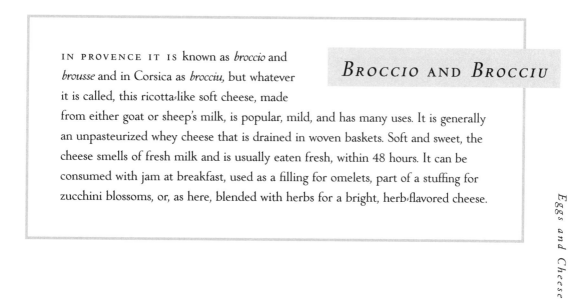

IN PROVENCE IT IS known as *broccio* and
brousse and in Corsica as *brocciu*, but whatever
it is called, this ricotta-like soft cheese, made

BROCCIO AND BROCCIU

from either goat or sheep's milk, is popular, mild, and has many uses. It is generally
an unpasteurized whey cheese that is drained in woven baskets. Soft and sweet, the
cheese smells of fresh milk and is usually eaten fresh, within 48 hours. It can be
consumed with jam at breakfast, used as a filling for omelets, part of a stuffing for
zucchini blossoms, or, as here, blended with herbs for a bright, herb-flavored cheese.

Eggs and Cheese

SERGE'S SPELT BREAD

CARPENTRAS MULTISEED BREAD

BLACK OLIVE FOUGASSE

BREADS

Les Pains

RAOUL'S KAMUT ROLLS

VAISON'S CANDIED FRUIT BREAD

QUICK POLENTA BREAD WITH ROSEMARY

A bread still life at Le Bistrot du Paradou in Le Paradou

SERGE'S SPELT BREAD

Pain d'Epeautre Chez Serge

In Provence, *épeautre* has long been called "poor man's wheat," for it will grow in poor soil, where more traditional wheat refuses to thrive. Traditionally, the tiny golden-brown grain—known as spelt in the United States and *farro* in Italy—appears often in hearty soups. More recently, modern chefs enjoy using the grain like rice, and today one finds many risotto-like creations. *Epeautre* has become a recent favorite of modern-day bakers, and it appears in both grain and milled form in *boulangeries* all over France. This nutty-flavored bread dough—which can also be used for making homemade pizza—comes from my friend Serge Boukassian, whose Carpentras restaurant/pizzeria is among my favorite local haunts.

EQUIPMENT: A heavy-duty electric mixer fitted with a dough hook; a nonstick 1-quart rectangular bread pan.

1 teaspoon active dry yeast

1 teaspoon sugar

1⅓ cups lukewarm water

1 teaspoon fine sea salt

1 cup spelt flour

2½ to 3 cups unbleached all-purpose flour, or more as needed

Restaurant Chez Serge
Serge Ghoukassian
90, rue Cottier
84200 Carpentras
Telephone: 04 90 63 21 24

1 In the bowl of the heavy-duty electric mixer, combine the yeast, sugar, and lukewarm water; stir to blend. Let stand until foamy, about 5 minutes. Stir in the salt.

2 Add the spelt flour, mixing at medium-low speed with the dough hook for 1 to 2 minutes, or until the flour is absorbed. Slowly add the all-purpose flour, a little at a time, mixing at medium-low speed until all of the flour has been absorbed and the dough forms a ball. Continue to knead at low speed until soft and satiny but still firm, 4 to 5 minutes, adding additional all-purpose flour as necessary to keep the dough from sticking. Transfer the ball of dough to a clean, floured work surface. Knead by hand for 1 minute. The dough should be smooth and should spring back when you indent it with your fingertip.

3 Clean the bowl. Return the dough to the bowl. Cover the bowl securely with plastic wrap. Place in the refrigerator. Let the dough rise until doubled or tripled in bulk, 8 to 12 hours. (This slow refrigerator rise will make for a more flavorful, well-developed bread.)

4 Remove the dough from the refrigerator. With a fist, punch down the dough. Cover the bowl securely with plastic wrap. Let rise at room temperature until doubled in bulk, about 1 hour. Punch down the dough once again and let it rise again until doubled in bulk, about 1 hour.

5 Punch down again. Form the dough into a tight rectangle. Place the dough in the bread pan. Cover with a clean cloth and let rise until doubled in bulk, about 1 hour.

6 Preheat the oven to 425 degrees F.

7 With a razor blade, slash the top of the dough several times, so it can expand evenly during baking. Arrange the oven rack in the center of the oven. Place the bread pan on the center of the rack. Bake until the crust is firm and golden brown, and the bread sounds hollow when tapped on the bottom, about 45 minutes, or until an instant-read thermometer plunged into the center of the bread reads 200 degrees F. Remove the pan from the oven. Turn the loaf out and place it on a rack to cool. Do not slice the bread for at least 1 hour, for it will continue to bake as it cools.

I LOAF, ABOUT 12 SLICES

VARIATION: For pizza, the dough—or portions of it—can be stored after step 3 in a sealed container in the refrigerator for up to 2 days. To use, simply punch down the dough after it doubles or triples.

ON SCORING OR SLASHING BREAD

I CONFESS THAT I LOVE kitchen gadgets, the smaller the better. A favorite gadget is a small, curved, double-edged razor blade with a yellow plastic handle known as a *lame*. It is used to slash or score bread before baking to release some of the trapped gas. The slash helps create a bread with an attractive finished look and also makes the bread almost levitate from the baking sheet or pan, a quality called oven spring. The cut is made with the tip of the blade, actually dragging it through the dough. An ordinary razor blade will do just as well, but that takes the fun out of having a kitchen gadget!

CARPENTRAS MULTISEED BREAD

Pain de Carpentras aux Graines

One chilly, blue-skied day in December I began my market day with a quick, successful tour of Carpentras's fresh black truffle market, then moved on down the allée Jean-Jaurès to the fruit and vegetable vendors that lined the main parking lot of the city. There were salty, sparkling, freshly cured black olives from Nyons; home-pressed olive oil of the fragrant, grassy Verdale variety, put up in Perrier bottles; and this bread, from a vendor who talked my ears off. He preached the virtues of vegetarianism and the powers of soy protein, all the while confiding that those virtues did not help him hold on to his wife, who had left him. He tried to convert me (like preaching to the choir) and convinced me to buy his incredible multiseed bread. I guess he was a successful preacher, for I have become totally addicted to this bread laden with everything from purplish black poppy seeds to huge greenish black pumpkin seeds and—my favorite—grayish brown sunflower seeds. Aside from the dense, seed-rich interior, this bread shines with a thick coating of the same symphony of seeds. The seed mixture is of my making, so feel free to change the variety of grains to suit your personal taste.

EQUIPMENT: A heavy-duty electric mixer fitted with a dough hook; a nonstick 1-quart rectangular bread pan.

1 teaspoon active dry yeast

1 teaspoon sugar

1⅓ cups lukewarm water

1 teaspoon fine sea salt

2 tablespoons poppy seeds

2 tablespoons sesame seeds

2 tablespoons pumpkin seeds

2 tablespoons golden flax seeds

2 tablespoons dark brown flax seeds

2 tablespoons sunflower seeds

1 cup rye flour

2½ to 3 cups unbleached all-purpose flour

1 large egg beaten with 1 tablespoon cold water, for egg wash

Marché de Carpentras (Vaucluse)
Allée Jean-Jaurès and throughout the center of town
84200 Carpentras
(20 miles east of Avignon)
Friday, 8 a.m. to noon

1 In the bowl of the heavy-duty electric mixer, combine the yeast, sugar, and lukewarm water, and stir to blend. Let stand until foamy, about 5 minutes. Stir in the salt.

2 Meanwhile, in a small bowl, combine all the seeds and toss to blend. Divide into two batches, reserving 2 tablespoons of the mixture for the topping and the rest for the bread. Set both aside.

3 Add the rye flour to the yeast mixture, mixing at medium-low speed with the dough hook for 1 to 2 minutes, or until the flour is absorbed. Slowly add the 2½ cups all-purpose flour, a little at a time, mixing at medium-low speed until all of the flour has been absorbed and the dough forms a ball. Add the larger batch of seeds and continue to knead at low speed until soft and satiny but still firm, 4 to 5 minutes, adding additional all-purpose flour as necessary to keep the dough from sticking. Transfer the ball of dough to a clean, floured work surface. Knead by hand for 1 minute to help distribute the seeds. The dough should be smooth and should spring back when you indent it with your fingertip.

4 Clean the bowl. Return the dough to the bowl. Cover securely with plastic wrap. Place in the refrigerator. Let the dough rise until doubled or tripled in bulk, 8 to 12 hours. (This slow refrigerator rise will make for a more flavorful, better-developed bread.)

5 Remove the dough from the refrigerator. With a fist, punch down the dough and form it into a ball again. Cover the bowl securely with plastic wrap. Let the dough rise at room temperature until doubled in bulk, about 1 hour. Punch down the dough again. Let rise again until doubled in bulk, about 1 hour.

6 Punch down the dough again. Form the dough into a tight rectangle. Place the dough in the bread pan. Cover with a clean cloth and let rise until doubled in bulk, about 1 hour.

7 Preheat the oven to 425 degrees F.

Bread sacks at the linen and antique shop Atelier
du Presbytère in the village of Vallabrègues

8 Brush the top of the dough with the egg wash. With a razor blade, slash the top of the dough several times, so it can expand evenly during baking. Sprinkle with the seeds reserved for the topping. Arrange the oven rack in the center of the oven. Place the bread pan on the center of the rack. Bake until the crust is firm and golden brown, and the bread sounds hollow when tapped on the bottom, about 45 minutes, or until an instant-read thermometer plunged into the center of the bread reads 200 degrees F. Remove the pan from the oven. Turn the loaf out and place it on a rack to cool. Do not slice the bread for at least 1 hour, for it will continue to bake as it cools.

1 LOAF, ABOUT 12 SLICES

WHY ONLY A TEASPOON OF YEAST? I am often asked why I use a tiny teaspoon of yeast, rather than a full package, when making certain breads. During years of bread making and experimentation, I have found that a tiny amount of yeast yields a huge amount of power, is plenty enough to give the bread a good rise, and allows the bread to develop a rich flavor of its own. For my taste, a full package of yeast will make the bread taste yeasty and will overwhelm the flavors of the flour, grains, and other ingredients.

BREAD HAS ALWAYS BEEN sacred in the French home, and over centuries great efforts were made to keep the bread as

OF BREAD AND FABRICS

fresh as possible. In the days when bread was baked at home, in wood-fired bread ovens, loaves were large (up to 5 pounds each) and dense to make for long keeping. These were the days before tidy, sturdy, airtight plastic bags, and so each family kept the bread wrapped in cloth. It was easiest to store the bread in a cloth bag secured with a drawstring, the most efficient method to keep the bread at hand and yet out of harm's way. Today the bread sack remains an integral part of the French kitchen, though more often than not the bread is first secured in an airtight plastic bag, then stored in the festive bread sack. In Provence, the sacks will likely be made of the popular printed fabrics (the best known are made by Les Olivades and Souleiado) known as *les Indiennes*. The story goes like this: In the 16th century, printed fabrics from India became popular in France. Mills around Provence began to copy the idea, but were shut down because of quality. Clever fabric printers moved their operation to Avignon, a papal territory that was not subject to royal sovereignty. The industry grew and thrived until 1734, when the agreement between the king and the pope was broken and all workshops were closed. Sixty years later, the laws changed again and the fabric printing industry returned to Avignon. It thrives to this day in the region.

BLACK OLIVE FOUGASSE

Fougasse aux Olives Noires

All my life, bread has held a certain fascination. When I was growing up, my mother baked bread every week, and I can still smell the fresh aroma of yeasty breads and rolls wafting from the kitchen each Saturday. As a young bride in the 1960s, I used to bake my mother's homemade refrigerator rolls whenever we had "company." Today I still love waking early in the morning to begin a batch of fresh bread, rolls, pizza dough, or this pizza-like Provençal flatbread known as *fougasse*. Much like an Italian *focaccia*, this flatbread can be seasoned with everything from olives to capers, fennel or tomatoes—just about anything that goes with bread! My favorite is made with my home-cured black Tanche olives, classified as the famed Olives de Nyons. I have added the little *truc* of brushing the dough with a wash of salt, water, and oil, which gives the bread a finished glaze and a pleasantly salty flavor.

EQUIPMENT: A heavy-duty electric mixer fitted with a dough hook; a pastry scraper; 2 baking sheets.

1 teaspoon active dry yeast

1 teaspoon sugar

1⅓ cups lukewarm water

1 tablespoon extra-virgin olive oil

2 teaspoons fine sea salt

About 3¾ cups (1 pound) bread flour

About 20 black olives, preferably brine-cured olives from Nyons, pitted and halved

THE SALT WASH:

2 teaspoons cold water

½ teaspoon fine sea salt

2 teaspoons extra-virgin olive oil

Fougasses *for sale at an outdoor farmers' market in Provence*

1 In the bowl of the heavy-duty electric mixer, combine the yeast, sugar, and lukewarm water, and stir to blend. Let stand until foamy, about 5 minutes. Stir in the oil and the salt.

2 Add the flour a bit at a time, mixing at medium-low speed until most of the flour has been absorbed and the dough forms a ball. Continue to knead at medium-low speed until the dough is soft and satiny but still firm, 4 to 5 minutes, adding additional flour as needed to keep the dough from sticking.

3 Cover the bowl tightly with plastic wrap, and place in the refrigerator. Let the dough rise in the refrigerator until doubled or tripled in bulk, 8 to 12 hours. (The dough can be kept for 2 to 3 days in the refrigerator. Simply punch it down as it doubles or triples.)

4 Preheat the oven to 450 degrees F.

5 Punch down the prepared dough. Gently knead the olives into the dough, trying to distribute them evenly throughout the dough. Divide the dough in half. Shape each piece into a ball. On a lightly floured surface, roll or simply stretch each ball of dough into a roughly shaped rectangle measuring about 10 by 15 inches. Using a pastry scraper, cut lengthwise slashes into the bread, with several slashes at the bottom half of the dough, in the center, and at the top, so that the slashes resemble the veins of a leaf.

6 Carefully transfer the rectangles of dough to the baking sheets. Gently pull apart at the slashes. Prick the dough all over with a fork. In a small bowl, whisk together the water, salt, and oil. Brush the salt wash over the dough. Cover the dough with a clean towel and let it rest for about 15 minutes.

7 Place the baking sheets in the oven and bake until the *fougasses* are firm and golden, 15 to 20 minutes. Remove from the oven and let cool about 10 minutes before serving. The *fougasse* can be eaten warm or at room temperature.

2 FLATBREADS, ABOUT 12 SERVINGS TOTAL

Breads

RAOUL'S KAMUT ROLLS

Les Petits Pains de Raoul

*R*aoul Reichrath is the chef-owner of a small local restaurant in the village of Roaix. Along with his Mexican wife, Flora, this young Dutchman offers a modern, personal cuisine with an emphasis on fresh and wholesome ingredients. He kindly shared the recipe for these golden homemade rolls, which are served at each meal at Le Grand Pré. I love the simplicity of the recipe, but mostly I adore the nutty, golden color and rich, almost buttery flavor of this amazing grain.

EQUIPMENT: A heavy-duty electric mixer fitted with a dough hook; two baking sheets.

2 teaspoons active dry yeast

2 tablespoons coarse sea salt

About 1½ cups bread flour

About 5½ cups Kamut flour (see box)

2½ cups water

1 In the bowl of the heavy-duty mixer, combine all the ingredients and mix at low speed for 3 minutes, stopping occasionally to scrape down the sides of the bowl with a spatula. Increase the speed to medium for 8 minutes, stopping occasionally to scrape down the sides of the bowl with a spatula. The dough should be golden, firm, and very flexible, with visible strands of gluten. Cover securely with plastic wrap and refrigerate overnight.

Le Grand Pré

Flora and Raoul Reichrath
Route de Vaison (D 975)
84110 Roaix
Telephone: 04 90 46 18 12
Fax: 04 90 46 17 84
E-mail: *legrandpre@walka9.com*

2 The next day, preheat the oven to 425 degrees F. Place a metal roasting pan filled with hot water on the floor of the oven to help create a steamy atmosphere.

3 Punch down the dough, and pull and stretch it into a rectangle about 1 inch thick and about 8 by 16 inches. Cover with a damp cloth and let rise for about 20 minutes in the summer and about 1 hour in the winter. Cut the bread into 40 squares, each about 2 inches wide. Place the rolls on a baking sheet. Place in the center of the oven and bake until a deep, golden brown, 20 to 25 minutes.

40 ROLLS

KAMUT IS A STRAIN of wheat that has not been cross-bred and hybridized as traditional wheat has, and because of its sweet flavor it is sometimes called the sweet wheat. The grain is an ancient relative of durum wheat, is twice the size of common wheat with 20 to 40 percent more protein (common wheat is 12.3 percent protein; Kamut wheat is 17.3 percent protein), and is higher in lipids, amino acids, vitamins, and minerals. The grain migrated to the United States from Egypt and has been used successfully by those with wheat allergies. Kamut, which is a registered trademark and is always grown organically, can be used like rice and cooked in a pilaf, and is most often ground and used in place of whole wheat flour in breads. It has a nutty, rich, buttery flavor and sometimes reminds one of cinnamon.

A bread shop in Eygalières, where bread is baked in a wood-fired oven

The grain's origins are intriguing. After World War II an American airman claimed to have taken a handful of grain from a stone box in a tomb in Egypt. Some of the grain was given to a friend who, in turn, mailed it to his father, a Montana wheat farmer. The farmer planted and harvested the grain and displayed it as a novelty at a local fair. Because they then believed the grain came from an Egyptian tomb, they called it "King Tut's Wheat." The novelty wore off and the grain was forgotten. In 1997, a remaining jar of the grain was obtained by T. Mack Quinn, another Montana wheat farmer. He and his son spent a decade propagating the humped-back kernels, and research revealed that the wheats of this type originated in the Fertile Crescent, which runs from Egypt to the Tigris-Euphrates basin. The Quinns coined the trade name Kamut, an ancient Egyptian word for wheat. Egyptologists claim the root meaning of Kamut is "soul of the earth."

In 1990 the USDA recognized the grain as a protected variety. Today Kamut is considered an important new crop for sustainable agriculture. The grain's ability to produce high-quality wheat without artificial fertilizers and pesticides makes it an excellent crop for organic farming. Kamut is available in health food stores or can be ordered through the Grain & Salt Society, telephone (800)867-7258, or via the Internet at *www.celtic-seasalt.com*.

Breads

269

VAISON'S CANDIED FRUIT BREAD

Pain aux Fruits Confits de Vaison

Denis Lefèvre opened his high-quality *boulangerie* on September 1, 1999, and for some serendipitous reason, I was his very first customer. I had in fact been watching the transformation of this former pizzeria/*boulangerie*, and was dismayed that the new baker was removing the wood-fired oven and replacing it with a more traditional electric oven. I happened to be marketing early that day, and was delighted to see that the new shop in town had opened its doors. One taste of Denis's fabulous breads and I didn't care what kind of oven he used, I just wanted him to stay in Vaison and be successful. He later explained that the wood-fired oven was fine for pizza or for baking an occasional loaf of bread, but not big enough for any serious bread baking. Besides, he loved the aura, the sheen, and the reliability of the 1950s oven he had purchased and installed in the little shop on the village's Place Montfort. I confess an addiction to many of his breads, including this one, a brioche-style loaf that is packed with colorful candied fruits, whole nuts, and raisins. It is rich, gorgeous, delicious. I especially love the aromas that fill my kitchen as the bread toasts to a golden, glorious brown. Spread it with a touch of butter or, better yet, some runny Saint-Marcellin cheese, and enjoy! This bread is always on the table the first night of my cooking classes, served with my favorite assortment of local goat, sheep, and cow's milk cheeses.

EQUIPMENT: A heavy-duty electric mixer fitted with a dough hook; two 1-quart rectangular loaf pans, preferably nonstick; an instant-read thermometer.

THE SPONGE:

⅓ cup whole milk, warmed

1 package (2¼ teaspoons) active dry yeast

1 teaspoon sugar

1 cup rye flour

1 large egg, lightly beaten

1 cup unbleached all-purpose flour

THE DOUGH:

⅓ cup sugar

1 teaspoon fine sea salt

2 large eggs, lightly beaten

About 1½ cups unbleached all-purpose flour

8 tablespoons unsalted butter, softened

1½ cups (8 ounces) raisins

1½ cups (8 ounces) minced candied or dried fruits

¾ cup whole unblanched almonds

1 Prepare the sponge: In the bowl of the heavy-duty mixer, combine the milk, yeast, and sugar and stir to blend. Let stand until foamy, about 5 minutes. Stir in the rye flour and the egg, and stir to blend. The sponge will be sticky and fairly dry. Sprinkle with the all-purpose flour to cover the sponge. Set aside to rest, uncovered, for 40 minutes. The sponge should erupt slightly, cracking the flour. After the 40 minutes, mix at low speed to incorporate the flour.

2 Prepare the dough: Add the sugar, salt, eggs, and 1 cup of the all-purpose flour to the sponge. With the dough hook attached, mix at low speed for 1 or 2 minutes, just until the ingredients come together. Still mixing, sprinkle in ½ cup more of flour. When the flour is incorporated, increase the mixer speed to medium and beat for 15 minutes, scraping down the hook and bowl as needed.

*Denis Lefèvre at his bread shop,
Le Pain des Moissons, in Vaison-la-Romaine*

3 To prepare the butter—which should be the same consistency as the dough—place the butter on a flat work surface and, with a dough scraper, smear it bit by bit across the work surface. When it is ready, the butter should be smooth, soft, and still cool—not warm, oily, or greasy.

Denis Lefèvre
Le Pain des Moissons
36, place Montfort
84110 Vaison-la-Romaine
Telephone: 04 90 36 03 25

4 With the mixer on medium-low, add the butter a few tablespoons at a time. When all of the butter has been added, increase the mixer speed to medium-high for 1 minute, then reduce the speed to medium and beat the dough for 5 minutes. The dough will be soft and sticky. Incorporate the candied or dried fruit and the almonds, mixing at low speed until the fruit and nuts are thoroughly incorporated.

5 Cover the bowl tightly with plastic wrap. Let rise at room temperature for 1 hour.

6 Punch down the dough. Cover the bowl tightly with plastic wrap. Let rise a second time at room temperature for 30 minutes.

7 Preheat the oven to 375 degrees F.

Breads

271

8 Divide the dough in half and place each half in a 1-quart loaf pan. Let rise at room temperature for 30 minutes.

9 Place the pans in the center of the oven and bake until the loaves are deeply golden and an instant-read thermometer plunged into the center of the bread reads 200 degrees F., 30 to 35 minutes. Remove the pans from the oven and place them on a rack to cool. Turn the loaves out once they have cooled. The bread is best eaten the day it is baked. It can be stored for a day or two, wrapped in a plastic bag.

2 LOAVES, ABOUT 12 SLICES EACH

TAKE YOUR BREAD'S TEMPERATURE:
If you bake bread regularly, it is a good idea to invest in
a small instant-read thermometer, a tool used regularly
by professional bakers. If you plunge an instant-read
thermometer into the center of the loaf and it registers
200 to 210 degrees F., you can be certain that your
bread is fully baked.

QUICK POLENTA BREAD WITH ROSEMARY

Pain de Polenta au Romarin

When I want bread in a hurry, I turn to this creation—one that is part bread, part main-course polenta. The bread is put together in minutes, and while still warm it can be cut into wedges and served with a spoonful of warm Spicy Tomato, Fennel, and Orange Sauce (page 318). Once it has cooled, serve it as a quick bread, a nice complement to a Provençal salad or soup.

1 Preheat the oven to 425 degrees F. Oil the cake pan and set aside.

2 In a medium bowl, combine the polenta, baking soda, and salt and stir to blend. In another bowl, combine the egg, buttermilk, and rosemary and whisk lightly to blend. Combine the polenta mixture with the egg mixture and stir until well combined.

3 Pour the batter into the prepared cake pan. Sprinkle with the cheese. Place the cake pan in the center of the oven and bake until the bread is firm and a cake tester comes out clean, about 15 minutes. Let sit for 5 minutes, then turn out onto a serving plate. Cut into wedges and serve warm or at room temperature.

8 TO 12 SERVINGS

EQUIPMENT: A 9-inch round nonstick cake pan.

1 teaspoon extra-virgin olive oil, for oiling the pan

1¼ cups instant polenta

½ teaspoon baking soda

¾ teaspoon fine sea salt

1 egg, lightly beaten

1 cup buttermilk, shaken to blend

1 tablespoon finely chopped fresh rosemary

½ cup (2 ounces) freshly grated Parmigiano-Reggiano cheese

The facade of an abandoned bread shop, Boulangerie Fournier, in the village of Villedieu

STRAWBERRIES FROM CARPENTRAS WITH YOGURT CREAM

DOMAINE ST. LUC'S ALMOND COOKIES

CHANTEDUC CHERRY CAKE

CHANTEDUC SWEET CHERRY SORBET

INDIVIDUAL CHERRY-HAZELNUT GRATINS

FRESH FIG AND HOMEMADE APRICOT JAM TART

LIGHT FLAKY PASTRY

WARM FIGS WITH HONEY, RASPBERRIES, AND FRESH CHEESE

COLD CAVAILLON MELON SOUP WITH BEAUMES-DE-VENISE
AND BUTTERMILK SORBET

RASPBERRY-ALMOND FINANCIERS

RASPBERRY SORBET

DESSERTS
Les Desserts

FRESH RASPBERRY SAUCE

CHÂTEAU PESQUIE'S WHITE PEACHES POACHED IN RED WINE

THREE-PEAR CAKE

CHEZ SERGE'S CINNAMON-APPLE TART

LEMON MOUSSE

LEMON CRISPS

WALTER'S CHILLED NOUGAT MOUSSE

BEAUMES-DE-VENISE SORBET

DARK CHOCOLATE SORBET

AUTUMN WALNUT CAKE DOMAINE DE LA PONCHE

A girl selling cotton candy, or barbe à papa, *at a village* fête *in Villedieu*

STRAWBERRIES FROM CARPENTRAS WITH YOGURT CREAM

Fraises de Carpentras à la Crème de Yaourt

Strawberries are a sign of hope: they arrive in the market at the middle of March, a sure signal that summer is not far behind. Long and oval, with a fine balance of tartness and sweetness, the strawberries of Carpentras are a personal favorite. This is a fine, simple preparation that demands a minimum of effort with maximized flavor results. The vinegar and sugar combination serves to bring out the color and flavor of the berries, while the yogurt cream provides just the proper lactic tang for a refreshing balance. A nice companion to this dessert is the Domaine St. Luc's Almond Cookies (page 278).

EQUIPMENT: 6 martini-style glasses.

1 pound strawberries, rinsed, stemmed, quartered lengthwise (cut jumbo fruit into sixths)

1 tablespoon best-quality vinegar (red wine, sherry wine, or balsamic vinegar)

6 tablespoons sugar

1 cup best-quality Greek-style yogurt, well drained

2 tablespoons heavy *crème fraîche* or cream

6 sprigs fresh mint, for garnish

1 Place the martini-style glasses in the refrigerator.

2 In a large bowl, combine the strawberries, vinegar, and 4 tablespoons of sugar. Stir gently. Cover securely with plastic wrap and refrigerate for 30 minutes to 1 hour.

3 At serving time, combine the yogurt and crème fraîche in a bowl and whisk gently to combine, adding the remaining 2 tablespoons of sugar to taste; the mixture should remain quite firm. Spoon the strawberries into the glass serving bowls and top with the yogurt cream. Garnish with a sprig of fresh mint. Serve.

6 SERVINGS

COME MID-MARCH, throughout
French fruit markets, you will find
the welcome sign *Les Fraises de
Carpentras*, a signal that spring has begun in earnest and an assurance that for the
next few months the sweet strawberries from the Provençal town of Carpentras
will be in the market. Since 1882, strawberries have been a specialty of Carpentras,
where the climate and soil are perfect for first-of-season, or *précoce*, varieties of
berries. Three varieties of early berries—the Ciflorette, Gariguette, and Pajaro—
are grown in Carpentras, with the finest being the Ciflorette, an elongated, orange-
red fruit with a flavor closest to the wild strawberry, or *fraise des bois*.

LES FRAISES DE CARPENTRAS

STRAWBERRY ADVICE:
Strawberries do not
ripen after picking,
so plan to consume
the fruits the day of
purchase. Rinse and
stem the berries just
before eating; never
stem or rinse earlier
or you will end up
with soggy fruit.

DOMAINE ST. LUC'S ALMOND COOKIES

Croquants aux Amandes Domaine St. Luc

*E*liane Cornillon, wife of our winemaker, Ludovic, offered these irresistible almond cookies at the end of a summer's lunch. I admit I don't have a huge sweet tooth, but I need a discipline of steel to stay away from these golden, almost taffy-like cookies with just the right amount of crunch. Not too sweet and full of pure almond flavor, they really hit the spot at the end of a meal. The cookies—actually more a cake cut into wedges—can be put together in a few minutes and baked for just 25 to 30 minutes in an oven that's not too hot. In the summertime when it is still cool in the morning, I make and bake these while I have coffee and breakfast, and the house stays cool all day long. (I just have to learn to stay out of the "cookie jar" on those days!)

EQUIPMENT: A 9-inch round nonstick cake pan; parchment paper; a pastry brush.

About 1 teaspoon almond oil or flavorless oil, such as canola oil

2 tablespoons lavender honey

½ cup sugar

1 tablespoon flour

1 egg white

8 ounces (2 cups) unblanched whole almonds

Wine Suggestion: Any good sweet wine, such as a Muscat de Beaumes-de-Venise or an Italian Vin Santo, would be ideal here.

1 Preheat the oven to 350 degrees F. Using the cake pan as a template, cut a round of parchment paper the same size as the pan. Place the parchment in the bottom of the pan. With a pastry brush, brush the paper and the sides of the pan with the oil. Set aside.

2 In a medium bowl, combine the honey, sugar, flour, and egg white. Beat vigorously with a whisk until the mixture is white and foamy, about 1 minute. Add the almonds and stir to thoroughly coat the nuts. Pour the mixture into the prepared cake pan.

3 Place the pan in the center of the oven and bake until an even, golden brown, puffy and fragrant, 12 to 15 minutes. (If your oven has hot spots, you may need to rotate the pan halfway through baking.) Remove from the oven and transfer the cake pan to a rack to cool and firm up, about 15 minutes. Carefully cut into 16 wedges. Place on a platter and serve.

THE PROVENCE COOKBOOK

LITTLE SWEETS—most often made with a honey base—are a specialty of Provence. Many villages are connected to the sweets they made famous (such as the nougat of Montélimar and Sault, the *calissons* of Aix-en-Provence). Here is a brief glossary of some of the treats, with addresses for some of the best purveyors:

NOUGAT Honey, egg white, and almonds—a pure Provençal triumvirate—make up the base of this popular, taffy-like treat that made the town of Montélimar famous. The town is considered the gateway to Provence, and nougat (which has been made there for centuries) was popularized in the 20th century when motorists traveling from Paris to Nice stopped along the Route Nationale 7 for their sweet fix. Nougat is symbolic of the holidays, when both *nougat blanc* (honey, sugar, almonds, and eggs) and *nougat noir* (honey and almonds) are often made at home.

Chabert et Guillot
Place de la Gare
9, rue Charles Chabert
26200 Montélimar
Telephone: 04 75 00 82 00

André Boyer
Rue Porte des Aires
84390 Sault
Telephone: 04 90 64 00 23
Fax: 04 90 64 08 99

CALISSONS The little diamond-shaped candies made of ground almonds and candied melon topped with a white sugar frosting are ubiquitous in Provençal pastry shops. Like some versions of nougat, the candies are set on a thin sheet of edible rice paper known as *hostie*.

Confiserie Brémond
16, rue d'Italie
13100 Aix-en-Provence
Telephone: 04 42 26 56 39
Fax: 04 42 38 01 70

FRUITS CONFITS Certainly because Provence supplied France with its most beautiful fruit, they searched for a way to preserve the fruit for the winter months. Since the 14th century, fruits have been preserved in a sugar bath, with each fruit cooked separately, sometimes going through eight or nine cookings until the fruit has absorbed enough syrup to allow for long preservation. Walk past any pastry shop, especially in winter, and you will see slices of melon, entire pears, and brilliant clementines sparkling in the windows. The best are prepared by the Lilamand family:

Maison Lilamand et Fils
5, avenue Albert Schweitzer
13210 St.·Rémy·de·Provence
Telephone: 04 90 92 11 08
Fax: 04 90 92 53 83

CHANTEDUC CHERRY CAKE

Gâteau aux Cerises de Chanteduc

We are blessed with an orchard of ancient cherry trees that each May produce an abundance of plump purplish·black fruits. The season is short—just a few weeks—and during that time I pick and pickle the cherries, turn them into sweet *confiture*, and make every variety of dessert possible: tarts and *clafoutis*, ice cream and sorbet. This very Provençal cake, made with half butter and half oil, is moist and golden.

1 Preheat the oven to 425 degrees F. Generously butter and flour the springform pan, tapping out any excess flour. Set aside.

2 In the bowl of the electric mixer, beat the eggs and sugar over high speed until thick and lemon-colored, about 2 minutes. Add the butter, oil, milk, and vanilla extract and mix just to blend.

3 Sift the flour, baking powder, and salt into a large bowl. Add the lemon and orange zests and toss to coat the citrus zest with flour. Spoon the mixture into the bowl with the egg and sugar mixture, and stir with a wooden spoon until thoroughly blended. Scrape down the sides of the bowl and mix once more. Do not overmix. Set aside for 10 minutes to allow the flour to absorb the liquids. Stir about three-fourths of the cherries into batter and blend. Spoon the batter into the prepared cake pan, smoothing out the top with a spatula.

4 Place in the center of the oven. Bake for 15 minutes, then sprinkle with the remaining cherries. Bake until the cake is golden and feels firm, 40 minutes more. Remove to a rack to cool. After 10 minutes, run a knife along the sides of the pan. Release and remove the side of the springform pan, leaving the cake on the pan base. Serve warm or at room temperature, cut into wedges.

8 SERVINGS

EQUIPMENT: A 9-inch springform cake pan; a heavy-duty electric mixer fitted with a whisk; a sifter.

Butter and flour for preparing the cake pan

2 large eggs, at room temperature

⅔ cup sugar

4 tablespoons unsalted butter, melted

¼ cup extra-virgin olive oil

⅓ cup whole milk

½ teaspoon pure vanilla extract

1½ cups unbleached all-purpose flour

1 teaspoon baking powder

Pinch of fine sea salt

Grated zest of 1 lemon, preferably organic, blanched and refreshed

Grated zest of 1 orange, preferably organic, blanched and refreshed

1 pound fresh cherries, rinsed, stemmed, and pitted

CHANTEDUC SWEET CHERRY SORBET

Sorbet à la Cerise Chanteduc

Our five ancient cherry trees at Chanteduc are so productive that we never get a chance to pick all their fruit. But during the three weeks in May that they offer the dark, shiny red fruits, we go to town! The variety is known as Burlat— what we would call sweet cherries. They are dense, deeply crimson, and ever so juicy. I often serve this gorgeous red sorbet as part of a dessert trio, along with the Chanteduc Cherry Cake (page 280) and a tiny glass of cherry *eau-de-vie*. Pitting cherries may seem like a chore to some, but I look forward to sitting in our courtyard, listening to the fountain bubble away and the birds sing as I contemplatively pit the ripe cherries one by one. Be sure to invest in a good-quality cherry pitter: the best ones come from Germany.

EQUIPMENT: A food processor or blender; a food mill fitted with the finest blade; an ice-cream maker.

¼ cup water

1 cup sugar

2 pounds fresh cherries, rinsed, stemmed, and pitted

In a medium saucepan, combine the water and sugar. Stir over low heat just until the sugar dissolves. Transfer the cherries and sugar water to the bowl of a food processor or blender and purée. Pass the mixture through the food mill. Refrigerate until thoroughly chilled. Transfer to an ice cream maker and freeze according to the manufacturer's instructions.

8 TO 12 SERVINGS

INDIVIDUAL CHERRY-HAZELNUT GRATINS

Mini-Gratins aux Cerises et aux Noisettes

*W*henever it seems fitting, I like to serve individual desserts: somehow a small gratin dish placed in front of a guest brings back childhood memories of having a dessert that is all your own. It's also a good form of portion control! These small gratins are baked with a nutty meringue-like topping and can be served warm or at room temperature. When cherries are not in season, I have prepared the same dessert with raspberries or apricots.

1 Preheat the oven to 425 degrees F. Butter and sugar the gratin dishes. Arrange the dishes side-by-side on the baking sheets.

2 Divide the cherries among the gratin dishes. Set aside.

3 In the bowl of the heavy-duty mixer, combine the eggs and sugar, and beat at the highest speed until thick and pale, 3 to 4 minutes. Add the hazelnuts and whisk until well blended. Pour the batter over the cherries in the gratin dishes.

4 Place the baking sheets with the gratin dishes in the oven. Bake until the gratins are firm and a deep golden brown, 20 to 25 minutes. Remove to a rack to cool. Dust lightly with confectioners' sugar. Serve warm or at room temperature.

6 SERVINGS

EQUIPMENT: Six 6-inch round porcelain gratin dishes; 2 baking sheets; a heavy-duty electric mixer fitted with a whisk.

Butter and flour for preparing the gratin dishes

1 pound fresh cherries, rinsed, stemmed, and pitted (or substitute raspberries or halved, pitted apricots)

2 large eggs

½ cup sugar

½ cup (2 ounces) finely ground hazelnuts

Confectioners' sugar, for dusting the gratins

Wine Suggestion: A tiny glass of cherry *eau-de-vie* or kirsch, if the gratins are baked with cherries. Otherwise the pleasantly sweet Beaumes-de-Venise is a good choice.

FRESH FIG AND HOMEMADE APRICOT JAM TART

Tarte aux Figues Fraîches et à la Confiture d'Abricots Maison

*O*ne September weekend I was making dinner in a hurry, and on the way from the herb garden I stopped to pick ripe figs from our tiny orchard. I had just prepared some stunning apricot jam (from a recipe shared with me by a Provençal friend, Maryse Jourdan, page 315), and there was pastry waiting for me in the refrigerator. This dessert all but made itself. Walter and I made short order of it, as well.

1 Preheat the oven to 425 degrees F.

2 With a spatula, evenly spread the jam over the pastry. Cut the figs crosswise into ¼-inch slices. Starting from the outside edge of the pastry, overlap the fig slices on top of the jam.

3 Place the baking sheet in the center of the oven and bake until the pastry shell is puffy and browned and the figs juicy and cooked through, about 15 minutes. Remove from the oven and dust generously with confectioners' sugar.

4 This tart is best served slightly warm. To serve, cut the tart in half lengthwise, then into even squares.

8 SERVINGS

EQUIPMENT: A nonstick baking sheet; a food processor or blender.

One 8 × 15-inch sheet of unbaked Light Flaky Pastry (page 285)

1 cup Maryse's Apricot Jam (page 315), pits removed and the jam puréed in a food processor or blender

About 1 pound ripe figs, rinsed

Confectioners' sugar, for garnish

LIGHT FLAKY PASTRY

Pâte Brisée Légère

This is a lighter version of a classic pastry, using 5 tablespoons of butter rather than 8. I find that despite the reduced amount of butter, one still obtains a pleasantly flaky crust. And that, after all, is the goal!

1 Place the flour and salt in the bowl of a food processor and process to blend. Add the butter and process until well blended, about 10 seconds. With the machine running, add the ice water and process just until the mixture resembles fine curds of cheese and almost begins to form a ball, about 10 seconds more.

2 Transfer the dough to a clean work surface, and with the palm of your hand, smear the dough bit by bit across the work surface until the dough is thoroughly incorporated. (This is called *fraisage*, the practice of mixing all the ingredients until every trace of water and flour have disappeared, at which point the mass becomes dough.)

3 Divide the dough into two even portions. Form each into a flattened round. Cover with plastic wrap and refrigerate for at least 1 hour and up to 48 hours.

4 On a lightly floured surface, roll each portion of dough into a 9-inch circle or into an 8 by 15-inch rectangle. Place on a baking sheet and refrigerate until ready to use. (The dough can also be rolled out and formed, then frozen. To use, take directly from the freezer to the oven to bake.)

PASTRY FOR 2 RIMLESS TARTS

EQUIPMENT: A food processor.

1 cup unbleached all-purpose flour

¼ teaspoon fine sea salt

5 tablespoons unsalted butter, chilled and cut into cubes

¼ cup ice water

WARM FIGS WITH HONEY, RASPBERRIES, AND FRESH CHEESE

Figues Rôties aux Framboises, Miel et Fromage Frais

When shopping in a French market, you don't have to think too hard and long to know what goes with what. In the springtime, beets and lamb's lettuce are always sold side-by-side, so you know that they go together. The ratatouille trio of eggplant, peppers, and tomato always share center stage on the vegetable man's table. And come August in Provence, cartons of plump and fragrant vermillion raspberries cuddle up to neatly ordered rows of ripe purple figs that taste as though they've been injected with honey. That's when this dessert becomes a favorite, night after night, as long as the season lasts. I love the fact that the figs can be cooked in advance and actually profit from a little marinade time, while the feast goes on under the oak tree.

EQUIPMENT: A large nonstick skillet; a pastry brush.

½ cup lavender honey (or substitute a favorite flavored honey)

⅓ cup dry white wine

24 ripe black figs, rinsed, stemmed, and halved lengthwise

1 pound Fresh Homemade Cheese (page 236), or *brousse*, or ricotta-style fresh cheese

8 ounces fresh raspberries, rinsed and drained

Wine Suggestion: A tiny glass of chilled Beaumes-de-Venise would be right at home here.

1 In a small saucepan, combine the honey and wine over low heat, stirring until the honey has totally dissolved with the wine. Set aside.

2 Heat the skillet over moderately high heat. With a pastry brush, brush the figs with the honey-wine sauce. Place the figs cut side down in the pan. Sear for 2 minutes, regularly brushing the figs with the honey-wine mixture. Remove the figs to a large bowl. Pour any remaining honey-wine sauce over the figs. Set aside. (The figs can be cooked up to 2 hours in advance.)

3 To serve, pour a scoop of fresh cheese into each of six small bowls. With a slotted spoon, transfer four figs to the edge of each bowl. Sprinkle with the raspberries. Drizzle with any remaining honey-wine mixture. Serve with Domaine St. Luc's Almond Cookies (page 278).

6 SERVINGS

Cold Cavaillon Melon Soup with Beaumes-de-Venise and Buttermilk Sorbet

Soupe de Melon de Cavaillon au Beaumes-de-Venise et Sorbet au Lait Fermenté

From early spring through late summer, ripe and fragrant Cavaillon melons fill the markets of Provence. There is always one (or more) in my refrigerator, ready to serve as a breakfast treat, a snack, or for making this quick and satisfying dessert. I love to serve it with a scoop of Buttermilk Sorbet, for the color contrast is astonishing and the flavor contrast just as stunning. We have lemon balm, or *mélisse,* growing wild all over the farm, so this is one place to put that mint-family herb to use as a festive garnish.

EQUIPMENT: A food processor or blender.

1 perfectly ripe cantaloupe (about 2 pounds)

¼ cup Muscat de Beaumes-de-Venise or other sweet white wine

Several sprigs fresh lemon balm or fresh mint

8 scoops Buttermilk Sorbet (page 290)

3 tablespoons fresh lemon balm leaves or mint leaves, cut into a *chiffonnade*

1 Halve and seed the melon. Cut the melon into slices, peel, and cut into cubes. Place the cubes of melon in a food processor or blender, and blend until totally smooth. Add the wine and blend again. Transfer to a bowl. Cover securely and refrigerate until serving time. (The soup can be made up to 8 hours in advance.)

2 At serving time, stir the soup to blend again. Pour into eight chilled, shallow soup bowls. Place a small scoop of sorbet in the center of each bowl. Garnish with the *chiffonnade* of fresh lemon balm or mint.

EIGHT ½-CUP SERVINGS

Desserts

287

CAVAILLON MELONS

MELONS HAVE BEEN known in the town of Cavaillon since the 15th century, when Charles VIII returned from the Roman papal village of Catalupo with a precious melon. From then until the end of the 18th century, the best corner of the Provençal vegetable garden was given to the prized melon, along with the equally rare artichoke and peach. By 1870, when the popular culture of *garance,* a plant cultivated for its bright dye, began to wane, the melon took its place on the rich, well-drained soil along the Durance River. The same year, the melon got another boost from the arrival of the P.L.M., the train that traveled the Paris-Lyon-Mediterranean route. Soon melons were transported to Paris and beyond, and the fame of the Cavaillon melons took root. Over the years there was never a single variety or size of melon that bore the name Melon de Cavaillon, and today the culture includes both the *melon brodé* (netted melons much like our cantaloupe or muskmelon) and oblong varieties with threadlike embroidery covering the skin, as well as the smooth-skinned varieties known as *écrits* (often the Charentais variety).

Some melon lore:

- The best melons are made up of ten ribs to form ten perfect slices. Those that slice easily into nine or eleven are likely to be less flavorful.

- When a melon is perfectly ripe, the stem detaches readily from the fruit.

- A great melon should smell great! Fragrance is always a sign of quality.

- At room temperature, a melon continues to ripen. Melons can easily be stored in the refrigerator for five or six days, hermetically closed in a plastic bag so as not to perfume the contents of the refrigerator.

If you are a melon lover, stop in to Jean-Jacques Prévot's restaurant, where in the summer months he features an all-melon menu, enjoyed amid his vast collection of melon-related objects.

Prévot
353, avenue Verdun
84300 Cavaillon
Telephone: 04 90 71 32 43
Fax: 04 90 71 97 05
E-mail: *jean-jacques. prevot2@freesbee.fr*

MELONS GROW on the ground, with the stem end toward the ground. The best flavor comes from the opposite end, which is

LA TRANCHE DE LA REINE— THE QUEEN'S SLICE

exposed to the sun, the light, the air. In Cavaillon, the slice from the sunny end of the melon is known as the queen's slice, or *la tranche de la reine*. So to best enjoy the flavor of a melon, cut a slice off the bottom of the melon (opposite the stem end), *then* cut the melon into slices, cutting along the ribs. You can sneak the *tranche de la reine* for yourself, or cut it into pieces to share with your guests.

"How should melon be eaten? Not with a spoon, as is usual in restaurants. . . .
The back of the spoon anesthetizes the taste buds! In this way,
it loses half its flavor. Melon should be eaten with a fork!"
—FROM A 1982 ARTICLE, "PROPOS DE TABLE,"
BY JAMES DE COQUET IN LE FIGARO

Melons from Cavaillon   289

BUTTERMILK SORBET

Sorbet au Lait Fermenté

I confess to a severe weakness for anything with a slightly lactic tang, and buttermilk is among those light and refreshing flavors that appeal to my palate. Buttermilk, which the French market as *lait fermenté*, is to my thinking an underutilized ingredient. It offers the pleasures of richer ingredients such as cream with much less fat. This sorbet goes with just about everything, so I serve it often.

EQUIPMENT: An ice cream maker.

⅓ cup freshly squeezed lemon juice

1 cup sugar

¼ cup light corn syrup

2 cups buttermilk, shaken to blend

1 In a medium saucepan, combine the lemon juice, sugar, and corn syrup. Simmer over medium heat until the sugar is dissolved. Cool to room temperature.

2 Combine the lemon syrup and the buttermilk, and stir to blend. Chill thoroughly. Transfer to an ice cream maker and freeze according to the manufacturer's instructions.

10 TO 12 SERVINGS

RASPBERRY⸱ALMOND FINANCIERS

Financiers aux Framboises et aux Amandes

*O*kay, which do I love better? The butter-rich almond *financiers* with their golden glow and tender crust, or those brilliant red fruits of the summer, raspberries? Well, one can get one's fill of both in these prized summer cookies, a delight when paired with a light Raspberry Sorbet (page 292). I make these first thing in the morning, when the house is still cool. The rectangular cookies should be made the day they are served, but can easily rest for about eight hours before serving. Plan on serving three *financiers* per diner, depending, of course, on appetites!

1 Preheat the oven to 450 degrees F. With a pastry brush, thoroughly butter the *financier* molds, using a bit of the melted butter. Arrange the molds side-by-side, but not touching, on a baking sheet. Place the baking sheet with the buttered molds in the freezer to re-solidify the butter (and make the *financiers* easier to unmold).

2 In a large bowl, combine the almonds, sugar, flour, and salt. Mix to blend. Add the egg whites and mix until thoroughly blended. Add the remaining melted butter and mix until thoroughly blended. The mixture will be fairly thin and pourable.

EQUIPMENT: A pastry brush; 21 1¾ × 3½-inch *financier* molds.

12 tablespoons (6 ounces) unsalted butter, melted and cooled (¾ cup)

1 cup ground almonds

1⅔ cups confectioners' sugar

½ cup unbleached all-purpose flour

Pinch of salt

¾ cup egg whites (5 or 6)

About 8 ounces fresh raspberries, rinsed and drained

3 Spoon the batter into the molds, filling almost to the rim. Place the baking sheet in the center of the oven. Bake until the *financiers* just begin to rise, about 7 minutes. Remove from the oven and carefully arrange four raspberries in a single row down the center of each. Reduce the heat to 400 degrees F. Return the *financiers* to the oven and bake until they are a light, delicate brown and are beginning to firm up, another 7 minutes. Turn off the oven and let the *financiers* rest in the oven until firm, about 7 minutes.

4 Remove the baking sheet from the oven and let the *financiers* cool in the molds for 10 minutes. Unmold. (Note: Wash molds immediately with a stiff brush in hot water without detergent, so they retain their seasoning.)

21 FINANCIERS

Financier molds can be ordered from:
Prévin Incorporated
Telephone: (215) 985-1996
Fax: (215) 985-0323

RASPBERRY SORBET

Sorbet à la Framboise

*I*f I had to limit myself to only three or four fruits, raspberries would be among them. In my childhood, we always had a huge raspberry patch in the backyard and would pick the ripe red berries for snacks morning and night. Our farmers' markets in Provence are laden with stalls offering plump berries, so I snatch them up whenever I see them. Serve this with Raspberry-Almond Financiers (page 290) and Fresh Raspberry Sauce (page 293) for a fine dessert trio.

EQUIPMENT: A food processor or blender; a fine-mesh sieve; an ice-cream maker.

6 tablespoons sugar

⅔ cup water

1 pound fresh raspberries (about 4 cups), rinsed and drained

1 In a medium saucepan, combine the sugar and water, then bring to a boil, stirring to dissolve the sugar. Set aside to cool to room temperature.

2 In a food processor or blender, purée the raspberries. Add the cooled sugar syrup. Pass the mixture through the sieve into a bowl. Transfer to an ice cream maker and freeze according to the manufacturer's instructions.

6 TO 8 SERVINGS

Fresh Raspberry Sauce

Coulis de Framboises

When fresh raspberries are in abundance, I always prepare some batches of this sauce, saving some for the winter months, when Walter's Chilled Nougat Mousse (page 302) is his (and, yes, one of my) favorite dessert. Of course, any time of year, frozen raspberries could be used here.

EQUIPMENT: A blender or food processor or blender; a fine-mesh sieve.

1 pound fresh or frozen raspberries (about 4 cups)

1 tablespoon confectioners' sugar

2 tablespoons freshly squeezed lemon juice

1 In a food processor or blender, combine the raspberries, sugar, and lemon juice and purée.

2 Strain the sauce through the sieve set over a large bowl to remove the seeds. Transfer to a container and seal tightly. The sauce may be refrigerated for 2 to 3 days, or frozen for up to 6 months.

ABOUT 2 CUPS

CHATEAU PESQUIE'S WHITE PEACHES POACHED IN RED WINE

Pêches au Vin Rouge Château Pesquié

*P*eaches poached in wine—red or white—is a classic Provençal dessert. This recipe was offered to me by Edith Chaudière of the fine Côtes-du-Ventoux winery Château Pesquié. It's a great recipe for entertaining when peaches are in season. The fruit is delicious warm as well as chilled the next day.

EQUIPMENT: A fine-mesh sieve.

4 ripe white peaches

Grated zest of 1 orange

2 whole cloves

1 cinnamon stick

10 black peppercorns

1 whole star anise

1 plump vanilla bean

½ cup sugar

1 bottle red wine

Château Pesquié

Edith and Paul Chaudière
84570 Mormoiron
Telephone: 04 90 61 94 08
Fax: 04 90 61 94 13

"An apple is an excellent thing—
until you have tried a peach."
—GEORGE DU MAURIER
(1834–1896)

1 Prepare a large bowl of ice water. Set aside.

2 With a small sharp knife, cut a cross at the stem end of each peach. (This will make them easier to peel.) Bring a large pot of water to a boil. Plunge the peaches into the boiling water and boil until the skins begin to peel away from the flesh, about 2 minutes. With a large slotted spoon, remove the peaches from the water. Immediately plunge them into the ice water. As soon as they are cool enough to handle, peel the peaches. Cut them in half. Remove and discard the pits.

ON PEACHES: The Romans called them *malum persicum,* or Persian apples. The French have always considered that the peach has aphrodisiacal qualities, and the names of peach varieties in France often make reference to a woman's breast. To this day, when someone has nice, soft skin, the French say that she has a *peau de pêche,* or "skin as soft as a peach."

3 Place the peaches in a large pot and add the remaining ingredients. Cover and let cook over low heat until the peaches are soft, usually just a few minutes. With a large slotted spoon, remove the peaches from the liquid and place in a bowl.

4 Over high heat, reduce the liquid by half, about 10 minutes. Pass the liquid through the sieve and pour over the peaches. Serve warm or chilled, in small glass bowls.

4 SERVINGS

ON KEEPING VANILLA BEANS MOIST: Have you ever gone to your pantry in search of a plump, moist vanilla bean only to find it dried to a shrivel? Long ago I began the habit of storing whole fresh vanilla beans in a small glass jar. I put about ½ inch of cognac or brandy in the jar, add the beans, and seal it well. I keep them in a cool, dark place in the pantry. The vanilla beans never dry out, and they help perfume the liquid, giving me a sort of homemade vanilla extract for flavoring desserts.

THREE-PEAR CAKE

Gâteau aux Trois Poires

One of the very first things I did once we acquired our farmhouse in the early 1980s was to plant a trio of espaliered pear trees. I had always admired the perfectly trained and tended trees in the Loire Valley, at Versailles, and in the Luxembourg Gardens in Paris, and I carried around a naively romantic view of my very own *verger*, or orchard. The trees were planted and staked, but somehow neither I nor Walter, nor any of the succession of gardeners we have hired over the years, seems to have the proper espalier pruning knack. The three different varieties of pears—Poire William, Passe Crassagne, and Bon Chrétien—have grown and grown and produce volumes of fruit, but in honesty, most people would not recognize them as espaliered trees. Also, never having grown pears, I had no idea how difficult it was to gauge their ripeness. Unripe, they totally lack flavor. But once they are ripe and fall from the trees, all manner of insects and critters come to devour their share. What I have finally learned to do is to pick them just before they begin to fall from the trees, store them in a dark, cool place to ripen, then begin cooking as many pears as I can in the

EQUIPMENT: A 9-inch springform pan.

Butter and flour for preparing the pan

½ cup all-purpose flour

⅓ cup sugar

1 tablespoon baking powder

⅛ teaspoon fine sea salt

½ teaspoon pure vanilla extract

2 large eggs, lightly beaten

1 tablespoon vegetable oil

1 tablespoon pear *eau-de-vie*

⅓ cup nonfat plain yogurt

Grated zest of 1 lemon

4 large pears (about 2 pounds), peeled, cored, and cut lengthwise into 16ths

THE TOPPING:

⅓ cup sugar

1 large egg, lightly beaten

1 tablespoon pear *eau de vie*

Grated zest of 1 lemon

Wine Suggestion: A pear *eau-de-vie*.

shortest amount of time! This is a variation on my popular Apple Lady's Apple Cake (see *The Paris Cookbook*). I have fiddled with it quite a bit, substituting yogurt for milk (which gives a more moist texture), highlighting the pear flavor with a touch of pear *eau-de-vie*, and boosting the acidity with a touch of lemon. I serve this with Buttermilk Sorbet (page 290).

1 Preheat the oven to 425 degrees F. Butter the pan and set aside.

2 In a large bowl, combine the flour, sugar, baking powder, and salt, and stir to blend. Add the vanilla, eggs, oil, *eau-de-vie*, yogurt, and lemon zest, and stir until well blended. Add the pears and stir to thoroughly coat the fruit with the batter.

3 Spoon the mixture into the prepared cake pan. Place the pan in the center of the oven and bake until fairly firm and golden, about 40 minutes.

4 Meanwhile, in a small bowl, combine the sugar, egg, *eau-de-vie*, and lemon zest and stir to blend. Set aside.

5 Once the cake is firm and golden, remove it from the oven and pour the sugar mixture on top of the cake, evening it out with a spatula. Return the cake to the oven and bake until the top is a deep golden brown and the cake feels quite firm when pressed with a fingertip, about 10 minutes more, for a total baking time of 50 minutes.

6 Remove to a rack to cool. After 10 minutes, run a knife along the side of the pan. Release and remove the side of the springform pan, leaving the cake on the pan base. Serve at room temperature, cut into thin wedges.

8 SERVINGS

Desserts

Chez Serge's Cinnamon-Apple Tart

La Tarte aux Pommes et à la Cannelle de Chez Serge

*L*eaving the weekly Carpentras market one icy Friday morning in December, I walked into my favorite restaurant in the town—Chez Serge—as the kitchen staff was putting the finishing touches on this apple tart. I am a regular at Chez Serge, so chef Philippe Lemaître eagerly shared all the details of this classic but simple French dessert. Atop the pastry, the chef spreads a thick bed of freshly made applesauce, then tops the applesauce with a layer of very thinly sliced apples. A sprinkling of sugar, a generous dose of ground cinnamon, and into the oven it goes. Once baked, the steaming tart is gently brushed with apricot jam, giving it a shine and sparkle that warms the heart on wintry, cold days. The tart is best served warm. As for apple variety, my preference is for a good, tart baking apple, such as Newton Pippin, Fuji, Criterion, Macoun, Jonagold, Stayman Winesap, or Northern Spy.

1 Preheat the oven to 425 degrees F.

2 Peel and core the apples for the sauce and cut into small cubes. In a medium saucepan, combine the apple cubes, water, sugar, and vanilla. Cook, covered, over low heat until the apples are very soft, about 10 minutes. Watch carefully so they do not scorch. Remove from

EQUIPMENT: An apple corer; a food processor or blender; a mandoline, electric slicer, or very sharp knife.

APPLESAUCE BASE:

3 baking apples

3 tablespoons water

2 tablespoons sugar

½ teaspoon pure vanilla extract

One rectangular 8 × 15-inch sheet of unbaked Light Flaky Pastry (page 285), on a baking sheet

THE APPLE TOPPING:

3 baking apples

2 to 3 tablespoons sugar

About 1 teaspoon ground cinnamon

About 2 tablespoons apricot jam

Restaurant Chez Serge

Serge Ghoukassian
90, rue Cottier
84200 Carpentras
Telephone: 04 90 63 21 24

the heat. Transfer the applesauce to a food processor or a blender and purée. Transfer the purée to a measuring cup: you should have about 1 cup of applesauce. Set aside to cool.

3 Once the applesauce has cooled slightly, spoon it onto the unbaked pastry shell, spreading the sauce out evenly with a spatula.

4 For the topping, trim and discard a very thin slice of each apple at both the stem and bottom ends. (This makes the apples easier to peel and creates more uniform slices.) Peel and core the apples. Using a mandoline, electric slicer, or very sharp knife, slice the apples crosswise into paper-thin rings.

5 Arrange the apple rings on the pastry shell: Beginning on the outside edge of the longest side of the rectangle, arrange a row of overlapping rings from top to bottom. Repeat for two more rows to completely cover the pastry shell. Sprinkle evenly with the sugar, then with the cinnamon.

6 Place the baking sheet in the center of the oven and bake the tart until the pastry shell is puffed and browned and the apples are a deep golden brown, about 25 minutes. Remove the baking sheet from the oven and brush the apples with the apricot jam. This tart is best served slightly warm. To serve, cut the tart in half lengthwise, then into even squares.

8 SERVINGS

VARIATION: My honey suppliers, Christine and Hubert Poquet, offered a fine variation on this ultra-thin apple tart: Substitute 2 to 3 tablespoons of lavender honey for the sugar in the topping, and do include the cinnamon. It's a dream!

Christine and Hubert Poquet
Route de Gap
26110 Condorcet
Telephone: 04 75 27 74 95
Open for visits April through September.

Our honey vendor, Hubert Poquet,
in the market in Vaison-la-Romaine

LEMON MOUSSE

Mousse au Citron

Light and airy, this lemon dessert is equally ideal in the winter (when lemons are about the only fruit in season) and in the summer, when you don't want to heat up the kitchen. I always serve this in individual ramekins or *pots-de-crème*. Serve with a cookie alongside, such as Lemon Crisps (page 301).

1 In the bowl of the heavy-duty mixer, beat the sugar and egg yolks until thick and pale yellow, about 2 minutes. Slowly add the lemon juice, whisking constantly. Whisk in the lemon zest. Set aside.

2 Pour the hot water into a small bowl. Sprinkle the gelatin over the water and stir until it dissolves. Whisk the gelatin mixture into the lemon mixture. Whisk the yogurt into the lemon mixture, blending thoroughly. Set aside.

3 In a second bowl of the heavy-duty mixer, beat the egg whites until stiff peaks form. Carefully fold the lemon mixture into the whipped egg whites. Ladle the mixture into the ramekins or *pots-de-crème*. Refrigerate until firm, about 3 hours.

12 SERVINGS

EQUIPMENT: A heavy-duty electric mixer fitted with a whisk; twelve ½-cup ramekins or *pots-de-crème*.

¾ cup sugar

3 large eggs yolks

½ cup freshly squeezed lemon juice

Grated zest of 2 lemons, preferably organic, blanched and refreshed

⅓ cup hot water

2¼ teaspoons (1 package) powdered unflavored gelatin

1 cup nonfat plain yogurt, drained

3 large egg whites

Wine Suggestion: Serve this with a pleasantly sweet dessert wine, such as a Muscat de Beaumes-de-Venise.

LEMON CRISPS

Petits Gâteaux au Citron

When I prepared these thin, light cookies with my students during a special fitness week in Provence, they quickly dubbed them "Cookie Wannabees." I guess they were expecting something chunky, rich, sweet, and filling, like a chocolate chip cookie. I love the light airiness of these ultra-thin sweets, prepared ever so quickly with lemons, sugar, phyllo dough, and a touch of butter. For years I dreamed of growing my own lemons, and finally our gardener, Jean-Paul Boyer, found Meyer lemon trees that would grow proudly in pots near the garden. They produce profusely in the summer months, and this hardy, compact variety of lemon gracefully finds its way into my kitchen at least six months of the year. In cooler months, we store the trees indoors, where the blossoms provide a fragrant winter perfume.

EQUIPMENT: A nonstick baking sheet; a pastry brush.

Grated zest of 1 lemon, preferably organic, blanched and refreshed

2 tablespoons sugar

2 sheets frozen phyllo dough, thawed

2 tablespoons unsalted butter, melted

1 Preheat the oven to 425 degrees F.

2 In a small bowl, combine the lemon zest and sugar. Place a sheet of phyllo dough on the baking sheet. With a pastry brush, brush the phyllo dough with half the melted butter. Sprinkle the dough with half the sugar mixture. Stack the second sheet of dough on top of the first. Brush the second sheet with the remaining butter. Sprinkle with the remaining sugar mixture. Cut the dough lengthwise into eight strips. Cut the strips crosswise in half.

3 Place the baking sheet in the center of the oven and bake until the cookies are crisp and golden, 4 to 5 minutes. Remove the baking sheet to a rack to cool. Serve with fresh fruit sorbets or ice cream.

WALTER'S CHILLED NOUGAT MOUSSE

Le Nougat Glacé de Walter

*S*tudded with nuts and candied fruit that shine like jewels, *nougat glacé* is a modern variation on the popular Provençal candy, the taffy-like nougat. This is one of my husband, Walter's, favorite desserts, and one on which he's become the expert. He orders creamy, chunky, chilled *nougat glacé* whenever it appears on a restaurant menu. While traditional versions of nougat are usually made with a blend of pistachios and almonds, I prefer to use almonds alone, or a mix of almonds and hazelnuts. Provençal markets offer an abundance of colorful, flavorful, preserved candied fruit, which bear no resemblance to the sticky, tasteless mixed candied fruits sold in bulk and destined for holiday fruitcakes. I always have a varied collection of fruits on hand, favoring strips of candied lemon and orange and whole candied kumquats. *Nougat glacé* knows no season, so is as welcome in July as it is in December. If good-quality candied fruits cannot be found, try using candied ginger (found in Asian markets) and then use any variety of good dried fruits, such as apricots, dates, figs, cranberries, or cherries. Likewise, if top-quality pistachios are available, use them half and half with almonds and/or hazelnuts. It's the quality of the ingredient, not the specific ingredient itself, that will make or break your dessert.

EQUIPMENT: 2 baking sheets; a spice grinder or food processor; a nonstick 1-quart rectangular bread pan, lined lengthwise with wax paper, leaving a slight overhang for "handles"; a heavy-duty electric mixer fitted with a whisk.

¾ cup (4 ounces) minced candied or dried fruit, cubed to the size of a raisin

¾ cup (3 ounces) whole unblanched almonds

1 cup heavy cream

⅓ cup sugar

2 large egg whites

3 tablespoons full-flavored honey, such as chestnut

2 cups Fresh Raspberry Sauce (page 293)

1 Place the pieces of cubed candied fruit in a single layer on a baking sheet and put in the freezer. (This will prevent the fruits from clumping up when they are mixed with the egg whites and cream.)

2 Preheat the oven to 400 degrees F.

3 Place the mixing bowl and the beaters of a heavy-duty mixer in the freezer. (This will help stabilize the cream and help it whip to maximum volume.) Place the almonds on a baking sheet. Toast in the oven until lightly browned, about 4 minutes. Cool. In a spice grinder or food processor, coarsely grind the almonds. Set aside.

4 In the chilled mixer bowl, beat the cream at high speed until soft peaks form, about 1 minute. Gradually add the sugar and beat until stiff peaks form and the mixture is glossy and smooth, about 1 minute more. Set aside.

5 In another mixer bowl, beat the egg whites at high speed until stiff, about 1 minute. Add the honey and continue whisking until the honey is incorporated.

6 Remove the bowl from the stand. With a large spatula, carefully fold the whipped cream into the beaten egg whites. Bit by bit, add the ground nuts and the chilled candied fruit, and fold one more time. Pour into the prepared pan, smoothing out the surface with a spatula. Transfer to a freezer until firm, at least 6 hours.

7 To serve, run the blade of a knife around the edges of the mousse and turn it out onto a clean work surface. Carefully pull away the paper. Cut into thin slices. Place each slice on an individual dessert plate, and spoon the raspberry sauce around the slice.

8 SERVINGS

BEAUMES⸱DE⸱VENISE SORBET

Sorbet aux Beaumes-de-Venise

Beaumes⸱de⸱Venise is a fairly sweet fortified wine from a nearby village, so we always have a few bottles on hand for a chilled aperitif or with dessert. It's also a great cooking wine, as its delicate fruitiness offers a perfect balance as a palate brightener at the end of a meal. The sorbet could also be made with Champagne, should you feel so extravagant.

EQUIPMENT: An ice⸱cream maker.

1¾ cups water

1 cup sugar

Juice of 1 lemon

2 cups Beaumes⸱de⸱Venise wine (or substitute Champagne or any good sweet white wine)

1 In a medium saucepan, combine the water, sugar, and lemon juice, and simmer over medium heat until the sugar is dissolved. Cool to room temperature.

2 Combine the sugar syrup and the Beaumes⸱de⸱Venise. Chill thoroughly. Transfer to an ice cream maker and freeze according to the manufacturer's instructions.

10 TO 12 SERVINGS

WINE WRITER JANCIS ROBINSON puts it so aptly: "Curiously, only one sort of wine actually tastes like grapes, and that is wine made from Muscat.... In every other case, wine taste quite different from grapes, even from those grapes from which it was made."

The famed, amber-colored sweet wine of the Côtes-du-Rhône village of Beaumes-de-Venise is made from the most renowned of the more than 200 different sorts of Muscat grapes grown in the world, the Muscat Blanc à Petits Grains. The small white grape offers very small yields and is difficult to grow, but when vinified with care, it yields a luscious, golden sweet wine that tastes of honey and a *confit* of apricots, with a bouquet of pineapple and tropical fruits and a truly long finish. In most instances, the wine labeled "Muscat de Beaumes-de-Venise" is a blend of small Muscat *blanc* and Muscat *noir*.

This wine is what's known as a *vin doux naturel*. Like Port wine, alcohol is added to the wine to fortify it and to stop fermentation. The sugar in the wine remains unconverted, and so the wine's degree of alcohol is strengthened, usually to a level of about 15 degrees.

During Roman times, the village of Beaumes was a spa town, thanks to the natural sulphur spring at nearby Montmirail, and though locals assume that the sweet wine was also made by the Romans, most Muscat vines date only from the 1950s. Today the wine is popular as a chilled, sweet aperitif, as an accompaniment to the melons of Cavaillon, and as a dessert wine.

A favorite comes from:
Domaine de Durban
84190 Beaumes-de-Venise
Telephone: 04 90 62 94 26
Fax: 04 90 65 01 85
Open Monday through Saturday, 9 a.m. to noon and 2 to 6 p.m.

Desserts

305

Dark Chocolate Sorbet

Sorbet au Chocolat Noir

*T*here is something about this rich and bitter dark chocolate sorbet that is both decadent and totally legal. Its deep, dark color and gorgeous gloss make you just want to dive into the bowl, and it has a smooth, elegant feeling on the palate, a feeling that somehow only chocolate can give. I adore the purity of this recipe and make it often, pairing it with the Autumn Walnut Cake (below).

EQUIPMENT: A sifter; a fine-mesh sieve; an ice-cream maker.

2 cups water

⅔ cup sugar

1 cup unsweetened cocoa powder, sifted

7 ounces bittersweet chocolate, preferably Valhrona Guanaja 70%, broken into pieces

1 In a large saucepan, combine the water and sugar over moderate heat. Stir to combine and to dissolve the sugar.

2 Carefully add the sifted cocoa powder in a steady stream. Off the heat, add the chocolate and stir until thoroughly melted. Set aside to cool completely.

3 Pass through the sieve into a bowl. (Be certain not to skip this step or the sorbet will be coarse and full of little chocolate bits.) Transfer to an ice cream maker and freeze according to the manufacturer's instructions.

10 TO 12 SERVINGS

Autumn Walnut Cake Domaine de la Ponche

Gâteau d'Automne Domaine de la Ponche

*O*ne chilly evening in November we gathered with students from my wine week in Provence for a festive dinner at one of our favorite local spots, Domaine de la Ponche. That night they presented us with a delicious and moist walnut cake, re-created here for those cold winter evenings. I like to serve this with a dark chocolate sauce and a sip of the local sweet *vin doux naturel,* a Port-like wine made from the Grenache grape.

1 Preheat the oven to 375 degrees F. Butter the cake pan and set aside.

2 Place the eggs and sugar in the bowl of the heavy-duty mixer. Beat at high speed until thick and lemon-colored, 2 to 3 minutes. Add the flour and whisk to blend. Add the butter and nuts and whisk to blend.

3 Pour the batter into the prepared cake pan. Place the pan in the center of the oven and bake until the cake is firm and golden, about 20 minutes. Remove to a rack to cool. After 10 minutes, run a knife along the side of the pan. Release and remove the side of the springform pan, leaving the cake on the pan base. Serve at room temperature, cut into even wedges.

4 While the cake is baking, prepare the sauce: Place the chocolate squares in a bowl. Pour the hot coffee over the chocolate and let sit for 5 minutes. Stir to combine.

5 To serve, place a wedge of cake on each plate and drizzle with the chocolate sauce. The cake is best served warm but can be served at room temperature.

8 SERVINGS

Domaine de la Ponche Hotel and Restaurant

Ruth Spahn, Madeleine Frauenknecht, and Jean-Pierre Onimus
84190 Vacqueyras
Telephone: 04 90 65 85 21
Fax: 04 90 65 85 23
E-mail: *domaine.laponche@wanadoo.fr*
Web: *www.hotel.laponche.com*

EQUIPMENT: A 9-inch springform pan; a heavy-duty electric mixer fitted with a whisk.

Butter for preparing the cake pan

3 large eggs

¾ cup sugar

¼ cup all-purpose flour

4 tablespoons unsalted butter, melted

2 cups freshly cracked walnut pieces, coarsely chopped

FOR THE SAUCE:

3½ ounces bittersweet chocolate (preferably Lindt Excellence 70% or Valhrona Guanaja 70%), broken into pieces

6 tablespoons hot brewed espresso coffee

Wine Suggestion: Serve this with a dessert wine, such as the Port-like *vin doux naturel*. My favorite comes from winemaker André Romero of Domaine la Soumade in Rasteau.

André Romero

Domaine la Soumade
84110 Rasteau
Telephone: 04 90 46 11 26
Fax: 04 90 46 11 69
Tastings Monday through Saturday 8 to 11:30 a.m. and 2 to 6 p.m. Closed Sunday.
U.S. importer: European Cellars, New York, NY. (212) 924-4949

ARUGULA SAUCE FOR FISH AND POULTRY

OLIVE PUREE FROM NYONS

OLIVE, CAPER, AND MUSTARD TAPENADE

PROVENÇAL HERB BLEND

SWEET GARLIC CONFIT

MARYSE'S APRICOT JAM

SWEET AND SOUR FIGS

MIREILLE'S TWO-TOMATO SAUCE

SPICY TOMATO, FENNEL, AND ORANGE SAUCE

TRUFFLE OIL

THE PANTRY

Au Garde-Manger

TRUFFLE BUTTER

PICKLED CHERRY TOMATOES

BASIL VINAIGRETTE LE GRAND PRE

BALSAMIC VINAIGRETTE

CLASSIC VINAIGRETTE

RED WINE VINAIGRETTE

HOMEMADE CHICKEN STOCK

HOMEMADE CURRY POWDER

Jars of freshly made confiture, *or jam, cooling on a table
at the Auberge d'Aiguebelle outside the village of Bonnieux*

Arugula Sauce for Fish and Poultry

Sauce à la Roquette pour Poissons et Volailles

When the bumper crop of arugula comes in, I prepare this spicy, refreshing sauce to have on hand for grilled or poached fish, roasted chicken, or just for spreading on toasted homemade bread. I particularly like this with Six-Minute Salmon Braised in Viognier (page 90). If you do not have access to arugula, substitute a mixture of soft-leaved herbs (mint, tarragon, and parsley leaves or chives are good) mixed with lettuce, sorrel, or other soft greens.

In the bowl of a food processor or blender, combine all the ingredients and process until well blended. Transfer to a small bowl. (The sauce can be refrigerated in a sealed container for up to 2 days.) Taste for seasoning. To serve, bring to room temperature and stir once again.

1 ½ CUPS

EQUIPMENT: A food processor or blender.

2 tablespoons best-quality sherry wine vinegar

2 tablespoons imported Dijon mustard

2 cups loosely packed fresh arugula, stemmed (or a mix of greens and herbs)

½ cup extra-virgin olive oil

2 tablespoons salt-cured capers, rinsed and drained

Fine sea salt to taste

Olive Puree from Nyons

Crème d'Olives Noires de Nyons

In Provence it seems that each week of the year brings a feeling of satisfaction as one sees a welcome return of seasonal fruits and vegetables. One of my favorite seasons begins in late November, when with a flourish the first crop of olives and olive oil floods the market stands throughout the region. One December Friday at the Carpentras market, I stopped at a charming little stand run by the folks from the Ferme Brès, just outside Nyons. Not only did they have the *best* black olives I have ever tasted—meaty, sparklingly black, not mushy but firm, and salted just right—but the *pièce de résistance* was this remarkably delicious olive purée. The purée consists of nothing but the very best black olives and the familiar dried herb mixture known as *herbes de Provence*. I find this a pleasant change from tapenade, which in addition to olives generally includes capers, mustard, anchovies, and olive oil.

EQUIPMENT: A food processor or blender.

2 cups best-quality French brine-cured black olives, pitted

2 teaspoons Provençal Herb Blend (page 313)

Domaine de la Blachette

Ferme Brès
Pied de Vaux
26110 Nyons
Telephone/Fax: 04 75 26 05 41

Sachets of dried herbes de Provence

In a food processor or blender, combine the olives and herbs. Blend to a thick paste. Transfer to a container and cover securely. Store, refrigerated, for up to 1 week.

1½ CUPS

OLIVE, CAPER, AND MUSTARD TAPENADE

Tapenade aux Olives, Câpres et Moutarde

One evening I was in a bit of hurry preparing dinner. Guests were heading up the hill and I hadn't yet made the spread to go with the local black olive crackers. I pitted some home-cured black olives, then added home-grown capers and touch of mustard for a perky version of the Provençal spread known as tapenade.

EQUIPMENT: A food processor or blender.

2 cups best-quality French brine-cured black olives, pitted

3 tablespoons capers in vinegar, drained

2 teaspoons imported French mustard, or more to taste

In a food processor or blender, combine the olives, capers, and mustard. Blend to a thick paste. Taste for seasoning. Transfer to a container and cover securely. Store, refrigerated, for up to 1 week.

1½ CUPS

PROVENÇAL HERB BLEND

Herbes de Provence

Herbes de Provence is a collection of native aromatic kitchen herbs from Provence, and the recipe varies from cook to cook. The choice might include some or all of the following: basil, bay leaf, rosemary, summer savory, thyme, marjoram, and sometimes even lavender. The mixture is always dried, and is used essentially as a seasoning for grilled meats and poultry. Here is Josiane Deal's recipe: she sells the fragrant mixture in her lovely cheese shop, Lou Canestéou, in Vaison-la-Romaine.

In a small container, combine the herbs. Cover securely and shake to blend. Store in a cool, dry place for up to 6 months.

3 ⅓ TABLESPOONS

2 teaspoons dried basil leaves, coarsely ground

2 teaspoons dried thyme leaves, coarsely ground

2 teaspoons dried summer savory leaves, coarsely ground

2 teaspoons dried marjoram leaves, coarsely ground

2 teaspoons dried rosemary leaves, coarsely ground

Lou Canestéou
Josiane and Christian Deal
10, rue Raspail
84110 Vaison-la-Romaine
Telephone: 04 90 36 31 30
Fax: 04 90 28 79 33

Sweet Garlic Confit

Confit d'Ail Doux

*T*his is a simple, all-purpose way to soften the flavor of garlic. I often add the sweet cloves of garlic to a sauce just before serving, as a lively thickener. Try it with the Fricassée of Chicken with Garlic and Sweet Garlic Confit (page 122). This is the kind of recipe that pleases garlic lovers and non–garlic lovers alike. Garlic lovers get their garlic, and those who consider garlic too strong will delight in the sweet, rich flavor of these whole cloves simmered gently in milk. While some cooks find it a chore to peel this quantity of garlic, I look upon it as a relaxing, calming task to be enjoyed with a glass of chilled rosé.

EQUIPMENT: A fine-mesh sieve.

4 plump heads garlic, cloves separated and peeled

1 quart whole milk

Place the garlic in a small saucepan. Cover with 2 cups of the milk. Bring just to a simmer over moderate heat. Immediately pour the garlic and milk through the sieve set over a large bowl. Discard the milk. Return the garlic to the pan, cover with the remaining 2 cups of milk, and simmer, uncovered, over low heat until the garlic is soft and a small knife inserted into a clove meets no resistance, about 20 minutes. Let cool in the milk. Drain the garlic, discarding the milk. Transfer to a container and cover securely. Store, refrigerated, for up to 1 week.

ABOUT 1 CUP

MARYSE'S APRICOT JAM

La Confiture d'Abricots de Maryse

*T*o me, this is unquestionably the world's greatest jam. I generally don't swoon over sweets, but the first time I tasted this homemade apricot jam I was taken in. Not too sweet, rich with the almond-like, faintly acidic apricot flavor, this jam is full of the fragrances and colors of Provence. The recipe was given to me by the Provençal housewife Maryse Jourdan, who lives in the village of Goult in the Lubéron. She is one of the best jam makers I know.

EQUIPMENT: An unlined copper *bassine à confitures* or a large-bottomed, heavy-duty stockpot.

2 pounds apricots, rinsed, halved, and pitted (reserve the pits)

1½ cups sugar

1 Crack ten of the pits to reveal an almond-like nut within. Reserve these nuts, discarding the remaining pits.

2 In the copper jam pot or heavy-duty stockpot, combine the apricots, reserved nuts, and sugar. Stir to dissolve the sugar. Cook over moderate heat, stirring regularly, for 1 hour. Do not allow the mixture to burn or to stick to the bottom of the pan. The mixture will turn very thick and bright orange, and most of the apricots will melt into a purée. Transfer to a bowl and set aside at room temperature for 24 hours. (This 24-hour aging period helps give the jam a greater depth of flavor.)

3 The next day, reheat the mixture in the jam pot or stockpot over moderate heat until very thick. Prepare four 8-ounce canning jars with lids by sterilizing them in boiling water according to the jar manufacturer's instructions. Transfer the jam to the hot sterilized jars, leaving ¼ inch headroom. Seal according to the jar manufacturer's instructions. Store in a cool, dry place for up to 1 year.

ABOUT FOUR 8-OUNCE JARS

SWEET AND SOUR FIGS

Figues à l'Aigre-Doux

I have a hard time getting through a day without cheese. Or without some sort of pickle. This fig condiment is a perfect way to get to the fruit, the pickle, the cheese. I like to serve it with all types of cheese—especially firm sheep's milk cheeses—after the main course. It is a perfect condiment and also helps one hold back, just a bit, on the cheese!

8 ounces dried figs

1 cup red wine

½ cup balsamic vinegar

¼ cup sugar

1 large sprig fresh rosemary

In a saucepan, combine all the ingredients and stir to dissolve the sugar. Bring to a boil, reduce the heat, and cook just until the figs are soft, about 10 minutes. Remove and discard the rosemary. Transfer to a serving bowl. Serve with cheese or as a condiment any time you would serve pickles.

ABOUT 2 CUPS

A village fête *in Villedieu*

MIREILLE'S TWO-TOMATO SAUCE

Sauce Mireille aux Deux Tomates

We are regulars at Mireille and Jean-Louis Pons's marvelous restaurant, Le Bistrot du Paradou in the village of Le Paradou, not far from Saint-Rémy. Mireille is a fabulous Provençal cook, and I never fail to stop by the kitchen before or after lunch to chat about the day's recipes. After yet another delightful meal I asked Mireille what she did to make her tomato sauce so rich and fresh tasting. She confided that she combined both fresh and canned tomatoes, since each offers different elements. The fresh tomatoes add, of course, that summery fresh flavor, while the canned variety adds a density and richness that is difficult to achieve with fresh tomatoes.

In a large skillet, combine the oil, onion, garlic, and salt and stir to coat with the oil. Sweat—cook, covered, over low heat until soft but not browned—for about 3 minutes. Add the canned and the fresh tomatoes, bouquet garni, and red pepper flakes (if using). Stir to blend and simmer, uncovered, until the sauce begins to thicken, about 30 minutes. Taste for seasoning. Remove and discard the bouquet garni. The sauce may be used immediately, stored in the refrigerator for up to 2 days, or frozen for up to 3 months.

ABOUT 1½ QUARTS

EQUIPMENT: A food processor or blender.

2 teaspoons extra-virgin olive oil

1 small onion, peeled, halved, and thinly sliced

2 plump cloves garlic, peeled, green germs removed, minced

Fine sea salt to taste

One 28-ounce can peeled Italian plum tomatoes in their juice, puréed in a food processor or a blender

2 pounds fresh tomatoes, cored, peeled, seeded, and chopped

1 bouquet garni: several parsley stems, celery leaves, and sprigs of thyme, wrapped in the green part of a leek and securely fastened with cotton twine, or in a wire mesh ball

Hot red pepper flakes to taste (optional)

Le Bistrot du Paradou
Jean-Louis and Mireille Pons
13125 Le Paradou
Telephone: 04 90 54 32 70

Spicy Tomato, Fennel, and Orange Sauce

Sauce Tomate Epicée au Fenouil et à l'Orange

This is one of the most versatile sauces I know. It is happily married to pasta or polenta, and is excellent as a base for any vegetable gratin. I love the addition of hot red pepper flakes, fennel seeds, and orange zest, which serve to heighten the flavor of the sauce and add a fabulous depth.

In a large skillet, combine the oil, onion, garlic, and salt and stir to coat with the oil. Sweat— cook, covered, over low heat until soft but not browned—for about 3 minutes. Add the puréed tomatoes, bouquet garni, red pepper flakes (if using), fennel seeds, and grated orange zest. Stir to blend and simmer, uncovered, until the sauce begins to thicken, about 15 minutes. Taste for seasoning. Remove and discard the bouquet garni. The sauce may be used immediately, stored in the refrigerator for up to 2 days, or frozen for up to 3 months.

ABOUT 3 CUPS

EQUIPMENT: A food processor or blender.

2 teaspoons extra-virgin olive oil

1 small onion, peeled and sliced

2 plump cloves garlic, peeled, halved, green germs removed, minced

Fine sea salt

One 28-ounce can peeled tomatoes in their juice, puréed in a food processor or a blender

1 bouquet garni: several parsley stems, celery leaves, and sprigs of thyme, wrapped in the green part of a leek and securely fastened with cotton twine, or in a wire mesh ball

Hot red pepper flakes to taste (optional)

½ teaspoon fennel seeds

Grated zest of 1 orange, preferably organic, blanched and refreshed

TRUFFLE OIL

Huile de Truffe

One January weekend, friends Alain Dumergue, Claude Udron, and Philippe Marquet spent two fabulous days with us just tasting and testing recipes with fresh black truffles. We were searching for the perfect homemade truffle oil and decided that this version—in which the peelings and oil are bathed together just until warm—most flattered that magical mushroom.

1 tablespoon minced truffle peelings

1 cup grapeseed oil

We also found that a good-quality grapeseed oil, which has no real flavor, allowed the truffle to shine. I love to drizzle this oil over pasta, toasted bread, or salmon, and of course use it in a vinaigrette. This is the only truffle oil I will allow in my house: the commercial variety is nothing more than perfume, contains no truffles, and is thoroughly indigestible, with an offensive, all-pervasive aroma.

In a small saucepan, combine the peelings and oil. Heat over low heat just until the oil becomes fragrant, 1 to 2 minutes. Cover securely and set aside at room temperature for up to 3 days. Check regularly to judge the infusing power of the truffle. After 3 days, filter the oil and use the truffle peelings for another use. Refrigerate the oil for up to 3 more days or freeze for up to 2 months.

I CUP

TRUFFLE BUTTER

Beurre de Truffes

*T*his incredible butter becomes an essential ingredient during the dreary winter months! It has unlimited uses. I like to make this with coarse sea salt, for it adds a pleasant crunch to the butter. Use it wherever you would use butter in a recipe—everything from omelets to cooked lentils to macaroni profits from this rich and intensely flavored concoction. And of course there's nothing to stop you from simply spreading this on toast!

On a small plate, mash the softened butter with a fork. Sprinkle with the truffles and salt, distributing as evenly as possible. Transfer the butter to a ramekin. Cover securely. Refrigerate for up to 3 days or freeze for up to 1 month. Serve at room temperature.

6 TABLESPOONS

4 tablespoons unsalted butter, softened

2 tablespoons minced truffle peelings

½ teaspoon coarse sea salt

PICKLED CHERRY TOMATOES

Tomates-Cerises à l'Aigre-doux

*U*se these tiny pickled cherry tomatoes as an appetizer (offering toothpicks to spear them) or as one would a pickle. I love to combine all different varieties of cherry tomatoes to make a rainbow-colored mix.

1 quart water

2 tablespoons coarse sea salt

1 pound firm cherry tomatoes (round and plum varieties of all colors can be used)

1 cup cider vinegar

2 tablespoons sugar

1 sprig fresh summer savory (or substitute tarragon)

6 black peppercorns

1 In a large bowl, combine the water and salt, and stir to dissolve the salt. Prick the bottom of each tomato with a needle. Place the tomatoes in the salt brine and allow to marinate for 24 hours.

2 In a large saucepan, combine the vinegar and sugar. Stir to dissolve the sugar. Bring just to a boil over high heat. Remove from the heat and cool thoroughly.

3 Remove the tomatoes from the salt brine and drain thoroughly. Discard the salt brine.

4 Carefully place the tomatoes in a large sterilized canning jar. Arrange the herbs around the edges of the jar. Pour the vinegar-sugar mixture over the tomatoes. Secure the jar tightly. Let sit in a cool, dry place—or in the refrigerator—for 3 weeks before tasting. Once opened, the tomatoes can be stored in the refrigerator for up to 3 months.

ABOUT 2 QUARTS

Basil Vinaigrette Le Grand Pre

La Vinaigrette au Basilic du Grand Pré

*T*his recipe was shared with me by Raoul Reichrath of Le Grand Pré, one of our favorite restaurants in the nearly village of Roaix. He serves this with his Seared and Roasted Salmon (page 94). I love the way the direct herbal aroma and flavor of the basil permeate this sauce. I enjoy having it on hand to boost the seasoning of salads, to stir into leftover rice or *épeautre,* or to simply drizzle over sliced fresh tomatoes.

In a small pan, combine the oils and heat just until warmed through. Add the basil and stir to coat. Cover and set aside at room temperature for 24 hours. The next day, add the salt and lemon juice, and transfer to an airtight container. Refrigerate for up to 2 weeks, removing from the refrigerator a few minutes before using. Strain as the oil is used.

About 1½ cups

¾ cup extra-virgin olive oil

¾ cup peanut oil, canola oil, or grapeseed oil

2 cups fresh basil leaves, tightly packed, cut into a chiffonade

¼ teaspoon fine sea salt

2 tablespoons freshly squeezed lemon juice

Le Grand Pré

Flora and Raoul Reichrath
Route de Vaison (D 975)
84110 Roaix
Telephone 04 90 46 18 12
E-mail: *legrandpre@walka9.com*

Balsamic Vinaigrette

Vinaigrette Balsamique

*W*hile I don't have a sweet tooth, I do sometimes like a vinaigrette that has a bit of a sweet tone. That's when I turn to balsamic vinegar, which gives just the right sweet-acid edge. I don't use an expensive aged vinegar, just a good-grade balsamic vinegar from Italy.

1 tablespoon best-quality sherry wine vinegar

1 tablespoon balsamic vinegar

Fine sea salt to taste

½ cup extra-virgin olive oil

Place the sherry vinegar, balsamic vinegar, and salt in a bottle. Cover and shake to dissolve the salt. Add the oil and shake to blend. Taste for seasoning. The vinaigrette can be stored at room temperature or in the refrigerator for several weeks. Shake again at serving time to create a thick emulsion.

ABOUT ¾ CUP

Classic Vinaigrette

Vinaigrette Classique

*T*his is the classic vinaigrette that sits on the counter in each of my kitchens. I make it ahead to make sure there is always some on hand when I want a quick salad.

2 tablespoons best-quality sherry wine vinegar

2 tablespoons best-quality red wine vinegar

Fine sea salt to taste

1 cup extra-virgin olive oil

Place the sherry vinegar, red wine vinegar, and salt in a bottle. Cover and shake to dissolve the salt. Add the oil and shake to blend. Taste for seasoning. The vinaigrette can be stored at room temperature or in the refrigerator for several weeks. Shake again at serving time to create a thick emulsion.

ABOUT 1¼ CUPS

The Pantry

RED WINE VINAIGRETTE

Vinaigrette au Vin Rouge

*T*his is a variation on my classic vinaigrette in which leftover bits of red wine are reduced and used in place of vinegar. The reduced wine adds a sweeter, less acidic quality to the dressing. Use any combination of leftover wines for this, including red, white, and rosé. Use this especially when you are serving a salad with cheese, for the dressing is very wine friendly since there is no hit of acidity to fight with the wine.

½ cup leftover red wine (or substitute white, rosé, or a mixture)

Fine sea salt to taste

1 cup extra-virgin olive oil

1 In a large casserole, bring the wine to a boil over high heat. Boil until reduced by half, 3 to 4 minutes. Set aside to cool thoroughly.

2 Place the reduced wine and salt in a bottle. Cover and shake to dissolve the salt. Add the oil and shake to blend. Taste for seasoning. The dressing can be stored at room temperature or in the refrigerator for several weeks. Shake again at serving time to create a thick emulsion.

ABOUT 1¼ CUPS

HOMEMADE CHICKEN STOCK

Fond de Volaille

Sometimes I buy a chicken just to make stock—
then, of course, I also have some poached chicken
left over for lunchtime! My freezer is always stocked
with containers of homemade stock, which I use
in soups, sauces, and sometimes "as is" as a nice
midday pick-me-up.

1 Place the chicken pieces in the stockpot and
cover with cold water by at least 2 inches. Bring to
a gentle simmer over medium heat. Skim to remove
the scum that rises to the surface. Add additional
cold water to replace the water removed and
continue skimming until the broth is clear.

2 Add the salt, vegetables, and bouquet garni.
Return the liquid to a gentle simmer and simmer
gently for 2 hours. Skim and degrease as necessary.

3 Line the colander with a double layer of dampened
cheesecloth and place the colander over a large bowl.
Ladle the broth into the colander; discard the solids.

EQUIPMENT: A heavy stockpot;
a large colander; cheesecloth.

4 pounds raw chicken parts
or raw or cooked carcasses

Pinch of salt

4 carrots

2 large onions, 1 stuck with
2 whole cloves

1 rib celery

1 leek, white and tender green
parts, halved lengthwise and
washed

1 bouquet garni: parsley leaves,
bay leaves, and celery leaves tied
with cotton twine, or secured in
a mesh wire ball

4 Refrigerate the stock, and spoon off all traces of fat that rise to the surface. The stock
may be safely refrigerated for 3 or 4 days, or can be frozen for up to 6 months.

2 QUARTS

HOMEMADE CURRY POWDER

Poudre de Curry Maison

One can always find varied curry powders in the spice shops, but I like to prepare my own, making the mixture as complex and spicy as I want to. This recipe is a simple blueprint; you can add or subtract spices, changing the intensity to taste.

In a small dry skillet, combine the peppers, coriander seeds, cumin seeds, mustard seeds, and peppercorns and toast over medium heat—shaking the pan often to prevent burning—for 2 to 3 minutes. Remove from the heat, transfer to a bowl, and let cool to room temperature. Add the fenugreek seeds. In a spice grinder or coffee mill, grind the mixture to a fine powder. Transfer to a small container. Stir in the ground ginger and turmeric. Store in an airtight container in a cool place for up to 3 months.

⅓ CUP

EQUIPMENT: A spice grinder or coffee mill.

2 small dried red chili peppers

2 tablespoons coriander seeds

1 tablespoon cumin seeds

½ teaspoon black mustard seeds

1 teaspoon black peppercorns

1 teaspoon fenugreek seeds

½ teaspoon ground ginger

½ teaspoon ground turmeric

Menus

A Springtime Dinner with Friends

Chanteduc Rainbow Olive Collection
Creamy Zucchini and Fresh Lemon Verbena Soup
Franck's Thyme-Marinated Leg of Lamb
Le Mimosa's Artichokes, Grilled Almonds, Lemon Zest, and Honey
Zucchini Blossoms Stuffed with Mint-Infused Fresh Cheese
Camargue Rice with Lemon and Pine Nuts
Raoul's Kamut Rolls
Chanteduc Cherry Cake

It's May and Time to Play

Niçoise Figs Stuffed with Fennel Seeds and Walnuts
Chanteduc Salad of Garden Sorrel and Fresh Mint
My Fishmonger's Tuna Daube with Green Olives and Red Wine
Spelt Salad with Peppers, Shallots, and Parsley
Strawberries from Carpentras with Yogurt Cream

It's Market Day—a Fine Tuesday Lunch

Quick-Cured Sardines
Salad of Tomatoes, Lemons, Croutons, Capers, and Basil
Six-Minute Salmon Braised in Viognier
Goat Cheese with Olive Purée from Nyons
Black Olive Fougasse

A Summer Vegetarian Feast under the Stars

Domaine St. Luc's Green Beans with Basil

Quick Polenta Bread with Rosemary

Spicy Tomato, Fennel, and Orange Sauce

Niçoise Figs Stuffed with Fennel Seeds and Walnuts

Fresh Goat Cheese with Freshly Cracked Black Peppercorns

Cold Cavaillon Melon Soup with Beaumes-de-Venise

Buttermilk Sorbet

It's Friday, It's Fish

Savory Rosemary-Parmesan Madeleines

Chilled Tomato Soup with Goat Cheese and Olive Purée

Le Grand Pré's Seared and Roasted Salmon with Sorrel Sauce

Château Pesquié's White Peaches Poached in Red Wine

June: A Summer Solstice Evening

Sunday Salad of Greens, Olive Toasts, and Mint-Infused Fresh Cheese

Guinea Hen Stuffed with Olives, Rosemary, Fennel, and Olive Leaves

Roasted Cherry Tomatoes

Raspberry Sorbet

Raspberry-Almond Financiers

A July Independence Day Festival

Raoul's Summer Truffle Salad

Roasted Chicken Stuffed with Rice and Figs

Russian Tomato Gratin

Quick Sautéed Green Peppers

Carpentras Multiseed Bread

Josiane's Fresh Goat Cheese with Provençal Herbs

Fresh Fig and Homemade Apricot Jam Tart

An August Dinner at Sunset

Tuna and Olive Spread

Salad of Tomatoes, Pine Nuts, and Basil

Tuna Fillet with Meyer Lemons and Summer Savory

Linguine with Saffron from Provence

Warm Figs with Honey, Raspberries, and Fresh Cheese

A Summer Luncheon under a Tent

Summer Herb Bread
Broccoli, Avocado, and Pistachios with Pistachio Oil
Mireille's Tomato, Green Pepper, Olive, and Anchovy Salad
Serge's Spelt Bread
Beaumes-de-Venise Sorbet

———

Sweet September, Indian Summer

Provençal Chickpea Spread with Cumin
Autumn Salad: Wild Mushrooms, Parmesan, and Arugula
Franck's Roasted Duck Breast with Green Olives
Chez Serge's Cinnamon-Apple Tart

———

Baby It's Cold Outside

Sautéed Almond-Stuffed Dates
Bistrot de France Garlic Salad
Pumpkin Soup with Truffles and Pumpkin Seed Oil
Forgotten Red Wine Daube
Three-Pear Cake

———

A Winter Truffle Feast

Black Truffle Open-Faced Sandwiches
Leek, Potato, and Truffle Soup
Brigitte's Squab Roasted with Honey
Cauliflower Gratin
Potato and Celeriac Gratin
Truffled Saint-Marcellin
Vaison's Candied Fruit Bread
Autumn Walnut Cake Domaine de la Ponche

Source List

Bread and Grains

Denis Lefèvre
Le Pain des Moissons
36 Place Montfort,
84110 Vaison-la-Romaine
Telephone: 04 90 36 03 25

Kamut and Epeautre:
The Grain & Salt Society
Telephone 1-800-867-7258
Internet: www.celtic-seasalt.com

Cheese

Lou Canestéou
Josiane and Christian Deal
10, rue Raspail
84110 Vaison-la-Romaine
Telephone: 04 90 36 31 30
Fax: 04 90 28 79 33
E-Mail: LouCanesteou@aol.com

Decoration for the Home

Scourtins (coco mats):
La Scourtinerie
36 Quarter La Maladrerie
26110 Nyons
Telephone : 04 75 26 33 52
Fax : 04 75 26 20 72

L' Atelier du Presbytère
(linens, antiques)
10, rue Presbytère
30300 Vallabreuges
Telephone: 04 66 59 37 37
Fax: 04 66 59 15 21

Fish and Shellfish

Poissonnerie des Voconces
Eliane and Aymar Berenger
6, rue Maquis
84110 Vaison-la-Romaine
Telephone: 04 90 36 00 84

Marée du Comtat Venaison
Arlette and Edmond Lafont
84500 Bollene
Telephone: 04 90 30 13 81

Honey

L'Apiarium
Christine and Hubert Poquet
Route de Gap
26110 Condorcet
Telephone: 04 75 27 74 95

Markets

Comité Permanent Promotion
    des Marchés
Telephone: 04 90 39 00 42
Fax: 04 90 39 00 43

Meat and Poultry

Boucherie La Romane
Franck Peyraud
13, rue de la République
84110 Vaison-la-Romaine
Telephone: 04 90 36 01 25
Fax: 04 90 28 75 11
E-mail: franck@laromane.com
Internet: www.laromane.com

Olives and Olive Oil

Moulin Jean-Marie Cornille
Rue Charloun-Rieu
13520 Maussane-les-Alpilles
Telephone : 04 90 54 32 37 and
04 90 54 38 12
Fax: 04 90 54 30 28
Internet: www.moulin-cornille.com

Domaine de La Blanchette
Ferme Brès
Pied de Vaux
26110 Nyons
Telephone/Fax: 04 75 26 05 41

Huilerie J. Leblanc
Anne Leblanc
6, rue Jacob
75006 Paris
Telephone: 01 46 34 61 55

Boutique Jean Martin
Jean-Louis Martin
Rue Charloun-Rieu
13520 Maussane-les-Alpilles
Telephone: 04 90 54 30 04
Fax: 04 90 54 40 79
Internet: www.jeanmartin.fr

Institut du Monde d'Olivier
40, place de la Libération
26110 Nyons
Telephone: 04 75 26 90 90
Fax: 04 75 29 90 94
E-mail: monde-oliver@wanadoo.fr

Pastries

Financier Molds:
Prévin Incorporated
Telephone: 215 985 1996
Fax: (1) 215 985 0323

Chabert et Guillot
Place de la Gare
9, rue Charles Chabert
26200 Montélimar
Telephone: 04 75 00 82 00

André Boyer
Rue Porte des Aires
84390 Sault
Telephone: 04 90 64 00 23
Fax: 04 90 64 08 99

Confiserie Brémond
16, rue d'Italie
13100 Aix-en-Provence
Telephone: 04 42 26 56 39
Fax: 04 42 38 01 70

Maison Lilamand et Fils
5, avenue Albert Schweitzer
13210 Saint-Remy-en-Provence
Telephone: 04 90 92 11 08
Fax: 04 90 92 53 83

POTTERY

Poterie Atelier du Sage
1, place Chateauras
26220 Dieulefit
Telephone: 04 75 46 35 25

Poterie d'Aigues-Vives
Richard Estéban
58, rue de l'Abattoir
30670 Aigues-Vives
Telephone: 04 66 35 18 79

Faïence d'Apt
Atelier Bernard
286, avenue de la Libération
84400 Apt
Telephone: 04 90 74 15 31
Fax: 04 90 74 30 51
Internet: www.faiencedapt.com

La Poterie de Cliousclat
Le Village
26270 Cliousclat
Telephone: 04 75 63 05 69
Fax: 04 75 63 05 13

Poterie Il Etait une Fois
Place de l'Ancien Collège
26220 Dieulefit
Telephone: 04 75 46 87 58

Lis Amélie
Dany et Robert Del Giudice
Pont de Monblan
13520 Mausanne-les-Alpilles
Telephone: 04 90 54 37 55
Fax: 04 90 54 21 03

Poterie Mont Rachas
Place Chateauras
26220 Dieulefit
Telephone: 04 75 90 63 25
and Commune aux Terres
26160 Poët-Laval
Telephone: 04 75 46 46 84
Fax: 04 75 46 45 80

Atelier Picot
Ponty RN 100
84220 Goult
Telephone: 04 90 72 22 79

Poterie du Plan des Amandiers
Pascale Mestre and Nils
    Descotes-Genon
84220 Gordes
Telephone/Fax: 04 90 72 36 32

Poterie Ravel
Avenue Goums
13400 Aubagne
Telephone: 04 42 82 42 00
Fax: 04 42 82 42 01
E-mail: poterie.ravel@wanadoo.fr

Atelier Soleil
Quai Saint Michel
04360 Moustiers Sainte Mairie
Telephone: 04 92 74 61 62
Fax: 04 92 74 61 71
E-mail: franck.scherer@wanadoo.fr.

PRODUCE

Le Coin Gourmande
Danielle and Alain Betti
14, rue Maquis
84110 Vaison-la-Romaine
Telephone: 04 90 36 30 04

Les Gourmandines
Josiane and Corinne Meliani
4, rue Paul Buffaven
84110 Vaison-la-Romaine
Telephone: 04 90 28 84 09

RESTAURANTS

La Beaugravière
Tina and Guy Julien
Route N 7, Quai Pont Neuf
84430 Mondragon
Telephone: 04 90 40 82 54
Fax: 04 90 40 91 01
Internet: www.beaugraviere.com

La Chassagnette
Route de Sambuc
13200 Arles
Telephone: 04 90 97 26 96
E-mail: restaurantchassa@aol.com

La Compagnie des Comptoirs
Laurent and Jacques Pourcel
83, rue Joseph Vernet
84000 Avignon
Telephone: 04 90 85 99 04
Fax: 04 90 85 89 24

Bistrot de France
67, place Bouquerie
84400 Apt
Telephone: 04 90 74 22 01

Le Grand Pré
Flora and Raoul Reichrath
Route de Vaison (D 975)
84110 Roaix
Telephone: 04 90 46 18 12
Fax: 04 90 46 17 84
E-mail: legrandpre@walka9.com

Le Jardin de Sens
Laurent and Jacques Pourcel
11, avenue Saint-Lazare
Montpellier
Telephone: 04 99 58 38 38
Fax: 04 99 58 38 39
E-mail: jds@mnet.fr

Restaurant Le Mimosa
Bridget and David Pugh
34725 Saint Guiraud
Telephone: 04 67 96 67 96
Fax: 04 67 96 61 15

L'Oustalet
Marlies and Johannes Sailer
Place de la Mairie
84190 Gigondas
Telephone/Fax: 04 90 65 85 30

Le Bistrot du Paradou
Mireille and Jean-Louis Pons
13125 Le Paradou
Telephone: 04 90 54 32 70

Restaurant Pic
Anne-Sophie Pic
285, avenue Victor Hugo
26000 Valence
Telephone: 04 75 44 15 32
Fax: 04 75 40 96 03
E-mail: www.pic-valence.com

Domaine de la Ponche
Ruth Spahn, Madeleine
    Frauenknecht, and
    Jean-Pierre Onimus
84190 Vacqueyras
Telephone: 04 90 65 85 21
Fax: 04 90 65 85 23
E-mail: domaine.laponche@
wanadoo.fr
Internet: www.hotel.laponche.com

Prévot
353, avenue Verdun
84300 Cavaillon
Telephone: 04 90 71 32 43
Fax: 04 90 71 97 05
E-mail: jean-jacques.prevot2@
freesbee.fr

Le Saint Hubert
84340 Entrechaux
Telephone: 04 90 46 00 05
Fax: 04 90 46 00 06

Restaurant Chez Serge
Sophie and Serge Ghoukassian
90, rue Cottier
84200 Carpentras
Telephone: 04 90 63 21 24
E-mail: ChezSerge@wanadoo.fr

Café du Village
Village des Antiquaires
84800 Isle-sur-la-sorgue
Telephone: 04 90 20 72 31

SAFFRON

L'Aube Safran
Marie and François Pillet
Chemin du Patifiage
84330 Le Barroux
Telephone: 04 90 62 66 91

The Spice House
Internet: www.thespicehouse.com

TRUFFLES

Plantin
Hervé Poron
841110 Puymeras
Telephone: 04 90 46 41 44
Fax: 04 90 46 47 04
E-mail: herve@plantin.com

VINEYARDS

Château du Beaucastel
Jean-Pierre and François Perrin
Chemin de Beaucastel
84350 Courthézon
Telephone: 04 90 70 41 00
Fax: 04 90 70 41 19
Internet: www.beaucastel.com

Cave de Cairanne
84290 Cairanne
Telephone: 04 90 30 82 05
Fax: 04 90 30 74 03
E-mail: inof@cave_cairannne.fr
Internet: www.CaveCairanne.com

Clos Chanteduc
Ludovic Cornillon
Domaine St. Luc
26970 La Baume de Transit
Telephone: 04 75 98 11 51
Fax: 04 75 98 19 22
Internet: www.dom-saint-luc.com

Domaine de Durban
84190 Beaumes-de-Venise
Telephone: 04 90 62 94 26
Fax: 04 90 65 01 85

Domaine les Goubert
Jean-Pierre Cartier
84190 Gigondas
Telephone: 04 90 65 86 38
Fax: 04 90 65 81 52
E-mail: jpcartier@terre-net.fr
Internet: www.terre-net.fr/
domaine-les-goubert

Domaine Gramenon
Michelle Laurent
26770 Montbrison-sur-Lez
Telephone: 04 75 53 57 08
Fax: 04 75 53 68 92

Château d'Hugues
Sylviane and Bernard Pradier
84100 Uchaux
Telephone: 04 90 70 06 27
Fax: 04 90 70 10 28

Domaine de la Mordorée
Christophe Delorme
30126 Tavel
Telephone: 04 66 50 00 75
Fax: 04 66 50 47 39

Château Les Palais
11220 Saint-Laurent-de-la
Cabrerisee
Telephone: 04 68 44 01 63

Château Pesquié
Edith and Paul Chaudière
84570 Mormoiron
Telephone: 04 90 61 94 08
Fax: 04 90 61 94 13

Domaine Le Sang des Cailloux
Serge L. Ferigoule
Route de Vacqueyras
84260 Sarrians
Telephone: 04 90 65 88 64
Fax: 04 90 65 88 75

Domaine Santa Duc
Yves Gras
84190 Gigondas
Telephone: 04 90 65 84 49
Fax: 04 90 65 81 63

Domaine la Soumade
André Romero
84110 Rasteau
Telephone: 04 90 46 11 26
Fax: 04 90 46 11 69

INDEX

Buttermilk
   sorbet, 290
   sorbet, cold Cavaillon melon soup with Beaumes-de-
      Venise and, 287

Cairanne, *cave coopérative*, 245
Cake
   autumn walnut, 306–7
   cherry, 280–81
   three-pear, 296–97
Candies, in Provence, types and shops, 279–80
Caper(s), 41
   fricassee of chicken with white wine, olives, and,125
   lentils with, walnuts, walnut oil, and mint, 174–75
   olivades: tomatoes, olives, mint, basil, and, 188
   penne with tomatoes, rosemary, olives, and,
      170–71
   potato salad with rosemary and, 223
   salad of tomatoes, lemons, croutons, basil, and, 40
   tapenade, olive, mustard, and, 312
Carrot(s)
   Provençal, osso buco, 212
   winter, and star anise soup, 72
Cauliflower
   anchovy dip with steamed whole, 210–11
   gratin, 209
Celeriac
   potato and, gratin, 228
   purée, 214
Cheese, 238–39
   Banon or goat, garlic salad, 28–29
   blue, Belgian endive, yellow pepper, fennel, and
      winter salad:, 47
   broccio and *brocciu,* 257
   goat, asparagus with, and salmon eggs, 186–87
   goat, Belgian endive, broccoli, and potato salad, 46
   goat, chilled tomato soup with, and olive purée, 60
   goat, fresh, with cracked peppercorns, 244–45
   goat, fresh, with Provençal herbs, 240
   goat, with olive purée from Nyons, 246
   goat, soufflé, 256
   homemade (fresh), 236–37
   homemade (fresh), warm figs with honey,
      raspberries, and, 286
   homemade or ricotta, cauliflower gratin, 209
   Gruyère, chunky zucchini gratin, 201
   Gruyère, hazelnut, and rosemary biscuits, 10–11
   Gruyère, potato and celeriac gratin, 228
   mint-infused fresh, 257
   mint-infused fresh, Sunday salad of greens, olive
      toasts, and, 36

   mint-infused fresh, zucchini blossoms stuffed with,
      200
   mozzarella, penne with basil, and pine nut oil,
      168–69
   pairing with bread and wine, 238–39
   Parmesan, savory rosemary-, *madeleines,* 6
   Parmesan, wild mushrooms, and arugula autumn
      salad:, 44–45
   Parmigiano-Reggiano, summer truffle salad, 32
   Russian tomato gratin, 189–90
   truffled Saint-Marcellin, 248–49
   various types, 241–43
   wines suggested for, 241–43
Cherry(ies)
   Chanteduc, cake, 280–81
   Chanteduc sweet, sorbet, 282
   individual, -hazelnut gratins, 285
Chicken
   fricassee of, with chorizo and peppers, 120–21
   fricassee of, with garlic and sweet garlic confit,
      122–23
   fricassee of, with white wine, capers, and olives, 125
   homemade stock, 325
   roasted, stuffed with rice and figs, 106–7
Chickpea(s)
   Provençal, spread with cumin, 19
   roasted Provençal, 18
Chili, vegetarian, 73
Chili peppers, pork stew with sweet and hot, 146–47
Chives, warm potato, and blood sausage salad, 232
Chocolate
   dark, sauce (*coulis*), 307
   dark, sorbet, 306
Cicadas, 124
Clams, 156
   spaghettini with mussels and baby, 156–57
Clos Chanteduc, 126–27
Cod
   poached salt, with vegetables and garlic mayonnaise,
      76–77
   six-minute, braised in spicy tomato sauce, 89
Cookies
   almond, 278
   lemon crisps, 301
   raspberry-almond financiers, 290–91
Couscous salad with mint, parsley, and tomatoes, 37
Crab, fresh, salad with lime zest, 92
Croutons, salad of tomatoes, lemons, capers, basil, and,
      40
Cucumber, Moroccan lamb meatballs with, and mint
      salad, 144–45